Rebecca Ruter Springer

Beechwood

Rebecca Ruter Springer

Beechwood

ISBN/EAN: 9783337139919

Printed in Europe, USA, Canada, Australia, Japan

Cover: Foto ©ninafisch / pixelio.de

More available books at **www.hansebooks.com**

BEECHWOOD.

BY

REBECCA RUTER SPRINGER.

PHILADELPHIA:
J. B. LIPPINCOTT & CO.
1873.

TO

THE KIND HUSBAND

WHO HAS EVER ENCOURAGED AND AIDED ME IN THIS AS IN
ALL OF MY LITERARY EFFORTS,

AND

THE LITTLE SON

WHOSE SUNNY HEAD FLITS EVER ABOUT MY CHAIR,

ALL THAT IS WORTHY AND ALL THAT IS BEAUTIFUL IN

This Little Volume

IS LOVINGLY INSCRIBED.

PREFACE.

With many hopes, and some misgivings, I start my little bark adrift upon the great sea of literature, feeling that some besides myself will watch its course with wistful eyes and prayerful hearts. It may be that, driven hither and thither by adverse winds, it will soon be engulfed in the waves, and so lost forever; or, being met by a favoring gale, it may be borne gently onward to a shore rich with luxuriant fields of waving grain. Whatever of golden sheaves, be they few or many, it may bring to me, shall be religiously devoted to the good of others, that in the great hereafter it may be said of me, as once it was said of another, "She hath done what she could."

THE AUTHOR.

BEECHWOOD.

May 12, 18—. To-day is my fifteenth birthday, and I have resolved, among many other things, that I will keep a journal,—a plain record of my life from day to day. I told mamma about it a little while ago, and she said she thought it a very good idea, as it would improve my handwriting, and also teach me to express my thoughts more readily. She gave me this nice little blank-book to use for that purpose, so that I would have an inducement, she said, to keep my diary neat and clean. I have the very best mother in the world. She never laughs at anything I tell her,—anything that is in sober earnest, I mean,—no matter how ridiculous it may seem, because, I suppose, she knows it makes me feel badly; and whenever any one else does so in her presence, she says, so sweetly, "Never mind, Nannie; they were once little, just like yourself, and, I doubt not, said just as many queer things." Ralph, my oldest brother, is a great tease; but then, you know, he is a boy, and boys always are such plagues! He resents our calling him a boy, however: he was nineteen last month, and already has quite a mustache. He is a real handsome fellow, too, though not quite so good-looking as Nettie Ray's brother Hal, I think; though Nettie thinks him much handsomer.

Dear me! what have I been writing? How Ralph would

plague me, if he could read this first entry in my journal! He thinks Nettie and I are nothing but children; while I am fifteen to-day, and Nettie will be sixteen in September. I do not suppose I have made a very sensible entry; but then, you know, old book, this is my first effort as a journalist, and could not be expected to be perfect. I hope I shall improve in time; I mean to, for I have made any number of good resolutions for the future to-day, all of which I meant to have copied into my journal; but I am so tired, I must stop for this time.

Well, who would have thought I would have written a whole page and a half the very first day? That is a pretty good beginning; although I am very much afraid Ralph would say there is very little sense in anything I have written.

May 13. Yesterday, after I quit writing, I went downstairs with my sewing, and sat with mamma. She asked me if I had written in my journal yet. I told her I had, but feared I had not succeeded very well. She encouraged me very much; told me no one could expect to do a thing just right the first time; to be perfectly simple and honest in all that I wrote, and never attempt to color anything to make it appear better than it was in reality; to let my diary be a true record of my life from day to day, and that if I lived to be a woman it might some day be a great comfort to me to read it all over. She told me, too, to be careful to record my faults also, as then I would be more watchful over myself, so that hereafter I need not be ashamed when I reviewed my life as recorded on these pages. Dear mother! I know too well the fault she had in mind when she told me that: my quick temper and ungovernable tongue. I do say such bitter things to those I love best when I am excited,—I will not say angry, although I am afraid sometimes it amounts to that. I am very sensitive, and often misconstrue the language and actions of those whose love I should never doubt. And then how terribly I suffer for it afterward, no one can tell. I feel as though I deserved to have the earth open and swallow me up for my sinfulness and ingratitude. Mother says I will surely overcome it, if I only watch myself closely and pray earnestly for strength from above. I do try so hard to follow her instructions; but I cannot be good like she is, ever. I often wonder if she ever has even a wrong thought, she is so mild and gentle always. Her reproofs never anger me, as do those of others, for she seems to feel so sorry when she has to reprove me; and every time I think I will be more watchful over myself, so that she will never have to do it again. But alas for good resolutions! they are made only to be broken at the first severe temptation. It was only yesterday—upon my birthday, too—that I yielded to one of these fitful moods in a manner I shall not soon forget. I was called from the library a moment, where I had been writing a letter to Aunt Katie, and with which I had taken great pains, for I was anxious she should see how hard I was trying to improve myself; and when I returned to the room, after a few minutes' absence, Ralph and Charlie and little Kittie were there, but my letter was nowhere to be seen.

"Where is my letter?" I said, trying to speak unconcernedly as possible, for I saw by the twinkle in Ralph's eye and his glance at Charlie that he knew more of the matter than he chose to admit.

"Her letter, Charlie. Pray, mark the dignity with which Miss Nancy Cleve asks us for her purloined letter. What an idea!" And he threw his curly head back and broke into a hearty laugh.

Now, Ralph knows if there is anything in this world I hate, it is to be called "Nancy." I often wish the old aunt, who insisted upon having me named for herself, had been any place in the world but with mamma when I was born. "Nannie" I can stand very well; but when it comes to *Nancy*, as some of the old ladies in the neighborhood will persist in calling me, it annoys me greatly. Ralph has discovered this weakness, and often turns it to good or bad purpose in teasing me. I tried very hard not to seem annoyed, for I remembered it was my birthday, and said to Ralph, "Please, Ralph, do give it to me; I want to finish it before dinner."

"Well, now, Nannie, I will," he said, "seeing you are so anxious about it; but on one condition only. I must first read it aloud, for the benefit of the company here assembled." And the saucy fellow mounted a chair and began :—

"My dear Aunt Katie" ["very good indeed, Nannie, if you only had not spelled the aunt without a u, which suggests to one the idea at once of an ugly little insect instead of our beautiful young relative"], "as this is my fifteenth birthday" ["a very mature young lady;" and he bowed to me from his perch with mock dignity], "I thought I could not better improve the time than by writing to you." ["Watch her, Charlie; I see that she is ready to spring, cat-like, upon her prey, which, of course, means her innocent young brother."] I had really sprung to him and tried to catch the letter from his hand, but he held it at arm's length, and continued : "I want to tell you how hard I am trying to overcome my hasty temper." ["Steady, Nancy; try and stick to your resolution."]

But I could endure no more, and broke from him, exclaiming, "You are a rude, unmannerly fellow; and I would rather have no brother at all than one whose only delight is to torment me so." And I sat down upon the hearth-rug and sobbed passionately.

Dear little golden-haired Kittie crept to my side, and, stealing her little bare arm about my neck, she said, tenderly,—

"Never mind, sister Nannie, he won't be naughty any more. Will you, brother Ralph?"

Ralph looked sorry, but half laughed as he threw the letter into my lap and said,—

"I did not think you were such a child, Nannie; and I am sure you did not mean what you said last."

"Yes, I did, and more too," I retorted, angrily, crushing the letter I had penned with such care in my hand, and throwing it into the grate.

Ralph looked grieved; and at that moment mamma entered the room. She looked as though she had heard all, as she doubtless had, the library opening into the drawing-room.

"My son," she said, very quietly, to Ralph, "this is scarcely the way I had hoped you would help Nannie enjoy her birthday. You cannot surely have forgotten how earnestly she tried to confer pleasure upon yours."

I knew she alluded to the care with which I had embroidered for him a very handsome pair of slippers as a birthday gift. The remembrance, instead of making me feel more unkindly toward him, softened my heart, and I was already beginning to feel ashamed of my violent outbreak, when Ralph, over whom mother has unlimited influence, as indeed she has over every one in the house, burst out impulsively,—

"Indeed I have not! I was a brute to tease her so. Will you forgive me, little sister?"

His arm was around me, and his hand softly wiping the tears that flowed so freely, though from a very different cause than those that fell so hotly a few moments before.

"It is I who should ask to be forgiven, dear Ralph, for

speaking to you so bitterly," I whispered, my heart sore at the remembrance of my hasty words.

"Never mind, darling; you did not really mean what you said, did you? It was all my fault for teasing you so."

"Oh, no, no, no!" I sobbed; and Ralph, kissing me tenderly, said,—

"I will try never to tease you again, dear; and, to show you that I did not really mean to be ugly, let me place this where it should have been an hour ago." He drew from his vest-pocket a tiny package as he spoke, and, unrolling it, showed me a beautiful ring, with "Nannie, from Ralph," engraven upon the inside, together with the date, and pressed it upon my finger. "I came in here to find you, for this purpose, but, spying your letter, my evil genius pointed to it as the means for a little fun, and I was weak enough to yield to his suggestions."

My heart was all broken up by his kindness, and I could only put my arm about his neck, and sob out,—

"I will never be ugly with you again, dear Ralph."

"Nor I with you, dear Nannie."

So the compact was sealed; and I will try and live up to it.

When we looked up, mother was no longer in the room, but I knew at once of what she was thinking when she told me not to hide the record of my faults. So I have written this all out as faithfully as I could, that whenever I look at it I shall remember the promise I then made, to be more watchful for the future.

May 14. To-day Gertie and I went over into the south meadow to look for flowers, and, not being very successful in our search, Gertie proposed we should go upon the hillside beyond the meadow. To this I was very willing; but when we came to the little brook that winds like a silver thread through the grass and bushes, we found it so swollen by the recent rains as to prevent our crossing.

"Oh, pshaw!" said Gertie; "how provoking to lose our nice walk, just for the little brook!"

"But we shall not," I said.

"How can we help it?"

"Wade!" was my response, as I sat down to unlace my boots.

"Oh, Nannie," said timid Gertie, "do you think we ought to?"

"Why not?"

"We are so big!" She did look so comical as she said this, with that perplexed look of doubt and desire combined upon her face, that I lay down in the grass and laughed till I cried. Then I said,—

"No one will see us, sis; and if they did, who cares?"

Now, I am always, I am sorry to say, getting Gertie, as well as myself, into all manner of scrapes, simply because I am so thoughtless and impulsive, and she is so easily led; so, as usual, she said no more, but sat down and untied her boots also. I said, "We will put our shoes and stockings in the basket, carry them over, and slip them on again on the other side,—it will only take a minute, you know."

Gertie assented, and we were soon laughing and talking and wading into the brook. Now, if we had gone straight through, as we at first intended, all would have been well enough; but I was ripe for a frolic, and so must needs propose wading up the stream a little way, to look for minnows.

"We will leave the basket on this log," I said, "till we come back." So off we went, splashing and laughing, and enjoying our frolic to the utmost; the pure cool water rippling over our bare feet and ankles delightfully. Just in the midst of our fun, we heard some one whistling; and whom should we see coming over the hill but Ralph, gun in hand, with half a dozen squirrels dangling by his side! Such a flutter as then took place.

"Quick, Gertie!" I whispered, "stoop down behind these bushes, and hide. If he sees us, he will never have done teasing us."

In our haste we both slipped, and I, of course, sat down somewhat suddenly in the water. I gave a little, smothered scream, and then we both laughed till the tears came. Whether Ralph heard us or not, he passed on, apparently unconscious of our presence, whistling "The Blue Bells of Scotland;" and when we thought him safely away, we emerged from our hiding-place.

But in a moment Gertie cried, "Oh, Nannie, he has taken the basket with our shoes and stockings!" And sure enough he had.

We looked at one another a moment in consternation, and then began to call Ralph, somewhat timidly at first, but growing louder and louder till we called with all our strength. But he was perfectly oblivious, walking rapidly away, his musical whistle rising and falling distinctly upon our ears after he himself had disappeared behind the orchard fence. We sat down upon the grass and looked at each other, and Gertie was just ready to cry, and I was beginning seriously to wonder what mamma would say to our mad frolic, and to wonder also if I ever would be anything but a foolish child, always getting myself and Gertie into scrapes and never getting cleverly out of them, when our ridiculous position broke on me with such force that I burst out laughing; and after a moment Gertie joined me, and then we got up without a word and started home.

"Nannie, what will mamma say?" said Gertie, presently.

This was a damper again; and I looked somewhat ruefully at my wet garments, but answered, bravely, "Nothing to you, sis; and she is used to my short-comings."

It was anything but a pleasant walk home with our bare,

tender feet; and more than once we stopped to examine sundry scratches and bruises, but finally reached the back-door, somewhat crestfallen to find mamma waiting for us with a face that tried to look serious, but smiled in spite of itself as she said,—

"My little girls are getting too old to indulge in such questionable frolics. Go quickly and change your clothes; if you have not both taken cold I shall be thankful." And, too glad of the chance, we escaped to our room.

At tea, Ralph's eyes twinkled maliciously as he spoke of having had rare sport hunting; but he did not otherwise allude to our adventure, for which I felt very grateful, and so I am sure did Gertie. For his forbearance in that respect we can almost forgive him for the trick he played so cleverly upon us. It was just like Ralph, and it is hard to feel vexed at anything he does.

May 16. I did not write in my journal yesterday, because it was Sunday; and I went to church so often that I had not time, unless I had neglected my usual Sunday reading. Our Sunday-school is in the morning at nine o'clock, and, as it is quite a walk,—nearly a mile,—we do not return before church, which is at eleven. We usually stroll through the church-yard or sit under the maple-trees in the grove opposite the church during the short intermission immediately before the services. Hal and Nettie Ray are usually with us, which, of course, means Ralph, Charlie, Gertie, and myself, and sometimes little Kittie. Hal thinks my ring is very pretty; so does Nettie. Gertie is nearly an inch taller than I am, although she is nearly two years younger. She was thirteen the 3d of March. Everybody says we never would be taken for sisters, we are so unlike. She is quite large of her age; has black eyes, and short curls of dark glossy hair all round her head; I think her very pretty. My eyes, on the contrary, are gray, and my hair, which I will not let curl (curls are such a bore, I think), but gather into a knot behind, lies, Hal says, "in golden ripples all over my head." But that is all nonsense, of course.

They (Nettie and Hal, I mean) had a young cousin with them yesterday, who is at present visiting them. His name is Ellis Ray, and he seems to be a very pleasant gentleman. I should think he was about as old as Ralph, or maybe a little older. He seemed greatly pleased with Gertie. I heard him tell Hal she had the finest head he ever saw. She did look very pretty yesterday, indeed: she wore her blue muslin, which is very delicate and of that peculiar shade of blue that is so becoming to a brunette, and indeed the only one that she can wear; and she and Kittie had been having a run down to the spring back of the church, which stands upon a beautiful green lawn sloping from it on every side but one, and that is the front; and when she came up to us her face was slightly flushed with the exercise, and her moist hair lay in innumerable rings around her head,—every hair that could escape making a separate little curl of its own. She looked very beautiful as she came toward us swinging her hat carelessly in her hand and chatting merrily with Kittie, and I was not at all surprised at the admiration she excited or the remark it called forth from young Mr. Ray. Gertie is so innocent too,—she is really the innocent child she seems, and so much like mother that every one must love her. Mr. Ray seemed to think Kittie was very pretty too, and kept her on his knee nearly all the intermission. Nettie says he is studying for the ministry. He is going to spend the greater part of his college vacation with them.

Father White gave us a most beautiful and touching sermon from the text, "Forgive us our debts, as we forgive our debtors."

I never understood so forcibly the meaning of those words as when I yesterday heard them explained by that good old man. I felt as though I never again could dare to repeat that beautiful prayer, that I learned when a little child at my mother's knee, until I had first looked closely into my heart to see if I had any wrong thoughts therein toward another. He warned us, so solemnly, to be careful how we passed hasty judgment upon others; showing us how much better it is to judge charitably, even though we should sometimes be deceived, than, by judging harshly, to wrong and wound one innocent person. He said we are too apt to attach undue importance to trifles; to let a thoughtless word or act outweigh hundreds of a contrary nature, and that, too, when the word may have been innocently spoken, or the act unwittingly done.

I could not help thinking of poor Mary Black, who lost her situation as seamstress in Mrs. Wood's family, and well-nigh lost her reputation for life, by stealing out at night, alone, to meet her worthless brother and give him her earnings. The only one who really knew the true circumstances, and could have set poor Mary right before the world, was a girl in the same house, who, through envy, kept silent, and let her traducers say the worst of her; so that she lost her situation, and for a time her character in the community, although her life had up to that time been blameless. Almost every one believed the evil of her, and forgot all her former goodness; and but for the illness and death of her brother she might to-day have been a blighted and heart-broken woman,—innocent before God, despised among men. Upon his death-bed her brother told of his own worthlessness and her devotion, thus giving her the character almost of an angel, instead of that of a depraved woman.

Ah, how lenient we should be in our judgments of those

around us! "Therefore thou art inexcusable, O man, whosoever thou art that judgest: for wherein thou judgest another, thou condemnest thyself; for thou that judgest doest the same things."

We read these words day by day, yet dare defiantly to set their authority aside and pursue the promptings of our own sinful hearts, thus plainly saying by our conduct, what we dare not assert with our lips, "Stand aside, for I am holier than thou!" May God forgive and help us!

May 20. Yesterday mamma told me that our new governess would be here to-morrow. How I do dread to see her! I know I shall not like her. It nearly broke my heart to have dear Miss Reid go away, for she has been with us ever since I was eight years old, and I know I shall never love any one half so well again. She disliked to go very much, but her mother's health was so frail she was obliged to go to her. Mamma says I must not allow myself to become prejudiced against Miss Lane, our new governess, just because I loved Miss Reid so dearly; and Gertie says she means to love her if possible. It is very easy for mamma and Gertie to feel thus, because they are always good,—but poor willful me! No wonder I dread the change, for I am always getting myself into trouble with some one; and I know Miss Lane will never bear with my impatient moods as did dear Miss Reid.

Uncle Ralph came yesterday again. He comes to see us every week, and sometimes much oftener, for he lives in the village, which is only three miles away. He is so handsome, and so good, and such a favorite with all the ladies. Mamma is very proud of him. She thinks anything Uncle Ralph does is sure to be right. He is not our "sure-enough uncle," as little Kittie says, although he is just the same to us as though he were. His mother, who was a widow, married Grandfather Clifford when Uncle

Ralph was only five years old and mamma was eleven. Mamma says she remembers so well the first time she ever saw him; upon the day grandfather brought them home. She says he was a beautiful little boy, with a head very much like Gertie's is now. Grandfather always loved him as his own child, adopted him and gave him his name, and I think, if there is any difference, mamma and Aunt Katie love him better than Uncle Ben even, who is their own brother, but who lives hundreds of miles away from us. He is very indulgent to us children, and since dear papa's death, which is now nearly five years ago, has taken all mamma's business into his own hands. I often wonder he has never married. He is six years younger than mamma, —who is just thirty-eight,—so he is getting to be quite an old bachelor by this time. I mean to ask him, some time, why he does not get married. I know almost just what he will answer. He will pull my ear and say, "How do I know, pussy, whether any one will have me or not?" But I know there are few ladies could resist Uncle Ralph, if he once tried to please them. He laughs heartily at my determination not to like Miss Lane. He says he is quite sure I will, for he has met her and she is a perfect lady. I told him that Ralph told me she was an old maid, who wore glasses and false hair, and never allowed herself to smile upon any condition whatever. He seemed greatly amused, but only said Ralph was a sad tease. I could not get him to describe her, so I must school my impatience till to-morrow; but I am a good deal more than half inclined to think Ralph told me the truth, and I sometimes almost hope he did, so that I may have a good excuse for not liking her.

June 12. Miss Lane has been here two weeks, and when I read the last entry in my journal I feel like cutting it out and destroying it. I would surely do so if I had not promised mamma never to mutilate my journal. How I should dislike to have Miss Lane read it! The first evening she came, I felt so condemned and ashamed I could hardly talk with her. I do not know that I can better describe her than by using Uncle Ralph's words, "She is a perfect lady." She is not beautiful, rather plain-looking than otherwise; has soft brown eyes and hair,—the latter of which she brushes back plainly from her forehead and wears in a heavy coil at the back of her head. She is small, not much taller than I am, and dresses in black, for her mother, who is recently dead. She seems quite young, though I cannot quite determine her age. She is very quiet and gentle, but I would as soon think of facing a whole regiment of soldiers as going contrary to her wishes, when she looks me so firmly in the eyes and says, "You will, if you please, do thus or so." Out of study-hours she is always ready to yield to our wishes in anything reasonable; but in the school-room her word is law, most emphatically. I like her all the better for that, and so does Gertie, I am sure. We are all going over into the grove, this evening, to gather flowers: so my entry is brief.

July 24. I am afraid I should never make a daily journalist,—there are so many trifles that keep me from writing. Here it is six weeks since I have made a single entry. First, the weather is quite warm, which makes one naturally indolent; but that, I strongly suspect, mamma would say is no excuse at all. Then it is a canter on the ponies, or a romp through the woods; or an interesting book; or to dress Kittie's doll, or mend her wagon for her; and a dozen other things, all trivial, but all demanding time; and so the diary is neglected. Well, to-day it is raining,—a dull, steady, quiet, rainy day; just such a one as every one loves, now and then, to have upon us, when the musical patter of the drops upon the roof, and through the thirsty leaves, soothes and quiets the restless soul and prepares it for retrospection and reflection. We only study two hours a day through the very warm weather, so I have a long day yet before me. Miss Lane and Gertie are in the library, playing chess; and I have resolved to devote the day to "writing up" my journal, as Ralph would call it. Several things of interest have occurred since I last wrote; some of which I would rather not record, but for my resolution never to screen myself.

About two weeks ago, one sultry morning, in the schoolroom, I allowed my hasty temper to gain the advantage of me, in a manner very humiliating to remember.

I detest algebra. It is one of the few studies that I cannot easily master. The "unknown quantity" confuses me; and it is only by the closest application and most careful study that I can master it at all. It always annoys me to go to a recitation without a perfect lesson; for I will not stand second-best in any class. Nettie Ray comes over and recites with Gertie and myself to Miss Lane, and of course we are all ambitious to excel. Well, upon this particular morning there chanced to be a problem in our algebra lesson upon which I had spent hours of hard study, but I could not bring the right answer. Upon all the rest I was perfect; but, to my no small annoyance, I found when the class was called I was as far from right as ever.

"Well," I thought, "after the recitation is over, I will get Miss Lane to show us where the trouble is;" for I knew Gertie and Nettie were as much in the dark as I, for they had both been to me for assistance, which I was unable to give. Just at this moment Uncle Ralph came in, as he often does when he is here during study-hours, and took a seat near the door, to listen to our recitation. Miss Lane bowed "good-morning" to him, and, accustomed to his presence, went on with the lesson as usual. Nettie and Gertie were already at the board, working at the problems assigned them; and, as I stood, book and chalk in hand, waiting, Miss Lane said,—

"You may work the 'twenty-third' problem, if you please, Miss Nannie."

I thought I should fly, for it was the hateful example over which I had toiled till my brain was a confused mass of "x's" and "y's," "unknown quantities" and "cube roots." Why had she, out of the whole six examples set for our lesson, given me the only one I could not work? And Uncle Ralph there, too! How should he know that I could work with ease any and all the others? The only one assigned me I could not do: how should he know it was not the same with all? A thought struck me, and I began to work rapidly upon the twenty-fourth problem, hoping Miss Lane would not notice the difference. But in a moment she said, "The twenty-third problem, I said, Miss Nannie." Then, in my blind anger, I felt that she knew I could not work it, and only did this to mortify me before Uncle Ralph. I did not even notice that she said, "Gertie is working the twenty-fourth." I turned upon her fiercely, and said, "You know I cannot work it; and you have no right to make me appear always to the worst possible advantage!" And I threw the book upon the desk before me, and burst into tears; but not till I had seen the sad, surprised look of reproof that Uncle Ralph threw upon me as he arose and left the room. He had never given me such a look before; and all because of Miss Lane. How I hated her! She had no right to mortify me so, and turn dear Uncle Ralph against me thus. These thoughts passed like lightning through my brain, while I sobbed with my head down upon my desk,—for the only reply Miss Lane had made to my violent outbreak was,

"You may go to your seat, Miss Nannie," and I had gone. Study-hours closed with this recitation, and Nettie and Gertie had stolen out, as I afterward learned, to find Uncle Ralph, and tell him how faithfully I had been trying to solve the problem, hoping it would be some excuse in his eyes for my offense. Miss Lane lingered a few moments, adjusting the books, and then she too went out, without a word, and I was left to my by no means pleasant thoughts.

After a little, my violent sobbing exhausted itself, and a calmer mood took possession of me. I began to wonder really what Uncle Ralph thought of my conduct. Then, from him I came to think of Miss Lane, and to suspect I had acted very unjustly toward her, instead of her toward me. I saw now, clearly, that she could not possibly have known that I had failed to solve that particular problem, for she had been busy in her own room all morning, until study-hours began. How very miserable I felt! At last I heard a light step, and Gertie stole to my side, with comforting words, and tried to coax me down-stairs; but my heart was still too sore.

"What does Uncle Ralph say, Gertie?" at last I ventured to ask.

"Very little, dear, only that he was grieved to hear you speak as you did to Miss Lane."

"Oh, it is all on Miss Lane's account, then," I said, a little of the old spirit returning in me. "And what does she say?"

"That she does not think you meant to be at all disrespectful, but spoke under strong excitement at the moment. She had no idea but that you were perfect in your lesson, as you always are. She told Uncle Ralph that you were the most accurate scholar she had ever had; and that except in this one instance your conduct had been above reproach."

"Did she really say that, Gertie?" I asked, with a pang of self-reproach.

"She did indeed, and begged Uncle Ralph to come and assure you of his pardon."

"And he would not?"

"No: he said the offense was too serious to be lightly overlooked, and bade me give you this," laying a little card upon the desk before me. "But, dear," she continued, "come and say you are sorry, and it will all be right."

"No, Gertie," I said, kissing her: "you are a good, kind sister to come to me thus; but I cannot go now. You go down, and I will come presently."

"Will you, indeed?"

"Yes, before dinner. Now go."

She left me reluctantly; and as soon as she was gone I took up the card, and read, in Uncle Ralph's bold hand,—

"He that ruleth his own spirit is greater than he that taketh a city."

How bitterly I cried again! It is very seldom Uncle Ralph ever reproves any of us, although since dear papa's death he has been our only guardian; and it seemed very bitter to me now, the more, since I felt it was not undeserved. I sat and thought a long while; and the more I thought, the more hateful my conduct appeared to me. Why could I not have frankly told Miss Lane I had tried faithfully but could not solve the problem? Why must I fly into such a passion, and disgrace myself, and make every one about me unhappy? Was this always to be? Gertie never got into any such troubles, while my unfortunate temper was always leading me astray. I could not help it, I reasoned. I did try, but could not overcome it. So I reasoned with myself a long time; while ever and anon, through it all, would steal the words, "He that ruleth his own spirit is greater than he that taketh a city." Then it could be done; else these words had never been written. Yes, it could be; and, with many tears, I resolved to be doubly watchful, and, if possible, conquer myself.

I went to our room,—Gertie's and my own,—and bathed my face and brushed my hair; but, for all I had made renewed resolutions for the future, I could not feel satisfied. I felt something more than this was required of me,—something that I would gladly have persuaded myself was not at all necessary. The future I had tried to prepare for; but what of the present? At last, after a severe struggle with myself, my resolution was taken, and then I began to feel easier. I put on a clean linen collar and apron, and went down-stairs. I saw through the open window, as I stepped a moment upon the veranda, that Ralph and Nettie and Gertie were grouped together near the mantel, talking eagerly about a picnic to come off in a few days. Miss Lane and Uncle Ralph were sitting near the window, talking; while mamma was showing Hal Ray a beautiful book of prints recently sent to her by Uncle Ben. I felt strongly tempted to fly back to my own room; and the tempter whispered, "That is a good excuse for not speaking now: wait and speak to Miss Lane in her own room." Then my better angel said, "No; you insulted her in the presence of others, let your apology be before them also;" and, I am glad to say, for once it triumphed, and I turned and walked resolutely into the room. I would much have preferred that Ralph and Hal should not have been there; but I did not mean to let their presence deter me from doing what I felt was right, whatever they might think of me for it. I expected Ralph would never have done teasing me for it; but I determined not to care. I crossed the room, half dizzy with excitement and embarrassment, to where Uncle Ralph and Miss Lane were sitting, and scarcely knew my own voice as I stammered out,—

"Miss Lane, I was both disrespectful and unjust to you this morning: I am sorry for it, and hope you will forgive me!"

I saw a look of such surprise and pleasure flush Uncle Ralph's face when I spoke, as fully repaid me for all I had suffered, and at the same moment heard Ralph say,—

"Why, the brave little sis! I didn't think it was in her!"

All this was so wholly unexpected to me, who had expected anything rather than commendation, that when Miss Lane rose, as she instantly did, and, putting her arm about me, said, very tenderly, "That I certainly will, dear Nannie, and hope you will think of it no more, as I certainly shall not," I laid my head upon her shoulder, and cried tears of happiness rather than sorrow.

When I looked up again, no one was in the room, besides Miss Lane and myself, but Uncle Ralph, and he stood with his back to us, at a distant window. I heard the others out on the lawn in front of the house, laughing and talking, and thanked them all sincerely in my heart for sparing me the embarrassment of their presence. Miss Lane kissed me as she said,—

"Never doubt me, Nannie: love me a little, if you can, and be sure that, next to your mother, I am your friend." She kissed me again, and whispered, "Now run and speak to Uncle Ralph, and I will brush my hair for dinner," and slipped out of the room.

I crossed the room timidly to where he was standing, and whispered, without looking up, "Have you forgiven me also?"

"Entirely, dear child," he said, smoothing my hair softly, as I leaned my head against his arm,—"entirely; and I am proud to see that this morning my little girl has gained a great victory over herself, and is truly 'greater than he that taketh a city.'"

"Oh, Uncle Ralph!"

"Yes, darling, you have acted nobly, and we all honor you for it. And I trust this morning's experience, bitter as it has been, will be a safeguard for the future, by warning you of the treacherous quicksands upon which you walk when you trust to impulse rather than reason."

Much more he said, in the few moments we stood there together, that I trust will help me in my endeavors for the future. Oh, if I only could be as good as he and dear mamma! Somehow, when I am with Uncle Ralph he compels me to do what is right, without ever saying a word to me. I told him so this morning; but he only laughed, and said that was an idea of my own,—that I could do right as easily away from him as with him; but I don't half believe it. Then mamma came to say dinner was waiting. We had been so busy talking that I had not noticed the bell; and she kissed me very tenderly, which meant more than many words. My talk with Uncle Ralph had made me myself again; and, somehow, they all were so kind that my embarrassment soon wore away, and the dinner passed much more pleasantly than I had feared. Hal and Nettie stayed; and after dinner we all went over into the beech-woods, and had a real royal time till sunset. Hal was with me nearly all afternoon, and was so gentle and kind. I knew he wanted me to know he thought I had done right. He is such pleasant company. We shall miss him sadly when he goes back to college.

Last Thursday our picnic came off, and such a pleasant day as we did have! Charlie, who has been in the country visiting with a friend for several weeks, came home the day before, which made us glad to start with. He is such a dear, good boy, and so quiet, too, one would never know he was about the house till he was stumbled upon, book in hand, in some out-of-the-way corner. I will except him from the generality of boys. He is no tease; he is so quiet mamma thinks he will be a minister; but he says himself he means to be a physician. He is two years younger than Ralph, and as unlike him as day is to night, both in appearance and disposition. He looks more like Kittie than any of the rest of us; he is a great student, and cares for little else, so that he has all the books he wants to read. But to return to our picnic.

Thursday morning rose bright and beautiful, and about nine o'clock we started to the Bluffs, which are distant about three miles. Uncle Ralph took mamma, whom we had finally persuaded to go, with Miss Lane and little Kittie, in his rockaway. Then Ralph and Charlie and Gertie and Ellis Ray (who is now visiting with Hal) and Sallie and Susie Reid from the village were stowed into the spring-wagon, together with sundry baskets of luncheon; and Nettie and Hal and I followed upon our ponies,—and such a merry party as we did make! We climbed the rocks and romped through the woods, seeking ferns and mosses and flowers, till we were tired; and then we had luncheon on the grass near a beautiful spring of water that trickles laughingly from the rocks. Mamma had provided a large tablecloth, and plenty of everything nice to eat, and I assure you we did full justice to the good fare. We did not reach home till nearly sundown. I had found seven different varieties of moss, and quite a quantity of beautiful ferns and flowers. Hal gave me what he had collected also, so that I was able to make quite an addition to my herbarium. Hal said it was, without doubt, the pleasantest day he ever spent, and I am sure I enjoyed it very much indeed.

July 31. To-day it rained so hard all day that we could not go to church; so, at mamma's suggestion, we all went into the library at ten o'clock, and Ralph read one of Mr. Wesley's sermons. When he was done, Miss Lane said she had been recently reading a very interesting sketch of his life, and if we would like, and Ralph was not too tired, she would get it for us. She did so, and Ralph read part of it; when, feeling a little weary, he gave the book to Miss Lane, and she herself finished it. She reads very sweetly indeed, and we all enjoyed it very much. What a good man Mr. Wesley was, and how much I should have enjoyed hearing him preach! Those were strange, troubled times in which he lived, and I sometimes wonder if people really felt as we feel now, they acted so differently. Mamma says grandpa has often heard Mr. Wesley speak; and she has heard him tell of the large crowds he would draw, and the breathless attention with which the people hung upon his words,—immense crowds coming across the fields at five o'clock in the morning, summer and winter, to listen to his teachings. After dinner we had some sacred music; and so the day we had feared would seem so long and dull has passed very rapidly and pleasantly. How much really depends upon ourselves whether or not our time is pleasantly and profitably spent! Some persons say that everything depends upon outward surroundings; but I believe the happiest person I ever knew was old Granny Grey, who lived near the river by Aunt Katie's. I always loved to visit her when I went to auntie's; for, although her little cabin was built of logs and had but one room, and very scantily furnished at that, she kept it scrupulously neat, and was always as cheerful and happy as though she had every wish of her heart. I asked her once if she never felt unhappy or lonely, and I shall never forget the story she then told me, or the look of submission and faith upon her face as she talked. I was so impressed with it that when I came home I wrote a little sketch, which I will copy here that I may preserve it,—not for its own merit, but in memory of dear old granny; for only a few weeks ago the angels called her, and I feel sad to think I shall never see her again.

OLD GRANNY GREY.

She sits in the sunlight, knitting;
  Her dress is faded and thin,
And a kerchief over her head is thrown
  And fasten'd under her chin.

Her face it is brown and wither'd;
  Her hair it is thin and gray;
And if roses ever were in her cheeks,
  They long have faded away.

Her hands are brown and harden'd,—
  They always were used to toil,—
But you need not fear their kindly touch
  Your daintiest robe would soil.

As she looks up from her knitting,
  Her eyes are faded and dim,
But they wear a meek and holy look,
  As she softly croons a hymn.

She lives in her little cottage,
  Adown by the river side,
So close you can always hear and see
  The rippling of the tide.

'Tis a tiny, moss-grown cottage,—
  One room comprises all,—
But the floor is white, and shining tins
  Look down from the snowy wall.

The grass and violets mingle
  Around the cottage door,
And roses cling to the lowly thatch,
  And clamber the casement o'er.

As I sit on the lowly doorstep
  And look in the kindly eyes,
I somehow think of the shadowy light
  When a summer evening dies.

And while she is slowly knitting,
  And the sun is sinking away,
I say, "Are you never lonely here,
  Dear Granny, Granny Grey?"

And the dim eyes smile so kindly,
    As she lays her knitting down,
And o'er her dress, so scant and thin,
    She folds her hands so brown.

And she says, " Dear little Nannie,
    I am never lonely now;
But there was a time, in the years agone,
    That I wept the long day through.

" I came to this little cottage
    A youthful and happy bride;
And my husband, a goodly man and true,
    Stood proudly by my side.

" And, one by one, three children
    God sent, as the years went by,
And I thought my happiness complete
    As I watch'd them sporting nigh.

" And they grew up fair and comely,—
    Two boys and a lovely girl,—
With laughing eyes, and hair that fell
    In many a sunny curl.

" And I thought that ne'er was mother
    So happy and blest as I.
It never enter'd my heart that God
    Could let my children die.

" One beautiful day in summer,
    Just thirty years ago,
My manly boys and their father went
    On the river here to row.

" And they were full of their frolic,
    As boys are wont to be,
And Jenny and I stood watching them
    And laughing at their glee.

" But in their frolic the boat upset.
    I saw them struggling,—and then—
The river is wide, and swift, and deep—
    They never came back again."

She stops in her simple story,
   And covers her face so brown
With her wither'd hands, while one by one
   The silent tears drop down.

A moment of silent weeping,
   In memory of her dead;
Then she resumes, in softer tone,
   The story's broken thread.

"Three sorrowful years I yielded—
   Forgetting all else beside—
To grief for my idols snatch'd away;
   Then Jenny grew sick, and died.

"And then I saw how sinful
   And selfish I had been,
And strove to take, with a cheerful heart,
   The burden of life again.

"And God helps my endeavors;
   For when I would sorrowful be,
His promises, full of love and hope,
   Seem spoken direct to me.

"And often here on the doorstep
   I sit, in the sunlight's glow,
And think of the shadowy river,
   With its ever solemn flow;

"For I know they all are waiting
   For me on the other shore;
And I know ere many years are fled
   I shall take the journey o'er.

"So I sit in quiet waiting,
   And never lonely am I,
For I know on their shadowy wings of light
   They are often hovering nigh."

She ceases. The sunset shadows
   Are lengthening over the lea;
And I think of the mystic river,
   And think of the "crystal sea."

> For the fading sunlight falleth
>   On the river's rippling flow,
> And I seem to hear, through the balmy air,
>   The murmur of voices low.
>
> And I say, "Good-night, dear granny;"
>   And, as she smiles on me,
> I think how like an angel's face
>   Dear Granny Grey's must be.
>
> And I know ere long the angels
>   Will breathe on the weary eyes,
> And fold the toil-worn hands, and bear
>   Her upward to the skies.
>
> And this simple, true inscription
>   Should be graven on her tomb,—
> "The angels found her waiting,
>   When they came to call her home."

I know this little poem is by no means perfect, either in rhyme or measure; but then, as Aunt Katie says, it was written by a little girl only fourteen years old, and you could not expect it to be anything very wonderful. In the future I hope to do better.

Aug. 1. "Oh, mamma! do see what Aunt Louise gave me," said little Kittie this morning, running into the drawing-room, half breathless with haste, her little white apron filled with beautiful flowers, and a tiny basket of most delicious peaches in her hand. She had just returned from Colonel Ray's, and, as usual, "Aunt Louise," as we all call Nettie's aunt, had given her all that she could carry home. She is quite a favorite there with all the household, and considers it a great privilege to be permitted to go over alone, as mamma occasionally allows her to do. "These are for you, mamma," she continued, setting the basket of fruit at mamma's feet and putting up her rosy lips for a kiss, "but these are all mine; Aunt Louise said so;" and she seated herself on the floor, and forthwith fell to weaving a garland of the beautiful buds and roses and jessamines and verbenas with which her lap was filled. A most lovely picture she made, too, as she sat there upon the soft carpet, her little dimpled arms and neck bare, her long sunny curls falling about her face and shoulders, as she bent over her task, and her little face aglow with pleasure; for she has a passionate fondness for flowers, as for all else beautiful.

"Aunt Louise is always very kind to my little girl," said mamma, caressingly.

"I believe she loves Kittie," she answered, with charming *naïveté*, "for she lets me do just as I please, always, when I am there."

"I don't think she is any exception in that respect," I said, laughingly.

Mamma shook her head warningly: she thinks Kittie is in sad danger of being spoiled by us all. I believe Kittie was too busy just at that moment to notice anything. Presently, however, she raised her head, and said, very earnestly,—stopping her work the while,—

"Oh, mamma, don't you think that John and Martha [the cook and coachman at Colonel Ray's] were real angry with each other, while I was there, and Martha threw a cup of water right in John's face, and then he was———"

"Stop a moment, Kittie," said mamma, breaking into her excited narrative, and holding up a warning finger. "Did Martha tell you to tell us this?"

"No, mammá," she answered, in surprise.

"Did John?"

"Why, no, ma'am" (still more surprised).

"Well, who did, then?"

"Why, no one, mamma. I only thought I would tell you about it; it was so ugly."

"Why should you tell me about it, Kittie?"

"Why, don't you want to know all about it, mamma?"

"Certainly not, darling. Mamma has no right to know what is passing in anybody's home but her own; nor has she any desire so to do. Mamma's duty is to keep her own little household straight, and allow every one else to do the same. When you are a little older, you will understand this better; now you must only remember that it is very wrong to repeat to another anything you see or hear that was not intended especially for yourself; and, above all, never speak of people's faults when you are away from them."

"Why not, mamma?"

"Suppose Nettie Ray had been here yesterday when you were naughty and cried because mamma refused to let you go to the meadow with Joseph when the shower was coming up. Would you have liked to have her go home and tell Aunt Louise and Colonel Ray how naughtily you had acted, in refusing to obey your mamma cheerfully?"

"Oh, no, indeed," she said, her sweet little face flushing, and her eyes half filled with tears.

"Well, little Kittie must learn to practice, as well as repeat, the golden rule."

"Oh, I know what that is, mamma! 'Do unto others as you would that they should do to you.' I learned that at Sunday-school."

"Well, dear, if you are unwilling to have others talk of your faults, you must be careful never to speak of theirs."

"Oh!" said Kittie, and relapsed at once into silence, and was soon again wholly engrossed in her flowers. Gertie and I had both been attentive listeners, and felt the lesson was not designed for Kittie alone. After a little, Gertie said,—

"Do you think I did wrong, mamma, in speaking of

Susie Lewis as I did, a little while ago? I am sure I did not mean any harm."

"That I can readily believe, Gertie," mamma answered; "but let us look at the possible results of your words, and then we can form a better idea of the right and wrong involved. Did you expect Susie would ever hear of your remark and profit by it?"

"Oh, no; of course I knew Nannie would never repeat it."

"Well, then, did you think Nannie needed the lesson herself, and hoped she would be benefited by the example?"

"Certainly not, mamma. You know Nannie is neatness itself" (a compliment for which I am entirely indebted to Gertie's blind partiality for her careless sister). "I do not really know why I spoke of it at all, only that Susie always looks so very untidy and careless, one cannot but notice the contrast between herself and others. Her collar is usually awry, her hair but half put up, her apron soiled and rumpled, and her whole appearance anything but neat."

"Neatness is surely a great virtue, but one that, under some circumstances, it is very difficult to practice. It seems, then, that it was only a little gossip you were treating Nannie to when you spoke of Susie's failings in that respect."

"I do not know what you would call it, mamma, only I am sure I cannot see what possible harm it could do," said Gertie, a little obstinately.

"Suppose Miss Lane, or any other stranger, had been present and heard your remarks, what impression would naturally have been received in regard to Susie?—favorable, or unfavorable?"

Gertie was silent, and mamma continued,—

"It is true you said nothing either harsh or untrue; still,

it was not calculated to impress a stranger greatly in Susie's favor. Is it not so?"

"I am afraid you are right, mamma," said Gertie, humbly; "but I really did not see it in that light before."

"We can never be too careful how we condemn others, even for trifling faults. Every life has its own peculiar trials, that often go a long way in extenuation of such failings. Even the capricious moods of our servants should be regarded with leniency, for they often have sorrows and trials that we know nothing of, and that, in their ignorance, are much harder for them to bear than they would be for us, whose minds should be better trained by education for endurance.

"And now, in regard to Susie's failing, which I agree with you is an unfortunate one in any young girl. Do you know anything of her home-life?"

"Only that her mother is an invalid."

"Yes, her mother is an invalid, and there are four children younger than herself, one of whom is very delicate and not yet two years old. They have a housekeeper; but the principal care of the children, and often of the mother, who is nervous and sometimes hard to please, falls upon Susie; and the poor girl has cares enough not only to make her appear careless in her attire but also care-worn in her face. Every morning she has the younger children to bathe and dress, for they are not very well able to have a nurse; and then the little one is rarely out of her arms when awake, so that it is not much to be wondered at that her collar is awry, her hair untidy, and her apron soiled and rumpled. Frequently she is called from the midst of her duties to go on some errand that her mother fancies no one but Susie can do, and hence her appearance on the street in that condition. Is not that some little excuse for the fault that seems so inexcusable?"

"Oh, mamma, how heartily ashamed I am of my thoughtless remarks! Had I known these facts, of course I should never have spoken as I did; but I thought it was only a careless habit into which she had fallen."

"Well, dear, it all helps you to see how careful we should be in our judgment of others. Could we look into the secret lives of every one, I doubt not we should almost always find something that would teach us to judge more kindly of them. But even were it not so, it ill becomes weak, erring mortals like ourselves to sit in judgment on the lives of those with whom we are surrounded. Our hands, hearts, and heads can always be employed in more useful as well as more pleasant work; and when we look into our own lives we will find we have ample work to do in order to make ourselves acceptable in the sight of God, and will have little time or inclination to search out the faults of others."

Here mamma left us to our own reflections, which I trust will benefit us for the future; for, without the least idea of doing wrong, we are so apt to criticise and condemn that which we do not like in others, without reflecting that this very habit is tenfold worse, ofttimes, than the fault we are condemning.

> "Oh, wad some power the giftie gie us
> To see oursels as others see us,"

I quoted, as, twining my arm about Gertie, I gently drew her from her work for a stroll in the garden, to which she responded, with a sigh and a wise shake of her head,—

"Ah, Nannie, how could we ever bear the mortification such a knowledge would produce?"

True for her,—how could we?

Aug. 2. When I came into the drawing-room this morning, a little while after breakfast, I found Uncle Ralph there with Kittie snugly quartered on his knee, and both evidently greatly interested in some proposition afoot between them. When I entered, Uncle Ralph said,—

"Here, Nannie, will you dress this little puss up her very prettiest? I have promised to take her to ride with me, and, as I shall probably meet some friends, I want her to look her best," pulling at Kittie's rosy little ear.

Kittie looked very wise, but said nothing; so I took her up to mamma's room and bathed her, dressed her in her new white India muslin that Aunt Katie sent to her, and that mamma only finished last week, looping up the sleeves over her white, dimpled shoulders with broad blue ribbons, tying her scarf to match about her waist, and dressing her dear little fat feet in her blue ankle-ties. Then, with her long, light curls newly brushed flying about her shoulders, she did look as pure and sweet as a little angel.

"You precious little darling," I said, as I kissed her again and again, "you look as though you were all ready to fly, if you only had the wings."

"I shall have those some day, sister, sha'n't I?"

"Not very soon, I hope, darling," I said, with a sudden pang at my heart at the thought of losing her. "Are you going to tell me where you and Uncle Ralph are going, or is it a great secret?"

"Oh, a very great secret!" she said, shaking her little head very wisely. "I should like to tell you very much; but do you think Uncle Ralph would care?"

"Certainly he would, dear, if you promised him not to tell," I said; for I could not take advantage of her sweet innocence, though I must confess to a little curiosity on the subject.

"Well, I mean to ask him to let me tell you," she said, as she threw her arms around my neck and hugged and kissed me impulsively; then she bounded away to find Uncle

Ralph. I followed with her hat,—a beautiful little white crape one, relieved with delicate blue trimmings,—and, as I set it upon her head and fastened the dainty tie under her rosy chin, Uncle Ralph said, admiringly,—

"Well, Nannie, you certainly have outdone yourself: she is perfect! Come, Pussy, it is time we were off."

So, with many kisses from us all, she was lifted into the rockaway, and drove off in high glee with Uncle Ralph, calling back to me, as they started, "I'll ask him, Nannie, if I may tell you."

Precious little blossom! she is truly the sunlight of our home, and has always been. Every one pets Kittie the more because the dear child never saw our father. He was drowned, while out boating, nearly three months before she was born. I don't know what would have become of mamma without her. Uncle Ralph and she returned about five o'clock; and she had many and wonderful things to relate. She had her little lap full of toys that different persons had given her,—Uncle Ralph himself having bought her a fine large picture-book. He says she ruled the day every place they went. I don't doubt it; she always wins hosts of friends. She slipped up to me soon after their return, and whispered, "Uncle Ralph says I must not tell you yet. He wants to see if I can keep a secret; but after awhile he will let me tell you everything."

"Well, dear," I said, "that will do nicely." And away she flew to find Ralph, who is her prime favorite, and soon returned, riding in triumph upon his shoulder.

"Oh, Kittie," mamma said, "you are getting too large now for that!" But Ralph pleaded,—

"Now, mamma, don't try to make her think she is not a baby! What will we all do if our kitten becomes a prim young lady?"

Everybody laughed, and Kittie kept her seat; and I saw

her little white arms clasp Ralph's neck—in gratitude, I suppose, for his defense—till his face grew quite purple. But he would think it all right were he unable to breathe, just so it was Miss Kittie's doings.

She is now asleep, her little arms thrown over her head, and her precious face flushed and happy even in her dreams. Some one has beautifully said, "Heaven lies about us in our childhood;" and I believe it is most emphatically the case with Kittie, for she is always happy. I shall never forget her coming in from the garden, where she had been playing, one day when she was about three years old, and telling mamma, her eyes wide open with astonishment and pleasure, that there was an angel in the garden; she had seen it fly down out of heaven; and it kept telling her something, but she could not understand what it was. We all went into the garden to solve the mystery, and there, in a tree, sat old Captain Wood's white parrot, chattering and talking at a great rate. Kittie insisted that it flew down out of the sky; and we had hard work to convince her it was only a bird. She looked terribly disappointed; said she thought that "maybe it was one of Dod's angels, come to tell her she might go up into the sky."

Ralph will never let her forget it. He calls every white bird he sees—(even to a white goose, I believe)—"one of Kittie's angels."

Aug. 5. We had a terrible hailstorm to-day,—the hardest, I think, I have ever seen. The wind blew a perfect gale, and the lightning was dreadful. We all went into the library, and mamma had the lamps lit; for we were obliged to close all of the shutters, the hail was so large and was blown with such violence against the windows. Many of the window-lights were broken before we could get the shutters closed. I was terribly frightened, and sat upon a little stool by mamma, with my face buried in her lap to hide the vivid flashes of lightning.) Ralph sat next to mamma, with Kittie in his arms; and Gertie and Charlie were upon the sofa with Miss Lane. All the servants came into the room also. Every one seemed awe-struck, the storm was so terrific. It lasted about half an hour; and one clap of thunder, more dreadful than any of the preceding, and coming almost at the same instant with a very vivid flash of lightning, caused several to spring to their feet. I was sure the house was struck. I clung in perfect agony to mamma; but she, though very pale, was perfectly calm. She said to me once, in the midst of my fear, "Remember, dear, who rules the storm and the tempest: we are in his hands."

At length it passed; and, on opening the doors and windows, what a scene of destruction met our eyes! All of our beautiful flowers beaten to the ground, many of them hopelessly broken, and a beautiful great apple-tree, full of fine fruit, was cleft from top to bottom,—doubtless by the bolt that alarmed us all so much. It did not stand more than fifty paces from the house. The hail was blown in great drifts about the doors and pavements; and we picked some from the ground as large as a hen's egg. Joseph, the groom, gathered up a large pailful, and they actually froze some most delicious ice-cream with it. I told Ralph I thought that was bringing the "farce" rather close upon the "tragedy." He said that once during the storm little Kittie crept up close to his ear and whispered, "Brother Ralph, is God angry, that he makes it thunder so loud?" And when he told her, "No; that it was the intense heat that caused it all," she seemed perfectly satisfied, and said, "Well, he'll take care of us, then, I know. I was afraid he was angry because we were not good enough." Oh for the beautiful faith of childhood! Why do I say "childhood"? My mother has the same faith; our Uncle Ralph has it likewise: oh that I might add the same of myself!

Aug. 8. Gertie and I have been taking German lessons of Prof. Murch, this summer. He comes out from the village three times a week to hear us recite. He has been quite sick for a week past, and Uncle Ralph has kindly heard our lessons himself, rather than have us miss them. To-day Gertie had a very bad headache, so I had to recite alone. After the regular lesson, Uncle Ralph read and translated for me some very beautiful passages from Goethe, some lines of which reminded me of my old wonder in regard to himself, and on the spur of the moment, with my usual impetuosity, I said, looking up suddenly,—

"Uncle Ralph, why have you never married?"

He did not answer me, as I had expected he would, in his usual light manner, but looked greatly surprised, and after a moment asked me, quietly,—

"Why do you ask the question, Nannie?"

"Simply because it has always, or rather of late, been a matter of wonderment to me. I know it is your own fault, for the young ladies are all half in love with you; and——"

"Nannie, Nannie!" he said, reprovingly, "do not speak lightly of these matters, child: they are beyond your comprehension." He looked at me searchingly a moment, and then rose and walked rapidly backward and forward, for several minutes, across the floor. I was beginning to fear I had done very wrong, never in my life having seen him so agitated before; when he resumed his seat in the easy-chair beside me, and, laying his hand, with his old caressing movement, upon my head, as I sat upon a low ottoman near him, said, half sadly,—

"Do you think, Nannie, that you are old enough to listen to a sad story, and keep it?"

"I am sure I am, Uncle Ralph; but do not tell it to me if it will pain you. I was thoughtless to speak as I did just now."

"No, dear; it was a very natural question; and the story you would doubtless one day hear,—perhaps as well now as at any other time."

He sat a moment thoughtfully, and then said, leaning forward with his elbows upon his knees, as though reading from the carpet beneath his feet,—

"Several years ago, when you were quite a little girl, Nannie, not more than four or five years old, and I myself was only about twenty-two, I met a beautiful young girl, who was a general favorite with every one, and whom I soon learned to greatly admire. I say she was beautiful; but her beauty consisted more in a rare combination of mental and moral qualities, than in perfect symmetry of form or features, although she was far from being deficient in either. She was very frail, and seemed scarcely more than a child in her simplicity, though she was really but three years younger than myself. Very slight in figure, although enjoying, in general, good health, she seemed too spiritual for earth. She was purity itself; and no one could look upon her sweet, childlike face without feeling an intense yearning in the heart toward her: at least I could not. It chanced that we were both invited, together with one or two other friends, among whom was your mother, Nannie, to spend several weeks at the house of a friend, a few miles from our home. It was in summer, and, as we were then living in the city, it was a very pleasant change. Thrown constantly into her society, my admiration soon warmed into the most intense love. She was never absent from my thoughts at any time, and when out of her presence for a few hours I was restless and uneasy until I had found her again. In spite of my love, I had carefully avoided manifesting any unusual preference for her society, lest I should startle her into avoiding me through delicacy of feeling. I had no evidence that my society was more to her than that of her other friends; although I had sometimes fancied that I detected a slight tremor in her voice when I unexpectedly addressed her, or a faint flush more than usual on her cheek when I approached her, especially if we chanced to be alone. But it was too indefinite for me to build much hope upon, and I determined to be patient and bide my time, for we were both still quite young, and I wanted to be sure I had reason to think she preferred me, before I incurred the risk of startling her by an avowal of my own strong attachment. How long things might have continued in this state, I am unable to say. We lay our plans with wise forethought, as we proudly think; but when we have, in our simple judgment, fully matured them, Omnipotent Power perfects or annihilates them by a single breath. So it was in this instance."

He stopped a moment in thoughtful silence, and a look of intense suffering passed over his face. I scarcely knew what to say, the silence continuing some minutes; but, softly stroking one of his hands as it lay upon his knee, I said, softly,—

"What was her name, Uncle Ralph?"

"The sweetest of all sweet names,—Caryl Carrington. It was drawing near the close of our visit, when I was, late one night, awakened from sleep by a feeling of suffocation. I sprang instantly from my bed, with a strange presentiment of coming danger, to find my room full of smoke; and, hurriedly drawing on part of my clothing, I ran into the hall into which my room opened, to find it dense with smoke, and to hear the unmistakable sound of burning timbers. The house was on fire, I knew instantly, and also that no time was to be lost, as it had evidently taken fire below, and the sleeping-apartments were all above-stairs. To arouse the family, and bid them flee for their lives, was the work of a moment.

"'Go quickly,' I said to Mrs. Blair, our hostess, who had started to Caryl's room, 'go quickly down-stairs; I will save Caryl;' and I flew to her room, which was in a distant corridor; your mother, who roomed with Caryl, was spending the night with a neighboring friend, and I knew she was alone. There was no time for ceremony, and, hastily throwing open her door, I rushed in, catching up a large blanket-shawl that lay upon a chair near the bed. She seemed to have been awake, but unconscious of danger; and when I entered, she rose in bed with a look of alarm upon her sweet face that I shall never forget.

"'Darling, the house is on fire! Will you trust yourself to me?' I cried,—all the tenderness in my heart for her forcing itself into my voice and manner in that hour of peril. She did not speak a word, but, stepping instantly from her low bed, turned to me with such a look of love and trust upon her face that I thanked God in my heart for the danger which had shown me thus her heart. I instantly enveloped the little white-robed figure in the large shawl, and, gathering her in my arms, ran with all haste back through the long corridor to the stairs near my own room. I noticed the rooms were all deserted as I passed, and felt thankful the family had escaped. We reached the stairs, but only to find them wholly enveloped in smoke and flames, through which I felt it would be worse than madness to strive to pass. The back stairway was our only hope. I darted into a side hall, and flew, rather than walked, with my precious, trembling burden pressed close to my throbbing heart. She had not once spoken, nor in any way impeded my progress or thoughts; and now, as the fear of a terrible fate forced itself upon me, I said, with a convulsive tightening of my arms about her, 'I will save you, my darling, or perish with you in the flames.' She still made no reply; but an instant after I felt the dear head move upon my shoulder, and the warm, fluttering lips were timidly pressed against my neck, sending a thrill through me that for an instant almost unmanned me. There was no need of words, had we even had the opportunity; the flimsy veil was torn aside, and each had read clearly the heart of the other. The stairway was reached; but, alas, was little better than the other. True, there was not quite so much flame, but the smoke was terrific. I felt it was our last hope, for before we could reach a window now it would be too late. I knew the floor must soon give way. There was one instant of irresolution as we looked at the perilous way; then I said, hastily, 'Shall we go?'

"'Yes,' was her reply. And we each read in the eyes of the other the belief that it would be useless,—that we could not escape; and with the thought our souls clung tenderly to each other, and our lips met in such a kiss as those who love passionately and know they are about to lose their idol alone can understand. Then I rushed down the burning stairs into the smoke and flame. When midway on the stairs, I felt them giving way beneath my feet, and sprang with my now helpless burden to the floor, that I could dimly see was not yet burned. As I did so I heard a crash behind me, and knew the stairs had fallen. Of all that afterward passed I have no recollection, the smoke so strangled and confused me. I must have sought blindly several seconds for the doorway, for they saw me from outside stagger to the entrance with Caryl still in my arms and sink down helpless beside it. They dragged us out, and after several hours' work finally brought me to consciousness; but my beautiful Caryl was dead, strangled by the smoke in my arms."

Poor Uncle Ralph's voice here became so husky that he buried his face in his hands and sat silent for several minutes. I had been quietly crying for some time, and felt that words could yield no comfort amid such tender memories. At last he raised his head, and said, with something of his old manner,—

"It is years since I have spoken of this before. Your question startled it all back into life again, and I felt that it would be a relief to tell it you. I do not say that I can never love again or that I will never marry; that is all hidden in the future. The past is now to me more like the memory of a painfully-beautiful dream than a reality; but it has left its influence upon my life. I could not yield to an unholy impulse or commit wilfully an unmanly act with the memory of her pure love hallowing my heart; nor could I admit to my heart and place side by side with her own the image of one in any way unworthy her companionship. This, doubtless, is one reason why I have never felt any disposition to marry. I could not marry one that I could not help contrasting unfavorably with the pure being who first taught me the sacredness of love. But how I am talking to you, Nannie! I forget you are only a child and cannot yet appreciate half of what I have said."

"Oh, Uncle Ralph, I do, I do!" I cried, earnestly. "How I wish I might become as pure and good as Caryl Carrington!"

"That you may, my dear child," he said, warmly.

"Oh, no, Uncle Ralph, never, never! Do you know I am really afraid I shall never be anything but the impulsive mad-cap I have always been? What shall I do with this hot temper and ungovernable tongue? Tell me, dear Uncle Ralph," I said, half tearfully, for my heart was full, not only from the recital of his story, but through the vivid contrast it presented to my own imperfect nature.

"'He that ruleth his own spirit is greater than he that taketh a city.' Remember, darling, it can be done," he said, as, rising, he dropped a light kiss upon my upturned forehead, like a benediction, and passed from the room. And a few moments afterward I heard the clatter of his horse's feet as he passed from the yard. Dear Uncle Ralph! how sad that he of all others should have such an experience! Why it is, God knows,—shall we ever?

Aug. 9. This morning at breakfast mamma said, "I have had a letter this morning from Aunt Martha Mossburn, saying she will spend part of the summer and fall with us, if convenient to us. What shall I say to her?"

"Capital!" said Ralph. And the rest were silent,—Miss Lane, of course, because she does not know her; and Gertie and I, because we always feel under so much restraint in her presence that I fear we are a little selfish when a long visit is spoken of from her. Charlie rarely offers an opinion. Mamma, I thought, looked a little pained at our silence; so I must needs come to the rescue in my usual abrupt style.

"Why, mamma, of course we will all be glad to have her come; only I do hope she won't take Gertie and me to task for every act of our lives, as she always does. I scarcely knew whether I dared call my head my own, or not, by the time she went away last. She did even take me to task for not cutting my hair off short like Gertie's; and I expect this time she'll want to put me back into pinafores and pantalettes."

"Oh, Nannie, Nannie!" said poor mamma; and I, conscience-stricken, persisted:

"Now, mamma, you know she even finds fault with you,—with *you*,—to say nothing of all the rest of us; ending with poor me,—whom she rarely lets see a peaceful hour!"

"Well, dear," said mamma, very softly, "we doubtless all need a little fault-finding occasionally, to keep us from having too high an opinion of our own perfections. And

I trust we will all make Aunt Martha's visit a very pleasant one to her, whatever it may be to us. Remember, she is old, and be very patient with her, for she is a good woman at heart, and means well."

"Oh, yes, mamma!" we all promised; and so it is settled Aunt Martha is to come. She is, as mamma says, a good woman, but a little old-fashioned, and thinks no one knows anything half so well as she does; and it always annoys me to hear her find fault with mamma,—(dear, patient, perfect mamma). She was Grandfather's Clifford's half-sister, so is really but little kin to us, though she visits us every year or two. Her husband died nearly forty years ago, but she speaks of him still very often. And now, Nannie Cleve, here is going to be a test—a grand test—for your patience; and I beg that you may profit by it, and keep that unruly little tongue of yours in due subjection. Remember, there is no glory in a victory where there has been no contest. Remember Uncle Ralph's proverb, and be the victor here. I will! I will!

Aug. 20. To-day was mamma's birthday; and we had each some nice little present prepared for her, as we always have on these blessed anniversaries, and were anticipating a pleasant day. Uncle Ralph came out to breakfast with us; and the day has indeed been one of unmitigated pleasure. Little Kittie awakened me, at a very early hour, with kisses and caresses, and a little pleading voice, saying, "Please waken, sister Nannie, and dress me."

"Well, Kittie, I am awake now," I said; "but what is the hurry? It is very early yet."

"Yes, I know, sister; but this is mamma's birthday, you know, and I heard Uncle Ralph come long ago; and —and—I do so want to see what he has brought mamma," with a comical look in her blue eyes.

"Oh, you funny little puss!" I said, as I drew the dainty

little night-gowned thing up into my arms, "maybe he has brought her nothing."

"Oh, yes! he has brought her something, I know,—at least I think so; because he always does, you know," with a wise little shake of her head. "Do please dress me, and let me go see. Uncle Ralph said you were to dress me to-day, just as you did the day I went to ride with him, first."

"Uncle Ralph, indeed! What does he know about dressing babies, I'd like to know? Put on your new India muslin before breakfast? What would mamma say?" And I laughed at the idea. "Your little pink shambra and white apron will be much more suitable, dear."

"Oh, no, no!" said Kittie, very earnestly. "Uncle Ralph said I must have on my white dress and blue ribbons. Only dress me, sister, and let me run down to him, and soon as you come down you may take my dress off again. Only I must have it on a little while, because you know—you know—well—Uncle Ralph said so!" And she stood with flushed cheeks and sparkling eyes before me.

"Well, I suppose Uncle Ralph's word is law. I see plainly there is another secret on hand, and I shall have to submit," I said, as I arrayed the little gipsy in the fancied dress; "but mind, if mamma scolds, you and Uncle Ralph are to take all of the blame!"

"We will! we will! (but mamma never scolds) Nannie."

"True for you, darling," I said, as I tied the last bow, and sent her away with a kiss.

A little while afterward, I went and found mamma, to give her my good-morning kiss and fasten her collar with the delicate little brooch I had purchased with my own spending-money. She was just starting to the library, whither she had been summoned, and where we found all the others waiting at the door with their congratulation and tiny love-offerings; all but Kittie. And, as we entered the room, there she sat, all curled up in a great easy-chair, with her tiny white kitten, Daisy, in her lap, and her little, sunny, ringleted head thrown a little to one side, and her great laughing blue eyes dancing with joy.

"Why, Kittie!" mamma began,—but stopped short in bewildering astonishment; for there, side by side with the original, sat another Kittie, encircled by a heavy gilt frame, so exactly the counterpart of the former it seemed almost impossible to tell the real from the ideal. The artist had indeed delineated faithfully his living subject. The same sunny head; the same clear, laughing eyes; the same dimpled shoulders; and the same rosy, saucy mouth, just ready to open with some pretty speech; even to the little white kitten in her lap, with its sleepy eyes half shut in infinite enjoyment of the present. Mamma stood a moment motionless, then gathered Kittie to her full heart in a silent embrace, and, after a little, turned to Uncle Ralph, with her sweet face all a-quiver, and her voice full of unshed tears, and said,—

"Oh, Ralph! I know to whom I am indebted for this great happiness. Rarest of friends,—best of brothers,—how can I ever repay you for your loving care?" And she fairly broke down, and leaned her head upon Uncle Ralph's shoulder, and took a quiet little cry, as he, with his arm about her, said,—

"I am repaid a thousandfold, dear Fannie, if it has brought you a moment's added happiness."

All of our hearts and eyes were full in sympathy with dear mamma, and I do not know but that there would have been a general break-down, had not Kittie at this moment slipped from her chair, with a puzzled look upon her face, and, stealing up to Ralph, said, in what was evidently intended for a whisper, but was heard all over the room, "Brother Ralph, what makes mamma cry? You said she would be so glad she would dance for joy!" This brought a smile to all faces, and restored our equilibrium, (as Ralph would say) and for the next half-hour Miss Kittie queened it most royally, to the evident satisfaction of herself and all concerned.

"So this is Kittie's and Uncle Ralph's grand secret," I said, "and accounts for the frequency of Kittie's long rides of late. Well, you can keep a secret, Pussy, and well too."

"Indeed she can," said Uncle Ralph; "and I shall know to whom to go with mine hereafter." Kittie looked justly pleased; for she has been a very paragon of secrecy through all these weeks.

"Well," said Ralph, "there is one question still I should like to have answered, before I eat my breakfast, lest my curiosity should overcome my appetite,— which would be deplorable, in view of the nice fried chicken and hot muffins I saw Milly preparing as I passed through the kitchen a few moments ago. There goes the breakfast-bell now! Quick, quick, tell me! how came Mr. Van Resslinger to paint Daisy-kitten so accurately without ever having seen her? The likeness is perfect. I even fancy I see, as well as hear, the musical 'purr' with which she expresses her infinite satisfaction at, and just appreciation of, the course events have taken!"

"Oh, Ralph, you are perfectly incorrigible!" said Miss Lane; but Kittie, more accustomed to his moods, answered, very demurely,—

"Oh, but he did see her, brother Ralph. She always went to town with us, under the seat of the rockaway!" This raised another shout of merriment, as Miss Kittie was swung aloft to her usual seat of honor, upon Ralph's shoulder, and headed the procession to the breakfast-room.

"I think Kittie has monopolized mamma's honors to-day," whispered Gertie.

"Yes," said Charlie, "and I think, from mamma's happy face, that she is very well satisfied it should be so." And then, in the enjoyment of the nice muffins and coffee, we relapsed into comparative quiet; and so mamma's birthday was ushered in. Oh that we may all assist in celebrating many such another!

Aug. 23. Aunt Martha came yesterday; and, as usual (after one of my hasty speeches,) I feel a little twinge of conscience whenever I look at her, as she sits so quietly knitting by the drawing-room window. She brought a pair of socks apiece to each of the boys, also to Uncle Ralph, and is now very busy knitting dainty little soft ones, of bright-colored wool, for Kittie's wear next winter. So far everything has passed very pleasantly and quietly; for I expect we are all unusually watchful to avoid annoyance. The only thing was, last evening, when she saw, through the open door, Kittie riding through the hall on Ralph's shoulder, she looked very gravely over the top of her spectacles, and said to mamma,—

"Frances, don't you think Catherine is getting quite too large to be lifted about like that upon the gentlemen's shoulders?"

"No one does it but Ralph, Aunt Martha," said mamma, pleasantly; "but she is getting rather large, I tell her, to be so much of a baby. But the children all seem afraid, I believe, that she will get beyond being their plaything, and so they encourage her in her baby ways. And Ralph is worse than any of them about it."

"Well, well," said Aunt Martha, "maybe they are right, after all. She will be a woman soon enough, anyway; but I wouldn't much encourage her climbing on to Ralph's shoulder that way, anyhow."

Mamma wisely changed the conversation, and Kittie still rules. Aunt Martha seems much gentler than she ever did before: her visit may be one of pleasure, after all. Can it be that my own resolution to be more gentle and forbearing myself could make me think that she is so? It may be so: who knows?

Aug. 24. We are all very busy these days getting Ralph and Charlie ready for college again. Their vacation began a month earlier than usual this year, on account of the smallpox being so bad in the neighborhood that mamma could not rest till their return. How lonely we shall all be without them! They both graduate a year from next June, and then we shall be so happy to have them home for good. How thankful I am that dear mamma prefers having Gertie and me educated at home! I could not bear this constant absence from her. The boys have only a few days more now to remain at home with us. Hal Ray goes at the same time. One blessing is, they are not so far but that we can see them for a day or two every little while. I promised mamma to help her pack the trunks; so my entry is brief.

Aug. 25. "Frances," said Aunt Martha to mamma this morning, "I think you do very wrong to allow those girls, Nancy and Gertrude, so much time for play. I notice them both spend two or three hours every day at the piano, singing and drumming, and running their fingers from one end of the keys to the other. They could have knit themselves each a pair of stockings apiece, since I have been here, just in the time they have spent in that way." My face flushed indignantly, and I whirled round on the piano-stool with an angry retort on my tongue, but met dear mamma's eyes fixed on me with such a pleading look that I "bottled my wrath," as Ralph would say, and resumed my practicing; while mamma replied, very quietly,—

"That is part of their studies, you know, Aunt Martha. They are required to spend at least three hours every day in practicing their lessons."

"Nonsense! They had much better be knitting stockings to keep their feet warm next winter. Music is a very good thing to dance by, in pleasant weather; but it will not warm and clothe one."

"I can buy them stockings and clothes, you know; but knowledge they must themselves acquire; and if the golden opportunity is lost in youth it is seldom, if ever, regained. Then, too, you remember, Aunt Martha, if they were ever compelled to support themselves in the future, they could do it much more easily by teaching music than by knitting stockings; though each, I confess, it is well to understand at the proper time. But it is useless to begin anything without endeavoring to become proficient in it,—from knitting a stocking to playing a piano. A superficial knowledge on any subject is almost worse than none at all, simply because one is apt to have wrong views on any subject that one does not perfectly understand, and consequently spoils many a nice thing through ignorance, as Nannie would inevitably do at present with Handel's oratorio, or with Kittie's little soft stocking, growing so steadily beneath your skillful fingers,—skillful, Aunt Martha, through long and patient practice with your needles. Hence I require the girls to practice patiently and persistently at their music; and so I shall also do when they learn to knit, as I mean to have them both some day."

"Well, well, I suppose you are right, Frances. I must say that you generally are, though at first it does seem you are altogether in the wrong."

How mamma's pleasant ways and gentle words do subdue every one! although she seldom yields a point she believes to be right. But she never storms, never scolds, never says impatient or hasty words for which she has afterward to "repent in sackcloth and ashes," but presents the matter in such a gentle, dispassionate manner in its true light, that before you have the least thought of being convinced, you see that she is right. Now, I should have stormed right out at Aunt Martha,—something, no doubt, very naughty,—have been called "an impertinent chit" for my pains, and very likely have gone to bed in disgrace. Why cannot I profit by this daily example of beautiful patience before me so constantly? I felt this all so forcibly, that my own ugly feelings were conquered; and rising from the piano, and sitting down on a little ottoman at Aunt Martha's feet, I said, very humbly,—

"I would so love to knit as beautifully as you do, Aunt Martha; and if mamma will let me learn, I will get you to teach me this very day, and will promise not to let it interfere with my studies, but knit when I have no other duties to perform. May I learn, mamma?"

"I certainly have no objection, Nannie, provided you do not undertake more than you can accomplish. If one undertakes too many duties at once, one is apt to neglect some of them."

. "Well, I will get up an hour earlier every morning and study; and that will give me an added one of leisure during the day, in which to knit."

. "That will do," said mamma. "But, remember, whatever you begin you must not abandon until perfected. If you desire to learn to knit, you must consider it one of your duties, and persevere faithfully until you understand it well. It is bad policy for young people to begin a thing to-day with great enthusiasm, and weary of it to-morrow, throwing it aside, all incomplete, for the purpose of taking up something else, which would be perhaps as soon abandoned for some other thing again. It teaches vacillation, which should never be encouraged in the young."

"Is that the reason, mamma, that you never would permit Gertie or me to begin a new dress for our dolls, when we were little girls, till we had finished the one we were already making?"

"I suppose so, dear."

"Well, I will promise not to abandon the knitting till I have completed a pair of stockings for Kittie, at any rate, that Aunt Martha's critical eyes will pronounce wearable."

"On those conditions you may learn."

"And now, will you really teach me, Aunt Martha?"

"Certainly, my dear. I am glad you are anxious to learn to be useful as well as accomplished,"—a sly thrust I did not think it best to notice. So to-morrow morning I am to take my first lesson in knitting, and feel that to-day I did much better than to have quarreled with Aunt Martha.

Aug. 26. In thinking over the conversation of yesterday, I cannot but notice how mamma and Uncle Ralph both give practical illustrations of a principle they wish to inculcate, instead of trusting to precept alone. I see now clearly why mamma was always so firm about our never beginning any new piece of work while another, still incomplete, was on hand. I remember so well how she nearly broke Gertie's heart once by taking a new doll-dress she had begun to make, and putting it away out of sight until she had completed a little bonnet she had begun the day before. Uncle Ralph always does the same way. I well remember the course he once took to break Ralph and me of our careless habits. Several years ago, he gave Ralph a beautiful little chest of carpenter's tools,—everything complete in its way, saws, hammers, gimlets, chisels, etc. etc.,—and had Joseph clear a space in one end of the farm workshop for his especial use. Here Ralph, delighted, spent several hours every day, fashioning little sleds and wagons and wheelbarrows for himself and Charlie, and innumerable bureaus and wash-stands and bedsteads for Gertie's and my own play-house. One evening he took Uncle Ralph out, after tea, to show him a wonderful little wardrobe he had made that day; and Uncle Ralph was unsparing of the praise bestowed upon his skill as a workman; but more than once I saw his eyes rest on the almost empty tool-chest,—for Ralph had a very careless habit of leaving his tools wherever he last chanced to use them,—and noticed him two or three times pick up little articles from the floor. The next day, when Ralph went to work at his bench, first his saw, then his hammer, and finally his rule and best chisel, were missing, and he was compelled to abandon work.

"What can have become of them?" he said to me, in his perplexity.

"Perhaps Uncle Ralph knows," I suggested.

"Pshaw! He wasn't in there but a minute, and never touched a thing."

It was several days before Uncle Ralph came again, and still the tools were lost, and the wardrobe of course remained incomplete. After tea he made some excuse to go to the workshop, and we children, always at his heels, of course accompanied him.

"Why, Ralph, how is this? your wardrobe still unfinished? Not tired of work, I hope?"

"Oh, no," said poor Ralph; "but I have lost some of my tools, and I cannot finish it till I find them."

"Lost some of your tools? How does that happen? Ah, I see!" glancing first at the empty tool-chest, and then searchingly around the room to where in different places lay chisels, augers, planes, and nails, just as it chanced to be; some half hidden under a pile of shavings, and others conspicuous amid chips and blocks and sawdust they had helped to create. "I see with regret that my boy lacks one of the most essential traits of a good workman, and one without which it is utterly impossible ever to become a perfectly successful man."

"Why, Uncle Ralph! I thought you told me I used my tools so well!"

"And so you do, my boy; but the most skillful workman that ever lived will never make a successful business man so long as he lacks order and system. You may set it down as an inevitable fact that the workman who allows his tools to lie scattered carelessly around after the work of the day is over, instead of carefully replacing them in his tool-chest, will live and die a poor man. Not only will he lose time in searching for them when needed, that would have made him many a dollar, but he is forming habits that will destroy his usefulness for life. System and order are the foundations of success. These little things may seem but trifles to you, Ralph; but believe me, trifles are the lower rounds in the ladder to honor and wealth, and you cannot climb to the top unless you begin at the very bottom."

Ralph's face had first paled, and then flushed scarlet, as Uncle Ralph proceeded, and he now began to carefully search for, and gather together, his different tools, and place them in his chest; and when he had found all but the missing ones, he stepped up bravely to Uncle Ralph, and, looking into his face, said, earnestly,—

"Uncle Ralph, I intend to try to make a successful man."

"Bravo, Ralph! Then you will be sure to be one, for few try earnestly and persistently who fail. Now let us look for these missing tools, and then I think I must tell you a little incident, that once came under my own knowledge, to show the importance of trifles."

He stepped to a drawer in one end of the large work-bench, and opened it, and there lay all of the lost tools so long and earnestly sought for.

"I remember," said Ralph, "the drawer stood open the last day I was working, and I must have laid them in it myself and then forgot all about it."

"Yes," said Uncle Ralph; "you laid them in it, and I, seeing your careless habits, shut the drawer, hoping thereby to teach you a lesson."

"And one I shall not soon forget, I am sure," said Ralph.

"Nor I!" I echoed. Gertie and Charlie said nothing, for they are both as particular as old maids, anyhow. Gertie used always to be talking to me about hanging up my clothes and keeping my work-basket in order.

"And now for the story, Uncle Ralph," said Charlie.

"Well, there were once two men who worked together in the same shop, both steady and industrious workmen, although very unlike each other in disposition. One was full of life and fun,—a great favorite with his fellows,—but unfortunately very careless in his habits, always losing and mislaying his tools and having to borrow from his neighbors; the other full of good humor also, but very orderly and systematic in all he did. Their work-benches were adjoining, and they were fast friends always, Dick, the thoughtful one, often talking to his friend Joe, and trying to get him to throw aside his careless ways, which he well knew would keep him back in life, in spite of his skill, for he was the best workman in the shop. Joe always laughed good-naturedly, and said he meant to become very systematic some day, but that these things were so trifling that he could not take time to attend to them now.

"'Why, Dick,' he would laughingly say, 'I get home and have a good refreshing bath by the time you have your tools gathered away and your bench in order for the night.'

"'Yes,' Dick would respond; 'and in the morning your bench is full of chips and shavings, and half of your tools mislaid, and I have had a good half-hour's work before you are ready to begin.'

"Well, one day the proprietor of the shop, who was a very good man, came in and said that he had had a call for one of his best workmen to go to a neighboring city and attend to some very choice work for a wealthy old gentleman who was a friend of his,—that the wages would be large, and he had resolved to let the workman upon whom it fell have the full benefit of it all. 'And now who shall it be?'

"'Joe! Joe! Joe!' came from all sides of the house.

"'Well,' said the proprietor, 'the call seems unanimous: so Joe, I suppose, is the fortunate man. Gather up your tools, my man, for the call is urgent, and the train leaves in half an hour. You can have whatever clothing you need sent you by express, for the old gentleman is very eccentric, and will not brook delay.'

"Joe stammered out his thanks, and began to gather up his tools hurriedly. But first he had a hunt for his square, then for one of his chisels, and finally he remembered he had taken his small plane and two or three other tools home, to do a little job for a neighbor, the night before, had got to talking, and had forgotten to bring them back. What was to be done? His home was full a mile from the shop, and he could not possibly go without them.

"'Take mine,' said Dick, generously; 'I will get yours to-night and use them until your return.'

"But to this the proprietor, who had been closely observing both men for some time, would not consent, but said,—

"'No: Joe must suffer the consequences of his own carelessness, which I have long observed is no trifling matter. Dick must go in his place.'

"Against this Dick stoutly protested, but to no avail; the proprietor was resolute; and in a few minutes he was on his way to the situation Joe had lost through his careless habits, while the proprietor said, impressively, as he left the shop,—

"'There is more truth than jest in the old maxim, "A good workman never loses his tools."'

"Dick found everything very pleasant at the old gentleman's for whom he was working, but he kept feeling that he had taken Joe's place, and, finding there was a great deal to do, he at last proposed having Joe come and assist him. To this the old man consented; and after a few days Joe came, full of life as ever, and, I am sorry to say, very little improved in his careless habits. 'It was only his luck,' he said; and laughed, and worked, and lost, and borrowed, much the same as ever.

"The old gentleman for whom the men worked was very eccentric, as I said, and spent much of his time with them while they were at work. One day a package came from home, by express, for Joe, and was brought directly to the shop for him. Joe cut the string, a narrow tape, and, unwinding it from the parcel, threw it upon the floor.

"'That is such a nice string, Joe; why don't you save it?' said Dick.

"'Oh, pshaw! don't bother me about such trifles,' said Joe, unwrapping a nice little book on architecture, for which he had sent. Dick quietly picked up the string, and, wrapping it into a little ball, placed it in his work-box. The old gentleman seemed much pleased with Joe's book, but did not fail to notice Dick's carefulness, which pleased him greatly.

"The weeks slipped by, and their work was nearly completed, when one day the old gentleman, in handling a very sharp chisel awkwardly, let it fall upon his foot, severing a large artery, from which the blood poured so profusely as to seriously threaten his life before medical aid could be procured.

"'Quick, quick, boys!' he said, 'bandage my leg above the wound,—don't wait to go to the house,—anything will do,—any kind of string! Surely there is one some place.'

"'No, there is nothing,' said Joe. 'I will run quickly to the house.' But Dick said, 'Wait a minute,—I have a string,' and drew from his tool-chest the identical string Joe had flung so contemptuously away. With this they tied a tight ligature above the wound, that checked in a measure the great flow of blood till they could carry him to the house.

"The loss of blood weakened the old gentleman greatly; and the doctors said but for the prompt manner of binding his limb he must have bled to death in spite of them. He was unable to leave his room for some time, and fancied no one could wait on him so cleverly as Dick. One day, after he had performed several little offices for him, he said,—

"'Dick, you have never told me anything of your parents.'

"'They both died years ago,' said Dick, reverently.

"'And your brothers and sisters?'

"'Have only one, sir,—a sister,—who was married last summer.'

"'Ah! well,' said the old man, with much apparent satisfaction, 'that settles it, then. How would you like, Dick, to live with me always and relieve me of my many cares? I am getting old, and need a trusty, careful, provident fellow—such as I am convinced by close observation that you are—to stay near me always and see after my interests. Will you come?'

"Dick was touched by the old man's kindly interest, and readily undertook the duties desired. And he so grew into favor by his industry and careful habits in all things that at his death a few years afterward the old gentleman left him joint heir with his only daughter—between whom and Dick had grown up a strong attachment—to all of his property, which was immense. He afterward married the daughter, and to-day is one of the wealthiest and most honored members in the community of C——."

"And all," said Charlie, "for taking care of his tools and saving a string!"

"All," said Uncle Ralph, laughing, "for acquiring habits of order and carefulness in his boyhood, and believing, as I do most sincerely, that there are no such things as trifles in our daily life. Those we account such are often the stepping-stones to the most important events in our lives, as, for instance, the saving of that string, without which the old gentleman would probably have died, and so, of course, Dick's future been altogether changed."

Uncle Ralph's talk had a great influence upon both Ralph and myself. I remember going directly to my room upon coming into the house, and hanging up my dressing-gown, which I had thrown, as usual, upon a chair, gathering up my slippers, one of which was under the bed and the other beneath a table on the opposite side of the room, and setting them in their proper place in the bottom of the wardrobe, and then sitting down to right my work-basket, a glance at which, Gertie said, would have been enough to have frightened a less resolute heart than mine. I did not conquer my careless habits without a severe struggle; but mamma says now I am almost as nice as Gertie about my things; and that is saying a great deal, for she is perfection itself.

Sometimes even yet, when in great haste, I feel disposed to throw a garment aside or leave a drawer disarranged till my return; but have learned to be very resolute with myself, and when even half-way down-stairs will stop short and say very resolutely to myself, "Now, Nannie Cleve, you may just walk right straight back to your room and leave it in perfect order before you go a step farther;" and then, you know, I am not half so apt to forget the next time. I do not know why I have written this out at length thus in my journal, only mamma's conversation yesterday recalled it all so forcibly to mind that I could not refrain from recording it here.

I don't know what mamma would say, either, if she knew I sat writing till after eleven o'clock at night, for she always desires us to retire by ten o'clock, and above all things to be punctual in our habits of rising and retiring. I must not thus infringe upon her rules again, for I know she is right in whatever she requires, however much we may desire to have it otherwise at the time. She makes but few rules for us; but those she always expects us to conform to without any questions.

Aug. 31. Ralph and Charlie left us yesterday, and the house seems lonely and deserted enough, now they are gone. One never knows how much they love their friends, I think, until they are separated from them. It seems to me now, if I could only have my brothers with me always, I should never feel impatient or irritable with them, no matter what they might do. Charlie did not seem quite well; and I see that mamma feels a little anxious about him, as the weather is very warm. Ralph seemed full of life as ever, though I noticed that he choked up a little as he unloosed Kittie's little fat arms from about his neck, at the last moment. They will be at home two weeks at Christmas: so that we live on that hope. Hal Ray started at the same time. He and Nettie came over and spent the evening with us the day before they started. They have been traveling part of the summer with their cousin Ellis Ray, so that we have not seen as much of them as usual for the last few weeks. Poor Nettie! How sorry I feel for her! for she has had no mother since she was ten years old. A maiden aunt keeps house for her father, who loves both Hal and Nettie dearly, but she is so quiet you would never know she was about the house unless you saw her. Oh, what would I do without my precious mother? If I ever do make anything of a woman, it will all be owing to her unfailing, untiring care. And how ill do I repay it all!

Sept. 12. Kittie—our dear little, bright, playful Kittie—is ill,—I fear, very ill. She was taken violently sick several nights ago, and though we called in the best medical aid at once, and have given her every care and attention, she seems to grow slowly worse, in spite of all we can do. I dare not think where it may end. Oh, Kittie! our precious little darling! what would home be without your presence?

I pray God to be merciful to us.

Sept. 19. Kittie is very low indeed. She has typhoid fever. The doctors encourage us to hope for the best; but it is evident they feel very anxious indeed. Poor mamma will not leave her a moment; and her pale, sweet face, though very calm, wears an anxious, yearning look upon it I have never seen there before. I asked her this evening if she did not think Kittie seemed a little better, and she shook her head sadly, and said she feared not. And when I sobbed out, in spite of myself, "Oh, mamma, what will we do if Kittie dies?" she grew very white for a moment, and then said, calmly, laying her hand upon my shoulder tenderly, "We must trust in God, Nannie, and never forget that he will not needlessly afflict us."

And as she stole back into Kittie's room, with that patient look of suffering upon her face, I dropped involuntarily upon my knees, and sobbed aloud,—

"O blessed Father! give me of that heavenly grace my mother has, that I may aid her to bear this terrible suffering, instead of increasing it by my own sorrow. Oh, take me, in the midst of my many imperfections, and make me a Christian, true and earnest."

I thought I was alone, until I turned to go from the room, when I saw Uncle Ralph, lying, with his face covered, upon a lounge, where he had evidently dropped for a little rest, for he stays with us constantly during Kittie's illness, and carries her nearly all night, which is her worst time, in his arms.

I hope he was asleep. Not that I am ashamed of what I said, but I do not wish him to think I could unveil my secret heart so in the presence of any one but God.

Sept. 21. Kittie begs so much to see Ralph and Charlie that mamma has concluded to send for them. I see they all fear the worst. She has had to lose all of her beautiful hair,—the fever affects her brain so much,—and now only innumerable golden rings cover her little head. As mamma cut the long, sunny curls off, one by one, today, that we all so tenderly loved, Kittie would take each one in her little thin hands, and look at it a moment, and then say, "That is for you, Gertie,"—or, "That is for you, Nannie," handing them to us; or, "That is for brother Ralph, or Charlie, when they come." And so she went on, giving each one present one, till poor mamma could stand it no longer, and the tears fell upon the dear, trembling hands, trying so hard to do their task. Kittie, intent upon her own sweet thoughts, did not at first observe it, and finally said, "There now, all the rest are for mamma," when, looking up, she saw the tearful face above her, and, with a half-grieved, half-surprised look, put up her little hands and wiped the tears away, and whispered, "Shouldn't Kittie have given them away, mamma?"

"Yes, darling. Mamma was very wrong to cry because she had to cut off your beautiful curls; she will be good now;" and in a moment she was her own brave self again. Kittie seemed only half satisfied; but as mamma's sweet smile, always ready for her, from time to time reassured her, she soon dropped off into a quiet slumber, from which we hope the best again. I have only now left her sleeping, mamma insisting that Gertie and I shall retire early every night, as we can do no good, she says, at present, and after awhile our strength may be needed. It is very hard for us to leave them thus, but mamma is positive, and promises to call us should she get much worse; so that we are constrained to obey. It surprises me to see how constantly cheerful mamma is, in the midst of the anxiety that I know is eating at her heart. She always turns a bright, happy face to Kittie, who watches her very closely all of the time; sings to her softly whenever she wishes it, as she often does, when restless; and is always ready to tell her cheerful little stories, in a low voice, whenever she has a little respite from suffering. How wonderful, how passing wonderful, is a mother's love!

Sept. 23. Ralph and Charlie arrived late this evening. They were both shocked and grieved at Kittie's changed appearance. She seemed considerably excited, and very glad to see them, and will not leave Ralph's arms a minute. She says to Uncle Ralph, half apologetically,—

"You know he has been gone so long, Uncle Ralph, and you have carried me so much."

She seems to feel easier when carried around than in any

other way: so Uncle Ralph has carried her, with her head upon a little pillow, on his arm, night after night, for hours. She will often beg him to lay her down, feeling how wearisome even her light weight must be, but he soon lifts her up again, when he sees the restless look of suffering on her face. Oh, he is so patient and good. And what a world of comfort he has been to us through all these weary days! so calm and strong, and at the same time so loving and tender. We all look to him, cling to him, as we could to no other. I do not think Charlie seems quite well, though he will not acknowledge that he is sick. It would be dreadful if he too should get sick, and Kittie so low. But, as dear mamma says, "God is merciful; let us not borrow trouble." I must try to rest and save my strength, for, as mamma truly says, "It may be needed."

Sept. 25. Dear little Kittie has failed sadly in the last few days. Her little face looks so wan and white, and her blue eyes so heavy. She talks very little, and eats almost nothing. Ralph and Uncle Ralph carry her almost all the time in their arms, except when mamma rocks and soothes her, with her dear little sunny head—so aching and so weary—pillowed upon her breast. We have her little bed in the sitting-room down-stairs since her illness; it is much pleasanter on many accounts. To-day she said to Uncle Ralph, very feebly,—

"Please carry me into the parlor, Uncle Ralph; I want to see Kittie."

He carried her, very gently, across the hall into the parlors, and she looked long and earnestly at the beautiful painting of herself,—Uncle Ralph's gift to mamma on her birthday; then she said,—

"It does not look like Kittie now, Uncle Ralph."

"It will when your curls grow long again, darling," he replied.

She did not answer him for a moment, and then said,—

"Will you please ask mamma to let me have that same dress on again?"

"When, Kittie? To-day?"

"No; not to-day. Some day, when God calls me. Kittie wants to look sweet when she goes to see papa and God."

"Oh, Kittie,—darling!" I cried; but Uncle Ralph checked me by a look,—we two were alone with her,—and said, very tenderly,—

"Kittie does not want to leave us yet, does she?"

"No; only I think papa wants to see me,—Kittie dreamed he did. I am so tired; please take me back to mamma;" and the little eyes drooped wearily.

He carried her away, and I sat down and cried bitterly. My darling little sister, our pride, our sunbeam, — my heart rebelled at the thought of giving her up. Presently Uncle Ralph returned, and, sitting down upon the sofa beside me, drew my head gently to his shoulder, and, smoothing the hair from my heated, tearful face, wiped softly the tears away, and said,—

"We must not grieve too much, darling, at the sad loss I fear we are all to sustain. God knows best, and he never needlessly afflicts."

"Oh, but she is so precious, Uncle Ralph," I sobbed; "so precious! so precious!"

"Yes, darling, very, very precious to us all; hence how tenfold so must she be to her mother's heart! We must try and be strong for her sake, or the burden may prove heavier than she can bear. This I am sure my Nannie can and will do; for God cannot fail to hear and answer, in part at least, the earnest, beautiful prayer that sprang so fervently from her heart a few mornings ago."

Then he had not been asleep,—had heard it all. I could

not answer him, did not try to; my present sorrow was too great to let me care for other things. He pressed his cheek caressingly against my forehead, as my head still lay upon his shoulder, and added, oh, so tenderly,—

"I am glad you thought yourself alone that day, else I should never have known how, from the very depths of her pure young heart, my darling desired to do right. And I am sure she will see this morning how necessary is self-control for that dear mother's sake, and how perfect submission to the will of our always-merciful Father will make this trial even tenfold lighter to herself. Look beyond the shadow, Nannie, look beyond the shadow to the beautiful land of love and light toward which the angels are so rapidly bearing our darling. I will not conceal it from you: dear little Kittie has but a few hours to live, and I have come to you now to prepare you for it, that you may be calm when the trial comes, for your precious mother's sake. Go to your room now and rest a little, my child; and will you ask our Father anew for strength? Will you try, darling, as you never tried before, to take from, instead of adding to, your mother's care?"

He had both of my hands in his, and looked me earnestly, tenderly, in the face. I answered him, as well as my trembling voice would let me, "I will, Uncle Ralph, indeed I will," and hastened to my room.

I went in earnest faith to our Father, and prayed as I never in my life prayed before; and, oh, how mercifully he has heard me! I arose, bathed my face and arranged my hair, and went below to mamma and Kittie; and all through this sad, anxious day I have felt a calm, a holy peace, such as never was given me before. It is such a sad pleasure, too, to see how Uncle Ralph relies on me; and the neighbors, who are in, come to me for everything, instead of disturbing dear mamma; and even she herself now says to them, "Nannie will show you," or "Nannie will see to it," instead of being afraid to have me around lest I could not control my sorrow. Oh, if we could only always remember that other sorrows are heavier than our own, we would not always, I think, be so selfish in indulging ourselves, but would partly forget our own grief in striving to lighten that of others.

Sept. 30. It is all over. We have no longer our little Kittie, for God has taken her. Said I, "no longer"? Oh, no, I did not mean that, for she is ours,—ours always, forever! As Uncle Ralph beautifully says,—

> "She has only cross'd the river,
> She has only gone before,
> To that land of light and beauty
> Where she suffers nevermore.
>
> "She has only cross'd the river,
> With its glittering, golden strand;
> And the sunlight fadeth never,
> Where the angel-watchers stand.
>
> "She has only cross'd the river,
> To the Saviour's loving breast,
> Where, secure from pain and sorrow,
> She for evermore shall rest.
>
> "There some day we hope to meet her,
> When the toils of life are o'er,
> When our feet shall pass the river
> That our loved one cross'd before."

She died at sunrise last Thursday morning, the day after my last entry. I begged so earnestly to be permitted to stay up that night that mamma at last consented to let me be awakened at one o'clock, which was done, so that I was near our darling during all her last hours. She slept till about three in the morning, and then opened her eyes and asked for mamma. She was lying in her little crib, for she had grown so weak she could not bear to be moved. "Here I am, darling," was mamma's quick response, for she was sitting close beside her. "What does Kittie want?"

"Where is papa? Kittie thought he was here."

"No, darling," said mamma, "he is not here."

"I dreamed he was carrying Kittie in his arms," she said, and dropped off again into a light slumber.

I saw mamma's features work painfully for a few moments, and hot tears fell silently over her pale cheeks, but she never spoke a word. I thought it would break my heart to see her suffer so. I went and sat down upon a low stool at her feet and pressed my lips upon her dear hand. She took my hand in hers and pressed it gratefully; and so we sat together, watching the precious little life slipping so surely away from our midst. I felt that it comforted mamma to have me there, so I did not move, although I felt sometimes as though I would die if I could not yield to my feelings, which I would not do in her presence.

At last the morning dawned. I watched the gray light through the open window, creeping up the sky and bringing out, faintly at first and then more and more distinctly, the different objects that before had lain in shadow, and little Kittie still slept. Then the first rosy tints crept up the horizon, and the fleecy, vapory clouds that slept in the east grew beautiful beneath its soft touch, and wreathed themselves into myriad fantastic forms that looked like the temples and domes and walls of a great city. I watched them changing and flitting, until my mind half sped away from our sorrowful home; and, as the first golden beams of the morning sun shot athwart the rosy splendor, tinting with a line of burnished gold the walls and gates of my imaginary city, I thought of the eternal city whose walls are of "jasper and gold." There was a slight movement in the crib; the little arms were thrown up a moment, the sweet blue eyes unclosed for a last look of earth, the dear lips tried to whisper "*mamma;*" then there was silence. Oh, such silence for a moment as death only brings!—broken, at length, by the low anguished wail, "My baby, oh, my baby!" As the terrible strain suddenly removed, mamma's head dropped forward upon the crib, almost as lifeless as the little form from which the pure spirit had fled upward, on the first ray of sunlight, to God.

And now she is sleeping—our precious Kittie—under the green sod, that every morning we cover with freshly-blown flowers,—sleeping peacefully and quietly in her little grave, so tiny, so precious! It is a very little mound, and the form it covers is almost a baby's; but oh! the place left vacant in our home and hearts, who can fill? Mamma was very ill for a few days after Kittie's death; but she is better now, and carries her pale face, in and out, about her daily duties, with a look that tells of patient submission as well as sorrow. When Uncle Ralph would have borne her from the room, the morning Kittie died, she rallied from her swoon, and begged for a few moments alone with Kittie, which I am sure she spent in prayer beside her. Then with her own hands she bathed and dressed our little darling for the last time; brushed the sunny curls that clustered about her waxen face; laid her, in an attitude of repose, half covered with lilies of the valley and tiny half-blown roses, first in her cradle-bed, and afterward in the casket prepared to receive the treasured form. This, Uncle Ralph had had softly cushioned, and lined with the purest white satin, and, unlike any I have ever seen before, made to resemble a dainty little cradle, so that the precious child looked as though she had just fallen asleep in her downy crib, and we were spared the sight of that rigid, unlifelike appearance that renders death so terrible. Mamma never speaks of Kittie; but when she chances upon a book or toy made sacred by the touch of little fingers, I have seen her hastily leave the room, with a look upon her face that, to those who know her well, tells of suffering in her own room, too sacred to be looked upon, save alone by God. She is always cheerful when with us, neglecting no duty, but conversing cheerfully and pleasantly on all topics that have interest for others. Ralph and Charlie yesterday returned to college. Charlie is evidently not well, and mamma was very unwilling he should go back; but I think he could not bear to see Ralph go without him, now that home is so desolate: so they have gone together.

Aunt Martha, too,—how can I write of her untiring care and kindness during Kittie's illness, and also while mamma was confined to her room? All her harshness was gone; and no one could have been more gentle and lovable than was she. Hereafter, change as she may, I shall always love and honor her, for dear little Kittie's sake. She constituted herself cook for the sick-room; and no wish the dear child could express was deemed too difficult for her to accomplish. And although her most delicate and tempting dishes were returned to her with scarcely a morsel touched, she was ready at any instant, day or night, to try again and again, if she might not tempt the capricious appetite. And dear little Kittie would eat nothing that Aunt Martha had not prepared. And as I have watched her bending over the hot stove at midday, above some delicate mixture, jealous if any hand but her own even touched the spoon, I have thought again and again to myself how little we may know of the heart from external manners or appearance, and blamed myself over and over for my former harsh judgment of Aunt Martha.

Oct. 2. "Sorrows, like ravens, never come singly." To-day Uncle Ralph had a telegram saying that Charlie was very ill; and he and mamma left on this evening train, to bring him home, if able to be moved; if not, to remain with him till he is better. I feel very anxious indeed. Now God forbid that death again enter our already broken home-circle! I am very miserable at the thought.

Oct. 5. Charlie is very ill indeed, Uncle Ralph writes, and mamma bearing up with the same wonderful strength she manifested all through Kittie's illness. Our home is very desolate. Gertie and I wander about the house and through the orchard and garden, unable to settle ourselves either at work or study. If it were not for Aunt Martha,— poor, misjudged Aunt Martha, once so disliked, now our only comfort,—I do not know what we would do. She has ever a word of comfort for us, and sees so kindly to the many things that in our anxiety we utterly forget and neglect. We cling to her almost as we would to mamma. Oh, if we only could know how dear Charlie is! How terrible is this suspense!

Oct. 6. I am utterly miserable to-night. No word from Uncle Ralph; and we know not whether to hope or despair. Gertie has more fortitude than I. She is so much like mamma. She bears her grief silently, while I burst out into impatient and sorrowful ejaculations. We have just been to dear little Kittie's grave, to place fresh immortelles upon the sod. Can it be our hearts are to be opened afresh?—that—oh, Charley, my brother!—I cannot write it! It is too dreadful to contemplate.

Oct. 10. Uncle Ralph writes us: "The crisis in our dear boy's life is at hand. He has had several days of raving and delirium, and now he has fallen into a deep sleep, which will probably last for hours, and from which, the physicians say, he will either awake to life, or sink rapidly. Let us pray, my dear girls, that it be not the latter. I have written you thus, that you may be prepared for either event. He is very low, very low indeed; but

God is merciful and powerful. All we can now do is to wait patiently and submissively, and pray that it be well. I will write you again immediately upon any change in his condition. Be brave and hopeful, and, above all, cheerfully submissive; nothing else will enable you to bear sorrow when it falls heavily."

Oh, how easy for Uncle Ralph so to write, but how hard for us to obey! We can do nothing but go from the house to the garden, from the garden to the orchard, and from the orchard back to the house again; and there we wander from room to room, aimless and desolate. The sun is shining brightly, and the pale autumn flowers are blooming; but a shadow comes ever between us and the sunlight; and the robin's song in the lilac near the window has a mournful cadence I have never heard before. I look at Gertie, and say, falteringly, "Oh! Gertie, Charlie may be dying." She turns her pale face toward me,—so much like mamma's,—and sobs out, "Oh! Nannie! Nannie!" and then we lay our heads upon one another's shoulders and sob convulsively. Ah! I hear Aunt Martha's voice; she is calling us. Can she have a letter? I dread to go, much as I wish to hear. I shrink from hearing what may be so full of sorrow.

Two hours later. Oh, joy that I may write it! my brother will live. Aunt Martha had a letter from Uncle Ralph. It read,—" The crisis is past; and, God be praised, our Charlie may yet be spared to us. He has awakened in his right mind, and his symptoms are all favorable. Fannie [mamma] is almost prostrated with the sudden reaction from despair to hope; but she will not give up for an instant, but hovers constantly about his pillow. She is an angel." Ay, Uncle Ralph, and none know it so well as the children she watches over so tenderly.

I cannot write; my nerves are all a-quiver. How good

God is to us! I feel that I can better bear dear Kittie's loss, since Charlie has so nearly been taken, and then restored to us again. Gertie sits by me so silently, thinking,—thinking. She has said very little; but I know by the pale face, with the blue circle beneath the eyes, that to-morrow all day she will lie quietly and suffer with one of her excruciating nervous headaches. I found her half an hour after the letter came, lying under the great apple-tree in the orchard, sobbing as though her heart would break, and all she could say was, "Oh, Nannie, I am so glad! so glad!" Just so I had found her, in the same place, the morning our little sister died,—away from all companionship, all love,—sobbing out her sorrow upon the cold earth; and when I raised her head and placed it on my shoulder, and said, "Why do you come here alone, Gertie?" she only sobbed, "You have all enough to bear, without adding my sorrow to your own." Precious Gertie, others are always her first care,—never self.

Oct. 12. We are all bustle and confusion; every one striving to accomplish as much as possible. Aunt Martha proposed we should have the fall cleaning all done in mamma's absence; and Gertie and I were only too glad to be released from our studies. Miss Lane has been absent nearly two weeks; called away by the illness of her father,—her only living relative. She returned two days ago, leaving him much better. In the midst of our work we had a letter from dear mamma herself, so full of gratitude and happiness at Charlie's speedy convalescence. He is improving so rapidly, they think they will be able to bring him home, by easy stages, in a few days. His illness was brain fever; brought on, or aggravated, doubtless, by the great mental anxiety and suffering, when he was already half sick, at the time of dear little Kittie's death. Now that we may look for them soon, we are all anxiety to have everything bright and cheerful when they come. It is Gertie's and my first experience in real house-work,—mamma always overseeing everything herself; but Aunt Martha said it would be good for us, we were so unsettled; and I think she was right. I half suspect, however, that we have been more bother than help; but she has been very patient with us, and professed to think we had assisted her greatly. I said Gertie and I had heretofore done no house-work; but we have always been expected, and required, to take care of our own rooms. Mamma has never permitted us to have a servant either to assist us in dressing ourselves or in taking care of our rooms; saying she never wished us to feel dependent upon others for comfort, in such trifling matters. But I am tired with my unusual exertions, and must go to bed, that I may arise with the lark in the morning,—for am I not housekeeper now?

Oct. 20. They have come. Charlie has borne the trip well; but, oh! the pale, thin face that looked out upon us from the carriage-window almost broke my heart. They arrived about ten o'clock this morning, and found everything bright and cheerful and ready for them. Mamma was greatly surprised at what we had done, and lavish in her thanks to Aunt Martha and praise and caresses upon Gertie and myself. We are all so happy to have Charlie with us again, that we are much more cheerful than I had thought we ever could be again without dear little Kittie. Mamma seems full of happiness and gratitude whenever she looks at him, and watches so closely that he does not over-fatigue himself. And Aunt Martha seems so happy in her post of self-appointed housekeeper, that mamma declares she must share it jointly with her in the future,—an assertion that makes Aunt Martha's face flush with gratified pride and pleasure.

Nov. 18. Dear old book, I only open you to write "Adieu." Charlie and I are going to Uncle Ben's, to spend the winter and see if the mild climate will not recruit his frail health. It is useless for me to take you with us; for amid the strange scenes and strange faces with which we shall be surrounded I am sure I shall find small leisure to devote to your pages. Uncle Ralph goes with us, but returns again immediately. My heart is full of sorrow at leaving dear mamma and Gertie, and not seeing Ralph at the holidays; but I cannot help feeling a young girl's eagerness at the thought that I am going to see something of the great world of which I have read so much and seen so little. When I return, I hope to have much of which to tell you that is pleasant; and I doubt not I shall often wish for an hour's quiet converse with yourself; for I have learned to come to you, as to an old friend, and unveil my heart, as I can do to no one living. Adieu, adieu.

Oct. 24. Ah, faithful old friend, you see I have returned to you, but after so long an absence. First, you must know, Charlie and I stayed at Uncle Ben's until May, and a happy, happy winter we all had together. Uncle Ben is splendid,—almost as good as Uncle Ralph,—and he and Aunt Emily (who is one of the best women in the world) did everything in their power to make us enjoy ourselves. Then cousin Ned, and cousin Fannie, who is mamma's namesake, are the best company in the world; and nothing they could do seemed too great, if it could add to our happiness in the least. So we went to concerts and plays, had sleigh-rides and carriage-rides, and, in the spring, pony-rides, till Charlie grew well and strong, and I in sad danger of having my head fairly turned by the kindness and attention I received from every one.

Fannie is three years older than I, and already engaged to be married to a gentleman of wealth and standing in the city where they reside. Ned is three years older than she is, and a very fair match for brother Ralph. Then dear little Ninette,—so much like our own lost Kittie, that more than once the tears started to my eyes at her sudden appearance. It would be useless for me to attempt to transcribe the events of our visit: they are too numerous and full of excitement to be narrated on paper at this late day. When we began to talk of our return, in the spring, Uncle Ben said he and Aunt Emily had been planning a nice tour for the summer months, in which he proposed we should join, and have mamma, Gertie, and Uncle Ralph meet us all at a given point, and, taking our time, visit leisurely several places of interest, and then proceed to "Old Yale" in time to see Ralph graduate. So we agreed to wait until we could hear from mamma, who, to our great joy, consented to the plan, on condition that the whole party then returned to Beechwood, which you know is the name of our own dear grove, and where also Aunt Katie and Uncle Harry and the little ones would come. To this they finally agreed, stipulating first for a few weeks' travel after Ralph's college time; and so all summer we have been flitting here and there, visiting many cities we had never seen before, spending a week at Niagara, and going from thence to Hartford, where we saw brother Ralph and Hal Ray graduate with the highest honors. It was a sad disappointment for poor Charlie, for his illness has thrown him a year behind his class,— they thinking it unsafe for him to return to college last term; but he bore it like a hero, and was as proud of Ralph's success as though it had been his own. Hal has improved wonderfully, both in appearance and manners. Fannie says she thinks he is the handsomest man she ever saw, except Uncle Ralph. Nettie and her papa were at Hartford, and she and Hal joined us in our travels from there. We spent about three weeks at the sea-side, and then flitted away to our own quiet home among the hills, where we have now been just a month; and to-day our friends have returned to their distant homes, whilst I, old book, have flown back to you for comfort, as in the days of the past.

I do not know why it is, but I do not feel as though I were the same little girl who sat a year ago by the open window and wrote a brief farewell in her diary. I seem to have grown years older, instead of months. I know not why, unless from having been so long with Fannie, and entering so fully into all her plans for the future, I have imbibed some of the feeling of womanhood myself. Let me see,— I shall soon be seventeen. Heigh-ho! I have not, truly, many more years in which to be a child. I hardly know whether to rejoice or be sad. I am really afraid, Nannie Cleve, your head has been not a little turned by the excitement of the last few months. A little while alone with Gertie and dear mamma, and you will return to the old feelings and the old ways, and be the little child you were when you started forth with Charlie, a year ago.

Oct. 25. Hal Ray walked home with Gertie and myself, to-day, from church. He expects to spend the winter in New York, attending the medical lectures at college. He has chosen the medical profession, much against his father's wishes, who would like him to go into the army. Nettie is very glad he has so decided; and so am I,—or rather would be, had I any interest in the matter, which of course I have not. He did not come in, but returned home from the door. We found Uncle Ralph, who always spends Sunday with us, and mamma, had reached home first. I felt tired and dispirited, though I do not know why I should, and, when I came down from my room, threw myself, with childish abandon, upon a little ottoman at Uncle Ralph's feet, and laid my head, child-fashion, upon his knee. Aunt Martha, who sat reading in the room, spoke up, somewhat tartly I thought,—"Nancy, you are getting too old to act the child so!" I started up, with an angry retort upon my lip, but thought of little Kittie, and was silent.

"Ah, Aunt Martha," said Uncle Ralph, gently, "do not try to make her think she is a woman. Let her remain a child while she may."

He laid his hand caressingly upon mine, as it rested upon his knee; but he did not draw my head back to its resting-place, as he used to do. Can it be that they both see the change in me, which I feel so acutely? Have I indeed left my childhood behind me?

Miss Lane says she thinks me wonderfully improved in my manners; but I fear she always thought me a little hoydenish, and is glad to find me more sedate than of yore. It cannot be that I do not love the dear old home and home-ties as much as ever, for I feel that nothing could induce me to leave mamma and Gertie again; but I feel constantly such a longing to steal away by myself, to hold communion with my own thoughts; and more than once Miss Lane has been compelled to chide me for inattention during our French hour. I must take myself in hand and overcome these follies, for follies I am sure they are.

Oct. 27. Gertie and I have just come in from a long stroll through the grove. Oh, how beautiful is autumn, when the woods are gorgeous in their many-colored robes,— when the ash flings its bright leaves of crimson playfully down, to mingle with those of the yellow maple and the many-tinted ones of the oak and beech and hickory! Nature is very beautiful; but it fills one ever with a tender melancholy to sit silently and watch the bright leaves fluttering slowly downward, covering the earth with a carpet of many hues, listening, meanwhile, to the chirp of the squirrel as he springs nimbly from limb to limb, laying up cheerily his store for the coming winter. Provident little fellow; what knows he of sorrow? The bright summer birds have all departed for a warmer clime; the cooing of the dove is sad and desolate; and the occasional fall of a nut to the ground startles one like the clods that fall upon the coffin-lid. A letter from Carrie Reed to-day tells me of the death of her only brother,—a bright boy of twelve years; and mamma has just told me that little Annie Wood, one of dear little Kittie's playmates, cannot possibly live till morning. She has gone to sit through the night with the grief-stricken mother. I sit me down in sadness, and write,—

AN AUTUMN SONG.

The summer has faded in beauty away,
Like the pale sunset shadows of lingering day;
The autumn winds sadly sigh over its tomb,
And its roses are flinging their dying perfume.

The song-birds are hast'ning from the wild-wood away;
The leaves slowly falling are bright with decay;
The forests are gorgeous with crimson and gold,
And the pale autumn flowers their soft leaves unfold.

Alas! since we gather'd the summer's first rose,
How many a fond heart has sunk to repose!
How many a dear form we oft have caress'd
We've laid with the flowers away to their rest!

There are graves in the churchyard, and graves in each heart;
O'er the first, leaves are falling and tear-drops oft start;
By the last, faithful memory keeps watch night and day,
Nor e'en in our slumbers turns tearful away.

And so will some summer fade over our tomb,
And sad winds low whisper that autumn has come;
Yet calmly we'll slumber, till forth from the skies
The glad shout shall greet us, " 'Tis springtime; arise!"

Nov. 6. I am startled out of my lethargy; yet how shall I write the records of the last few days? It seems impossible that this is really myself, little Nannie Cleve, who sit here so demurely writing. Like "Die kluge Else" in the story we to-day had in our German lesson, I feel like crying out, "Bin ichs, oder bin ichs nicht?"

Well, to begin at the beginning, old friend, last Monday Hal came over early in the morning to invite Ralph, Gertie, and myself to join an impromptu riding-party they were just getting up at Mr. Ray's,—Nellie having some friends visiting her from the city for a few days past. Of course we were eager to go, and, having gained mamma's consent, donned our habits, had the ponies brought to the door, and were soon cantering away in high spirits to join the rest of the party. So ever recklessly we rush out to meet the future, knowing so little what it hath in store for us. We found the others waiting for us at the great gate that leads into Colonel Ray's lawn,—Nettie and her friends Mollie and Susie Shaw, together with their brother Albert and Ellis Ray, who had only arrived late the night before. We lacked one more gentleman to make the company complete; but Nettie protested that she would ride with no one, but be impartial in her favors. So they paired off as suited them best, Ralph with Mollie Shaw, Ellis Ray with Susie, Albert Shaw with Gertie, and Hal with Nettie and myself; for, somehow or other, I felt that I could not be alone with Hal, and persuaded Nettie to ride with us. But, as luck would have it, whom should we meet, as we turned into the high-road, but Uncle Ralph riding leisurely along on Racer on his way to Beechwood? And Nettie, at once darting away, claimed him as her captive, and, wheeling him into rank, rode off beside him in triumph. Then away we all cantered, through pleasant lanes and groves and beside murmuring brooks, limpid and beautiful,—away,

away, till our spirits rose jubilant in the clear, bracing air; and we chatted and laughed and tossed back and forth merry jests and witty repartee, until our ponies too caught the infection and dashed away quite cheerily with their merry loads. Hal and I brought up the rear; and, as we were compelled to stop a moment, in order to adjust the girth of my saddle, the others were a little in advance of us, when Hal remounted, and away we dashed faster than ever, in order to overtake them. And herein lay all our trouble; for, as we turned rapidly a quick bend in the road, a goat sprang suddenly from behind the hedge, and in an instant Hal's horse, which is none too gentle at best, sprang from under him, and, the movement being so unexpected, he was off his guard, and was thrown violently upon the ground. When I saw he did not rise, I sprang from my horse and ran to him. I found him stunned and senseless, and, I feared, dying. Blood was slowly trickling from a cut in his forehead, and he was ghastly pale.

"Oh, Hal," I cried, piteously, "are you killed?"

He did not answer me, and I ran to a little stream by the roadside, and, wetting my handkerchief therein, began to bathe his face. The cool water seemed to revive him, for he opened his eyes, looked up a moment wistfully into my face, over which the hot tears were streaming as I bent above him, and whispered, faintly,—

"I believe I am dying, Nannie. Kiss me once, darling, and remember——" And he relapsed into insensibility.

I was terribly frightened. I had never seen any one faint in my life but once,—that was dear mamma when Kittie died; and I really believed he was dying. My face tingles now with the hot blood while I think of it; but there came rushing all through me such an agony as I never before have felt, and trust I never shall again,—an agony that told me, by its intensity, that his life was dearer to me than my own; and I unhesitatingly bent forward and pressed my lips tremblingly upon his pallid face. The clatter of horses' hoofs reassured me, and I sprang up just as the rest of the party came dashing back,—Hal's frightened horse having apprised them of the accident by flying riderless into their midst. Uncle Ralph, fortunately knowing more of such accidents than we, soon assured us that he thought nothing more serious than a sprained arm and a few bruises would result to Hal from his fall.

A carriage was procured from a farm-house near by, and Hal, who by this time was much better, was helped into it and made as comfortable as might be, and we started homeward. I kept far in advance of the carriage, riding rapidly with Gertie and Mr. Shaw; and a quivering heart and flaming cheek were my companions all the way. As soon as we reached home I made my escape to my own room, where I threw myself upon the bed and gave way to passionate weeping. Gertie tried to comfort me; but how could she, when she knew not the embarrassing position in which I had placed myself? How could I tell her of it? My heart shrank from exposure even to precious Gertie. How could I acknowledge to her what, until that miserable day, I had never for an instant confessed to myself? And that kiss! What must Hal think of me? Easily won,—almost unasked. My face burns at the thought, and impatient ejaculations spring from my lips!

Ah, Nannie Cleve, Nannie Cleve! under what star dawned your natal day? A meteor surely,—so erratic and troublesome has been your life, from the cradle up. One thing is certain, Hal shall never see me again. He may pride himself on the knowledge he has gained, but he shall never take advantage of it. Thank goodness, it is only a month until he leaves home; and I surely can avoid him that little while without attracting notice. See him I will not. That is settled. He was quite ill for two or three days after his fall, but is able to walk around again now.

Nov. 7. Hal has been here. He called to-day with Nettie, in the pony-chaise. Fortunately, I saw them from my room-window in time to make my escape. I flew to the attic,—a place where I was least likely to be sought,—and remained there during their call, although I heard Gertie searching for and calling me everywhere. Through the little window I watched them depart. How handsome Hal looked as he helped Nettie into the chaise! I almost wish I had gone down, but avoided speaking alone with him. But no; how could I have met his eye? It is better as it is; only next time I will not run away so, but beg to be excused. I wish him to know my non-appearance is not accidental. They have only been gone a few minutes, and now I hear Gertie running up-stairs, and I must prepare myself to meet her inquiries as to my whereabouts during their call.

Nov. 10. Hal has again been here, and this time asked expressly to see me. He left his compliments, and regrets the last time when I failed to appear. This morning he asked to see me, if only for a minute; but I begged to be excused on the plea of a bad headache. Gertie said he looked much annoyed when she delivered the message, but was too kind to express a doubt as to its sufficiency. He left a message from Nettie to the effect that she would look for us all there to tea this evening, with her friends. But I again begged to be excused, for the same reason I had before urged.

"Do go, dear," said Gertie, who I think half suspects the true state of the case; but I was resolute.

"Indeed, my head aches too badly, Gertie." And I spoke truthfully; for the present excitement had set it to throbbing fearfully.

"But it will be better by evening, Nannie."

"No, dear! indeed, indeed I cannot go. You must not urge it," I pleaded. And Gertie, ever yielding, said no more.

So now, as I write, she and Ralph are there, having, I doubt not, a merry time, while I sit perched up here in my chamber alone, like a forlorn little maiden as I am, feeling very lonely and desolate. Well, well, it serves you just right, miss, and it will teach you to be a little more circumspect in the future with young gentlemen who are thrown from their horses.

Nov. 12. Gertie had much to tell me, upon her return, of the pleasant evening they had spent, and also of a nutting-party planned for Thursday,—that is to-day.

"Now, darling," said Gertie, "you will go to the picnic, won't you?"

"No, dear, I cannot," I said, resolutely; although it was a hard trial to me, for the beautiful Indian summer is upon us, and I know of nothing that would afford me such infinite pleasure as a day spent nut-gathering in the forest. But then how could I run the risk of being alone with Hal? No; I would rather deny myself forever than meet the contingency. Gertie looked troubled, and I saw the time had come when I must tell her of my grief. So, with many blushes, and a few hysterical sobs and tears, I related the scene on the day of our ride through the forest. She was all sympathy, of course; when was she not so with me? Then she said,—

"But, Nannie, if he loves you, it is not so bad."

"But he does not, Gertie, or at least———"

"Ah, but," she interrupted, eagerly, "I am sure he does; he looks so distressed, always, when you refuse to come down."

"Man like,—he wants to feel his power."

"No, no," she began; but I interrupted her with,—

"But even if he did, Gertie, what would mamma say? I am too young to have a lover. No; it is better so, I am sure."

But my heart gave a great twinge, even while I spoke; and for the first time in my life there was a glimmering doubt as to whether mamma might not, just once, be mistaken. Gertie was silenced; but so was not the little doubt in my heart. The "Why not?" recurred very often; but that I tried very resolutely to set it aside will be evinced by the fact that I persisted in pleading indisposition and remaining at home from the picnic. I will not deny that I shed a few quiet tears after Ralph and Gertie were gone, for the morning was very beautiful; but I soon dried my eyes, and betook myself to the library, which in the morning is deserted, and set myself resolutely to work upon a picture I was sketching for Ralph's next birthday. I had so sat for half an hour perhaps, working, striving hard to forget the gay party after which my heart had gone, when I heard a step in the hall. The door was thrown open, and I heard Annie, our little housemaid, saying,—

"Please walk in; Miss Nannie is in the library."

I arose to meet my guest, and confronted—Hal. For a moment the blood forsook my heart, then surged back in such a hot torrent that I thought I was going to faint. But I am not easily overcome, and almost instantly recovered myself sufficiently to say gayly, as he advanced eagerly to meet me,—

"Why, how is this? How happens it that so loyal a knight is not in attendance upon the ladies this beautiful morning?"

"They have sent me for you, and say I must not return without you."

They had sent him. Then he had not come of his

own free will. The thought made me perfectly myself again.

"It is impossible," I said, coldly. "I sent word by Gertie, this morning, that I was not well enough to go."

"But you see we will not take 'no' for an answer," he persisted.

"I am afraid you will have to," I replied, politely, but frigidly.

A moment's silence, in which I could hear my heart beating violently, and wondered if it was possible he could hear it also,—which thought did not in the least tend to soften its throbs,—and then Hal said,—

"What have I done, Nannie, to offend you? Why do you refuse to see me so often, and now treat me so coolly? Is the remembrance of our ride so unpleasant to you?"

"You have no right to question me thus," I began, haughtily,—when our eyes met; and then—well, it doesn't matter what more was said,—only *I went to the picnic* after all, and to-day has been the very happiest day of all my life. Hal says he has loved me ever since I was a little girl; and indeed I am half inclined to think I have loved him fully as long. To-morrow he is to come and talk with mamma and ask her consent to our engagement. How strange it seems, but how happy, how happy I am!

Nov. 13. Hal came this morning as we had planned, and, after half-an-hour's chat together, the nature of which I need not tell you, I went to mamma, and told her, with many blushes and conscious looks, that Hal had something he wished to say to her in the library. Mamma looked a little surprised at my evident embarrassment, but nevertheless went at once to Hal, and I made my escape up-stairs. After what seemed to me a long, long while, I heard the library-bell ring, and then Annie came up to say that my presence was desired there. Oh, how I dreaded to go! What would mamma think and say? I hesitated a moment, with my hand upon the door-knob, then I turned it and went in. The prospect was not encouraging. Mamma looked perplexed and anxious, I thought, and Hal was unmistakably flushed and annoyed. He arose instantly and set a chair for me near mamma, and then stood beside me, and after a minute's hesitation said,—

"Your mamma thinks, Nannie, that I have been very precipitate in declaring my feelings for you, which may have been the case, as I am not yet settled in business. She fears a long engagement will be embarrassing to us both, but will not hear of our marriage under two years. I have urged every reason I can possibly bring to bear upon the subject, and can now only trust to you to convince her that we do really look to each other for happiness in life."

I glanced timidly at mamma, and she met my glance with a reassuring smile, but said,—

"Hal has stated the case just as it stands, Nannie, and I really am at a loss what to say or do in the matter. I do not wish to be severe; yet, my dear child, you are so young to enter into any such engagement, which, once entered into, should last for life."

"It would, mamma, indeed it would," I said, hastily, looking at Hal. And then we talked, or at least Hal talked, and I supported the most that he said; until at last mamma said,—

"Nannie, are you sure, my child, that this is not an impulse? Remember, you are very young, and an engagement of this kind should not be lightly entered into."

"Mamma," I said, half pained that she could doubt it, "I do love Hal with all my heart, and always shall."

"Bless you for those words!" I heard Hal whisper, fervently. Then, finally, mamma consented to the engagement, on condition that for two years it should be only nominal. If at the end of that time we still both desired it, she would urge no further objection; but if, on the contrary, either felt it would be best otherwise, they must feel perfectly free to so say. Hal and I both smiled at the idea of such a thing; but, although Hal pleaded hard to have the time limited to one year, mamma was resolute, and he was forced to be content.

"You will let us write to each other in my absence?" said Hal.

"Yes," answered mamma, "provided no promises are given or exacted, other than I have said; and not oftener than once a month, unless in sickness or trouble."

To this we had to consent; and then Hal rose to go. "I shall see you to-morrow," he whispered, as he bent to say "good-by." Then he thanked mamma politely and warmly for her concessions, promised to do all in his power to merit her favor, and withdrew.

As soon as he was gone, I laid my head upon mamma's shoulder, and whispered,—

"Have I done wrong, mamma?"

She kissed me very tenderly, as she answered,—

"No, darling; only you are so very young and inexperienced that I cannot bear to have you bind yourself by any such engagement yet. I admire and love Hal very much, and two or three years hence should have no objection to your choice; but I am very sorry it has been made so soon. I am in no haste to lose my daughter. I do not know what Uncle Ralph will say to it."

"Oh, mamma, must you tell him?"

"Certainly, dear. It would not be right to keep him in ignorance of such a fact."

While we were yet speaking, we heard the clatter of his horse's hoofs on the pave, and his cheery voice in the doorway, a moment later, with Aunt Martha. I made a hasty escape to my own room, where I remained till the first dinner-bell rang. Then I went below, determined to have the matter over with Uncle Ralph before dinner, if possible; but Uncle Ralph was not to be seen; and, upon inquiry, I was told he had been gone more than an hour. I found mamma, and learned from her that he was very angry when she told him; more so than she ever remembered to have seen him.

"But never mind, dear," she said; "Uncle Ralph is a good man, and it will be all over before he comes again."

Gertie told me that she went into the library, not knowing they were there, and found Uncle Ralph striding back and forth through the room, and mamma crying upon the sofa. They did not notice her, but, as she slipped away again, she heard Uncle Ralph say, "I am a brute, Fannie, to distress you so; but my feelings sometimes gain the mastery over me." She ran hastily away, and heard no more; but wondered what had annoyed him so, till I told her of Hal's interview with mamma.

"Oh, I am so glad for you, darling," she said; "for though two years seem a long time, they will soon slip away, and then you will be so happy."

"Thank you, dear," I answered; "but I cannot conceive why Uncle Ralph should be so angry. He has always seemed to like Hal, has he not?"

"Oh, yes; you know how kind he was to him the day he was hurt. It is only because you are so young."

And I suppose it is; but it is very hard to feel that the event that has brought so much happiness into my life has caused so much annoyance to those who are so dear to me.

Nov. 18. The days slip by, very full of happiness. I see Hal almost every day, for a little while. We seldom are alone together long, but he always manages to whisper something to me that gives me food for pleasant thoughts and dreams when he is gone."

Mamma was right about Uncle Ralph. He did not come again for several days; but, when he did, he was only a little more grave than usual, and never once alluded to Hal, though I expected every moment he would do so. The only thing that could have any bearing upon the subject was that just as he was going away he turned to me and said, "Do not let excess of happiness cause you to neglect your daily duties, Nannie." He looked at me a moment, as though he were going to say something more, but only added, "God bless you;" and went down the steps.

To my great surprise, Aunt Martha is my strong ally. She says she has always believed in early engagements (she was married at seventeen), and reminds mamma how "Jonas," her husband, always favored "Charles"—dear papa—when he "came a courtin'." She tells Gertie and me, nowadays, long passages in the courtship of herself and the beloved "Jonas," for whom, never having seen him, I may be excused from having any very profound reverence. Ralph says he once saw a picture of him that was said to be a lifelike likeness. He was very small, according to Ralph's account, with light-blue eyes, and red hair, and his face covered with enormous freckles. To dear Aunt Martha he was a paragon of beauty. She loved him, and his imperfections became beautiful in her eyes. I doubt not he was a very good man, though not possessed of either great beauty or profound intellect. What a blessed thing is love, and how truly, like charity, doth it "cover a multitude of sins"! How precious the thought that, in the dull prison-house of life, love, like the little flower "Picciola" in the prisoner's gloomy cell, can beautify and bless that which else were only gloom and darkness!

> "The greatest blessing that our life can give
> Is to be loved for self, and love again :
> By loving truly do we learn to live,—
> And he who ne'er has loved has lived in vain."

Nov. 27. I read over my last entry, and my mind reverts to Uncle Ralph; poor Uncle Ralph! I go back to the sad story he told me once in the library, and think of the anguish it must have cost him to lose, by such a dreadful casualty, the lady he had learned to love so tenderly. How did he ever bear it? Oh, if anything should happen to Hal, I am sure, quite sure, I should die too! I never could live an hour, if the hope of spending life with him were taken from me! But that will never be, unless death comes between us. The thought of our waiting two years to see if either of us will change! The waiting is all well enough, for I am in no hurry to leave dear mamma, but I would trust him, and I am sure he would me, if we were separated wide as the two poles. Poor Uncle Ralph! I wish he could be as happy in his love as I am. I wish he could find some good, good woman to love, who would make life a paradise for him. And yet, come to think of it, I would much rather have him always remain an old bachelor than marry, if he can be just as happy so. How strange it would seem, to have some lady monopolizing all of his time and thoughts, leaving us precious little of either! I am quite sure I should not like it at all. How selfish I am growing! Suppose Nettie had so thought of Hal, where would have been my happiness to-day? But then we are so much younger than he, and he has the memory of his beautiful love to live upon.

Dec. 1. Only three more days till Hal goes to New York. How can I bear the parting for so long a time? He has become inexpressibly dear to me of late; almost to the exclusion of everything else. I think of him, dream of him,) but cannot talk of him, even to Gertie; and there are times when, in the midst of my happiest hours, a shadow, fleeting but darksome, flits over my heart, till, did I believe in presentiments, I should fear sorrow was in store for one or both of us. But away with these fancies!—I will not yield to them. It is only the intensity of my love which makes me fear evil.

Only three more weeks till Charlie, our student-brother, comes for Christmas. My heart leaps at the thought. He has not been home since he left in August, so intent is he this year upon his studies. I trust we shall enjoy the holidays greatly. How I wish Hal could be here also! but it is useless wishing for impossibilities. Ralph is at home so little, too, nowadays. He is studying law with Uncle Ralph, and only spends Sunday with us, and rides out for a little while once or twice a week. Uncle Ralph says he will make a good lawyer. I am sure he is smart enough, and witty enough, for anything. He is much more quiet since dear little Kittie's death; indeed, I think we are none of us quite the same that we were before that sad event. She was so precious, the life of the whole house, and it is as though the sunlight had been suddenly withdrawn from us, and in spite of all our efforts the shadows will steal into our midst. Her beautiful picture is the greatest comfort we have, and but for Uncle Ralph's thoughtful love we should not have had that. How interwoven he does seem with all of our blessings, and has been ever since I can remember. He says Ralph has but one really serious fault, and that is procrastination. He will put off duties that do not seem urgent, thereby frequently causing himself much after-annoyance and chagrin. He came very near losing a very important suit for Uncle Ralph, last week, by neglecting to copy at the proper time some papers he had given him to transcribe. He did not mean to neglect them, but thought he would have ample time the day following to write them all, and so rode out home in the evening. But the next day, when he set himself to the task, he found it was no light matter, and only completed it in time by missing his dinner and writing into half the night. Dear Ralph, he would not willingly harm a fly, much less neglect a duty, but he always was the greatest procrastinator imaginable. I do not think he ever went walking or riding with Gertie or myself that he did not keep us waiting at the door while he performed some little duty that might just as well have been done an hour before. Ah me! how few of us are born into this world faultless! and I am the last one who should speak of the faults of others, for it does seem to me that a double portion of the miserable little commodities have fallen to my share.

Dec. 24. Hal has been gone nearly three weeks, and so busy have we all been, preparing for Christmas, that not one word have I written in my diary. It seemed very strange and lonely, at first, for the days to come and go and bring him not; but mamma soon had me so engrossed —heart, soul, and body—in her plans for Christmas, that the days slipped by almost unnoticed. First of all, though, I had a long, dear letter from Hal; so long and so beautiful that I can well live on it for a month. He says, if we cannot write but one letter a month, it must be long enough to answer for three or four. I answered it the same day that I received it; and every night before I lay my head upon the pillow I read his letter all over again, and it furnishes ample food for pleasant dreams. Gertie laughingly says she wonders if she will ever be so completely enthralled as I? I tell her to bide her time; that it surely will come. But she only shakes her curly head, and says, laughingly, that there must always be one old maid in every family, and that, as I have stolen a march upon her, she must e'en "make a virtue of necessity," and submit to her fate with as much grace as may be. Gertie an old maid! I look at her now, as she lies sleeping so peacefully, —for it is late at night as I write,—her fair cheek pillowed upon her little hand, the short curls tangling themselves willfully all round her white forehead, and the bright lips wreathing themselves into a smile at some pleasant fancy in her sleep, and I laugh outright at the thought. No, no; in the years to come, she is destined to be the light of some happy home, the idol of some manly heart; and none could be more worthy to fill such a place than she.

But to return to our Christmas work. There are several families of poor people scattered among the hills back of us, and mamma gave Gertie and me permission to go and ask all the children, some thirty or forty in number, to come to the house at seven o'clock Christmas eve. So for the last three weeks we have been all working, working like bees; and now a great Christmas-tree stands, ready to be lit, in the large dining-hall, loaded with all kinds of useful and amusing presents for the little ones. There are dresses and aprons and warm flannels; and cloaks and hoods, all made up ready for use; stockings and mittens (over which Aunt Martha has nearly worn out her blessed old fingers, I fear), and scarfs, and shoes; and cloth for jackets and trousers for the boys; a new dress for each of their mammas; and a warm flannel gown for poor old sick Granny Weir, and an armful of things for her little granddaughter, Lizzie, who nurses her so tenderly. Then there are picture-books, and dolls, and tiny work-baskets, for the girls; and skates and sleds, and fire-crackers in abundance, for the boys; to say nothing of candy-bags and tiny nut baskets; and every shape of fancy cookies, made by Millie's skillful hand, in profusion. The tree is loaded down with the lighter articles, while the more weighty ones are arranged tastefully at the foot of it. Uncle Ralph has, as usual, shared largely in the expenses of the thing; and Charlie, who is home for the holidays, and well and happy, and Ralph, have taken all the heavy work off of us,—arranged the tree beautifully, and hung the presents with great taste upon it.

It will be such a treat as I trow the little ones have rarely had before. Miss Lane has been of great assistance. Nettie Ray, too, has entered, heart and soul, into our plans, and spent the greater part of her time with us for the last three weeks. She is coming over this evening, to stay until after Christmas. Oh, if Hal—my Hal—could only be here too!

Dec. 26. Well, Christmas is past; and such a merry, happy time as we did have. First of all came our Christmas-tree. Promptly at the hour appointed, the little ones came thronging in, all washed and dressed clean, but many of them very forlorn-looking indeed. Uncle Ralph was unanimously chosen president of our little meeting, and after the drawing-room doors had been thrown open, and we had all joined in a Christmas anthem, he made a pretty little impromptu speech to the children, and then began the distributing of the gifts. He took them down, one by one, from the tree, read the name of the recipient aloud, and passed it to Ralph or Charlie, who, in turn, passed it over among the crowd of eager expectant little faces, always accompanied with some witticism, that kept up a perpetual glee among them. Then we found, too, that many precious little gifts had been slyly smuggled on to the tree, so that we all came in for a full share of the spoils, as Ralph would say, and many a little shout of merry surprise and pleasure went round as, one after one, these articles were handed down. A volume of Lalla Rookh, from Miss Lane, Schiller's complete works, from Charlie, coral bracelets, from Ralph, a work-box, from Gertie, a picture, from mamma, of herself, in a most exquisite case (more precious to me than all the rest), a soft, warm sleighing-hood, from Aunt Martha, knit by herself, and last, but not least, the most exquisite little watch I ever saw, from Uncle Ralph, fell to my lot. Mamma's and Uncle Ralph's presents to Gertie were the same as mine; and, indeed, none of us have any right to complain of the visit of Santa Claus this year; for I am sure all are equally favored and equally delighted. The little ones all ran home with happy hearts,—if bright eyes and smiling faces are any index thereto. Then we drew our chairs about the cheery grate in the drawing-room, and talked of past Christmases, and looked forward with hope to future ones, till tea was in. Then some one proposed that we all should drive to the village and hear the Christmas anthem in the old church. The sleighing is excellent, so the proposition met with universal acclamation from the young folks. Mamma demurred a little at first, it would keep us out so late, and she knew we must be tired. But we overruled all of her objections, till at last she consented, on condition that Uncle Ralph would drive us,—and when did Uncle Ralph refuse to do anything that would give us pleasure? So, a little before eleven o'clock, the ponies and sleigh were brought to the door, and, well defended from the cold by warm wraps and hoods (I christened my new one), and completely enveloped in buffalo robes, we started. The night was calm and clear, and the stars looked down upon us as brilliantly as though their light had not already shone for centuries upon just such merry groups. As we whirled along over the spotless snow, so pure, so beautiful, with not a sound breaking the stillness of the night, save the soft crunching of the snow beneath the horses' feet, and the musical jingle of the silver bells, we all, by common consent, relapsed into silence; and I doubt not our thoughts were not widely different. For my own part, they were full of untold interest. My mind ran eagerly back to the time, a little more than eighteen hundred years ago, when doubtless, on just such a night as this, the shepherds of Judea, watching beside their flocks, beheld the angel descending from above, who came to bring to earth the "glad tidings of great joy." A great calm seemed to fall upon me, as in fancy I beheld it all, and then an intense longing to one day visit the very spot where the news was first proclaimed to man. Full of the thought, I said, very softly,—

"Uncle Ralph, will you some day take me to Palestine?"

I was nestled up close beside him as he drove, and he turned and looked down upon me in the starlight a moment, earnestly, and then said,—

"I would love to, little Nannie, dearly; but how can I now?"

His tone brought to my recollection that I was no longer my own, and had no right to travel in future with any gentleman but one,—not even with Uncle Ralph,—and I relapsed into silence, to think the rest of the way of Hal.

We reached the church about half-past eleven, and found it already densely crowded. The lights were turned so low that only a dim outline could be seen of anything. We found seats after some difficulty, and waited in silence and darkness for about half an hour. A profound silence was over all; we could almost hear our own heart-throbs. I could distinctly hear the breathing of a gentleman who sat just behind me. At length the old clock in the belfry, that for more than a century has rung the hours, struck the first midnight chime. Instantly, as though by magic, the whole church became a blaze of light; the bells in the tower, and of all the surrounding churches, rang forth a joyous peal; the grand old organ woke its most heavenly strains, and the whole congregation arose as by one impulse to their feet, while the grand Christmas anthem broke forth with a power I had never heard equaled before. It seemed as though "the glad tidings" had indeed but then been spoken, and the world of darkness had sprung into light and joy at the sound.

As we passed from the church, a tall, dark figure stepped up to me on the church steps, and said, in a low tone,—

"Will you not wish me 'a merry Christmas,' darling?"

And both my hands were caught and held in a warm grasp by Hal. Oh, what a great, glad throb my heart gave when by tone and touch I recognized him! My Christmas had already begun. He had run down from the city just to spend Christmas day with us, had reached the village on the half-past-eleven train at night, and was on his way to the hotel, to remain till morning, when he saw us enter the church. Of course his plans were all changed, and he himself went to the church. We took him with us into the sleigh; and I did not sit by Uncle Ralph going home. Gertie took my place, and I sat by somebody else; and our ride home in the clear starlight, that Christmas morning, is one I shall not soon cease to remember. We set Hal and Nettie down at their own gate, Nettie of course preferring to remain at home, now that Hal had come; but they both promised to come over early the next day, which they did; and such a pleasant, pleasant day as we did have. The only drawback to it was that, for the first time since I can remember, Uncle Ralph failed to be present at our Christmas dinner. He told us at breakfast that he was compelled to go to town; and the burst of indignation with which the announcement was met was enough to have appalled and conquered a less resolute heart.

"But, Ralph," said mamma, appealingly, "you will surely return to dinner?"

"I am afraid I cannot this time, Fannie," he answered; and he and mamma exchanged glances that, for the life of me, I cannot understand; and mamma said no more.

We all used every endeavor to get him to remain; but he persisted in saying that he had acquired Ralph's habit of procrastinating in his business, till he was compelled to work hard on Christmas in order to be able to take up a case the next day.

"Cannot I help you, Uncle Ralph?" asked our Ralph, who is very sore over the matter of procrastination.

"No, my boy; it is no fault of yours, but my own neglect, that has caused the disappointment: so for once you must eat your Christmas dinner without me."

"Humph!" said Charlie. "A Christmas dinner at Beechwood without Uncle Ralph is like a plum-pudding without any plums!"

In the general laughter that followed this sally, Uncle Ralph made his escape; but it was a sad disappointment to us all not to have him with us. We missed him everywhere, and the day seemed incomplete without him.

We all went to church in the morning, a merry sleigh-load, and listened to a fine discourse from the words, "We have seen his star in the east." The minister, a stranger to us, treated his subject with great skill, and spoke with a beautiful and touching pathos of the birth and sufferings of the Saviour, and with sublime trust of that wonderful hope for the future that the humble follower of Christ may always attain. He pointed us all to the glorious Star in the East, whose promise is ever to the faithful, and exhorted us never to rest until by faith we had looked upon it in its beauty.

Returning, we all sat down to a regular Christmas

dinner, such as only mamma's skill can produce. Nettie stayed all night with us, and Hal allowed himself barely time to reach the ten-o'clock train that night. How kind and good of him to come all this way just to spend one little day at Beechwood! He brought me a most delicately beautiful pearl ring, which he slipped upon my finger Christmas morning as we rode home together in the starlight. Dear Hal! how strange it seems that he should love me so dearly! He says he likes New York so well that he thinks he will make it his home in the future. That makes me sad; it is so far from Beechwood and mamma.

Dec. 27. What a way Uncle Ralph has of making one see one's own faults in the right light! About two weeks ago he said one day to Ralph,—

"I see that a lot of fine horses are to be sold at B——" (mentioning a little village about seven miles north of us), "and the beautiful filly you admired so much yesterday is among the number. I have been thinking it would be a nice ride for us, Ralph, to go over on the day of the sale: who knows but we might strike a bargain for the little beauty?"

Ralph of course was all animation at the thought, and asked, eagerly,—

"When does it come off, Uncle Ralph?"

"There is a private sale on the 21st, and all that are not disposed of that day will be knocked down by the auctioneer the day following."

"Oh, she will go by private sale, of course," said Ralph; "she is too pretty to go begging."

"The filly? Yes, I suppose so, unless the sale should not be generally known. I guess we had better be there the first day, anyhow."

"By all means," said Ralph; and so it was settled.

Well, on the day appointed Uncle Ralph came out at a late hour in the morning (Ralph was spending that week at home, helping us with our tree), and in reply to Ralph's inquiries said a friend had come into the office the day before and prevented his attending to some important writing on hand, so he was compelled to finish it that morning, and in consequence they would that day be too late for the sale. "Besides," said he, "I see Racer has lost a shoe, and it would ruin him to ride over that rough road shoeless. I only rode out to tell you what caused the delay, and to say that we must ride over bright and early in the morning. I met a gentleman who had been to the sale, as I came along, and he told me the filly was still there."

Ralph swallowed his disappointment as best he might; and Uncle Ralph, refusing to come in, hurried away, saying that he must go back and have Racer's shoes looked to. The next morning Ralph was "booted and spurred" soon after breakfast, and never was loyal knight so impatient to see his lady-love, as was he for Uncle Ralph's appearance.

"What in the world can keep him?" he had asked, impatiently, at least a dozen times before he came. At last, about ten o'clock, he came hurriedly, saying it was too bad, but he had thought the smith could fasten Racer's shoe in a very few minutes, and had neglected having it done the night before, and found in the morning it needed more than he had thought; and hence he had been greatly delayed.

"It is too bad, Ralph," he said; "but I guess we can be there in time;" and away they dashed at a spirited pace. About four o'clock they came back, very leisurely, and I knew at once by Ralph's disappointed looks that they had been too late. He was too generous to complain; but I knew it had been a sad disappointment to him; for I doubt not he had dreamed of that beautiful filly, sleeping and waking, (almost as much as a young girl dreams of her lover.) Uncle Ralph did not dismount, nor did we see him again till Christmas eve. That night, after the gifts from the tree had been distributed, he said to Ralph,—

"It is too bad, Ralph, I declare, about that filly. I fully intended she should have been your Christmas-present, and but for my negligence she would have been. As it is, you see, I have found nothing worthy to supply her place." There had been nothing for him from Uncle Ralph on the Christmas-tree, while Charlie, the book-worm, had a complete edition of the British Encyclopædia, over which he now gloats, night and day.

"If it had been your fault that we missed the sale," he continued, "I should have read you a regular lecture on the evils of procrastination; but as it was mine, you generously suppress all words of blame."

"Ah, Uncle Ralph," said he, "I trust you will never have to lecture me on that miserable failing again; for I here swear, by the head of that beautiful nag, that should have been mine to-night, and is not, that I will from this hour adopt for my rule of action, 'Never put off till to-morrow what can be done to-day!'"

"Bravo!" cried Uncle Ralph. "Now I am sure you will indeed make a successful man. I believe punctuality the only essential quality you lacked to insure success."

Ralph flushed with pleasure at these words of praise, and answered, earnestly,—

"Thank you, thank you, Uncle Ralph; I ask no better Christmas-present than your sincere commendation."

Tea at this moment was announced, and the subject dropped; but early the next morning Ralph went, as was his custom, to the stables, to take a look at the ponies, and in an incredibly short space of time came hurriedly in, with a countenance in which surprise, delight, and gratitude were unmistakably blended, and, seizing Uncle Ralph by both hands, said, eagerly,—

"How am I ever to repay you for your untiring interest in, and unfailing kindness to, me?"

Uncle Ralph tried hard to look surprised at this outburst, but Ralph continued:—

"All my life long I have been trying your patience with my mad pranks, and never more than by my careless neglect of duties of late; and now, as always in the past, you repay my faults by gratifying the first wish of my heart."

"Nay, nay, Ralph; it is the promise of amendment I repay, not the faults," said Uncle Ralph, laughing; and mamma said,—

"What has Uncle Ralph been doing now, I wonder?"

"Doing?" cried Ralph. "What has he been doing? Come and see." And he led the way to the hall door, before which we found Joseph, the groom, leading slowly backward and forward the most beautiful little filly I ever saw. She is a beauty, and no mistake. I am no judge of horseflesh, but I should single her out among a thousand: a dark bay, slightly dappled, with the trimmest little body and limbs imaginable, two white ankles, two black ones, and a heavy, black, flowing mane and tail. How beautifully she arched her glossy neck, and spurned the ground as lightly with her pretty feet as a delicate lady could have done! I did not at all wonder that Ralph was in love with her. A card was attached to the pretty bridle that encircled her head, upon which was written, in Uncle Ralph's well-known hand, "Something that I trust will prove a pleasant daily reminder to Ralph of the good resolutions he made on Christmas eve."

"Is she not a beauty?" said Ralph, fondly patting her glossy neck, while she tossed her head coquettishly, as though conscious of the admiration she was exciting. "Is she not a beauty? I think we will have to name her 'Di.'" Then, suddenly turning to Uncle Ralph, he said, earnestly, "If ever I do forget, or fail to keep, the resolution expressed last night, I shall be worse than a traitor to myself, and deserve to lose every friend I have." And he never will.

Jan. 4. The holidays are past. Charlie has gone back to college, Ralph to his law-studies in the village, and Gertie and I have settled ourselves resolutely to our studies. I mean to apply myself unremittingly to my books for the rest of the winter, to the exclusion of everything else,— even you, old book. I mean to make myself, if possible, worthy of Hal's love. He is so talented and clever, so well read in every department of literature, that I have to strain every nerve to make myself a suitable companion for him. Nettie says he thinks me almost perfect. How strange that any one could think so of poor imperfect me! But if he does think so, I will do my very best to fill his ideal. It would be terrible for him to feel some day that he had made a great mistake, and that I was not his ideal love after all. What would he do, I wonder, in such a case?—tell me of it, or suffer for his self-deception in silence? The latter, I fear; he is so noble and generous. But I will not allow myself to think of the possibility of this. He has surely known me long enough to know me well; and if he already loves me as I now am, with all my faults, he will surely love me better when he sees how hard I try to become more perfect for his sake.

Jan. 19. The tranquil stream of our daily life is again disturbed by a ripple. Cousin Minnie Norris has come to live with us. She is the only child of papa's half-sister, who died about three years ago. Last year her father married again, and shortly afterward himself died; so poor Minnie was doubly orphaned. It seems that her step-mother and herself did not get along very well together, and a few weeks ago Minnie wrote to mamma, and complained so bitterly of her lot that mamma, who has always loved her very tenderly, wrote at once inviting her to make her home with us, and also wrote to her step-mother kindly offering to relieve her of all future care, as she (mamma) was really more of kin to Minnie than herself. Mrs. Norris replied very courteously, and thanked mamma in a very ladylike manner, confessing that it would be a great favor to be relieved of Minnie, as, having known her such a little while before her father's death, she had failed to acquire control over her and felt the responsibility to be very great. So she came to us two days ago. She is just my age; is a pretty, delicate-looking little thing, and perfectly charming in her childish simplicity. She says her step-mother was very strict with her, allowing her to see no company, and frequently withholding letters that were written to her. Poor child! she seems so frail and delicate. I trust she will be so happy here that we will soon see the roses again upon her cheeks. Mamma has given her the room adjoining ours, and she is soon to begin studying with us also. Gertie and I are very happy to have her with us, and will, I am sure, fulfill mamma's injunction to do all we can to make her happy.

Feb. 20. Another long, dear letter from Hal. He steals a few days from the month every time. "Oh, Nannie," he writes, "the months go by so slowly that, when I think that there are still twenty-one to pass before I can claim you before the world, I feel half desperate. Why is this long delay necessary? I am sure we have enough to live upon if I should never make a dollar by my profession, which, however, I mean to follow resolutely and steadfastly. I have no notion of being a drone in this work-day world of ours; but it would be so sweet to feel that I had some one else to work for besides myself, and that one my beautiful darling. I confess I cannot see the point to this delay. Is it to test our affections? Surely, darling, we are not children, that they need fear we do not know our own hearts. I suppose when the two years have expired they will think it necessary for another to pass before we can marry, after our engagement has been proclaimed. I protest against this long delay! What shall we gain by it? Only two or three years snatched from the happiness of life. You are mine, and I want you, I need you; and I really think one year's probation is all that should be expected. Can we not by protest or strategy overcome your mamma's and Uncle Ralph's scruples? What say you, my darling?" And with my heart pleading strongly all the while for my absent darling, I have yet listened to reason rather than love (perhaps because I was sure mamma would not listen a moment to our proposition should it be made), and have written him thus in reply:—

"It does seem a long while, dear Hal, for us to wait, since you expect to spend most of your time in New York, and therefore we can see so little of each other; but I am quite sure mamma would never listen to any proposed change in the time. We must try and be patient, and live on the hopes of the future. And indeed, dear Hal, I have so much to learn still, before I can hope to be worthy of your great love, that the time, long as it seems, will be all too short in which to accomplish it. Three months have already gone, and although I miss your welcome step and voice, and the clasp of your dear hand, daily, still I live so much in the future, and am trying so hard to be better prepared to meet it when it comes, that the days come and go almost before I am aware of their presence. Let us be patient and hopeful, dear Hal, for if faithful to each other nothing but death can come between us in the future. I read the last sentence over, and feel half tempted to erase it, it seems so much like admitting the possibility of either proving unfaithful, than which I know nothing could be more impossible. But let it stand; it will do for us to laugh together over in the future."

What more I wrote is not even for you to know, old friend; such things must ever be too sacred for any eyes but the dear ones that will look upon them to-night in a distant city..

Minnie improves greatly upon acquaintance. She is very sparkling and interesting, though, Miss Lane says, she is not so good with her books as either Gertie or myself. Poor child! I guess she has been more of a pet and plaything all her life to her parents, than anything else; and since their death she must have been very lonely and desolate. She seems at times very bright and happy,—indeed, is generally so; but again she will be depressed and troubled; and I have more than once found her in tears, of which she always seemed much ashamed, and would allow me to offer no sympathy or consolation, asserting ever that it was only one of her "blue days." I wish she would not be so reticent; I sometimes fear she has a sorrow of her own, unknown to any of us. Truly every "heart knoweth its own bitterness."

Ralph and Minnie are great friends. He makes a great pet of her; but indeed we all do that, she is so confiding and childlike, and withal so pretty and delicate. Even Aunt Martha calls her "darling;" something of which she has never been guilty toward either Gertie or myself. Ralph calls her his humming-bird (and indeed she does remind one of that beautiful little bird,—so airy and delicate), and seems more like the Ralph of old times than he has since Kittie died. He came in yesterday with a pet squirrel he had purchased from a boy at the door, and seeing Aunt Martha sitting in her usual place by the window, knitting, her back toward the door, he quietly deposited the squirrel upon the back of her chair, and passed on to a seat by Minnie. Aunt Martha was busy, at the moment, "taking up a stitch" she had dropped in her knitting, and was not aware of the proximity of the squirrel till it leaped upon her shoulder and ran briskly up her neck on to her head.

"For the land's sake!" (her favorite expression when startled,) "what is the matter with my head?" she cried, dropping her knitting, and striking vigorously about her head and shoulders, one well-directed blow sending the squirrel flying into the middle of the floor, where he sat, doubtless greatly surprised at his somewhat abrupt dismissal from such pleasant quarters.

"Are there any more?" she inquired, anxiously, still brushing about her head and shoulders.

"No, Aunt Martha, there are no more," mamma hastened to say; and everybody in the room laughed merrily except herself, not excepting Aunt Martha, who peered over her spectacles at Ralph, as she carefully adjusted her snowy cap, considerably disarranged by the vigorous brushing it had received, and said, laughingly,—

"Ah, you are a sad rogue, Ralph; I don't know what we are to do with you!"

"With me, Aunt Martha?" ejaculated Ralph, as though greatly surprised at the insinuation,—which called forth another merry peal of laughter from us all.

"Mamma looks grave," said Ralph; "she thinks me incorrigible, I fear."

"I was only wondering," said mamma, quietly, "whether my son would never lay aside the pranks that are barely excusable in a half-grown schoolboy."

"You will have to place him in the navy, Aunt Fannie," laughed Minnie: "that is the place for incorrigibles!"

"Or under a woman's administration!" said Ralph, maliciously, looking at Minnie.

Mamma made no reply to either remark, but quietly resumed her reading, which had been interrupted by Ralph's entrance.

"Now, mamma thinks that to all my other faults I have added that of disrespect to the best mother that ever lived. Am I past all redemption, dear mamma?" said Ralph, throwing himself with a child's abandon at her feet, and nestling his curly head lovingly in her lap.

"No, my son," mamma at once kindly answered, stroking back the curls from his white forehead, "no; you have many noble qualities, of which I am justly proud, and few of which I am ashamed; but it always pains me to see you forget the respect ever due to age, or to hear you speak flippantly or lightly of the sex to which your mother and sisters belong."

"Oh, mamma," cried Ralph, "you make me most heartily ashamed of myself. I will apologize at once to Aunt Martha; and as to the other, I am quite sure you will never have cause to reprove me again; for I cannot forget that all that is good or lovable about me, if anything there is, has been instilled, through years of untiring patience, by the best of women,—my mother." And he arose hastily, kissed mamma tenderly, and turned at once frankly to Aunt Martha, who, anticipating the apology, held up both hands deprecatingly, and cried,—

"No, no, Ralph; have your fun. Boys must be boys; and I think Frances entirely too severe upon such innocent follies."

"No, Aunt Martha; my mother is right, as she always is; and if you will not hear my apologies for the past, you must at least accept my promises of amendment for the future. You shall see what a good boy I can be when I try," he added, roguishly; "and, to begin, let me hold that yarn for you to wind, for I see that yours is just exhausted." And he sat patiently, to Aunt Martha's great satisfaction, through the tiresome ordeal, telling her laughable stories all the time, which greatly retarded the process of winding.

Minnie seemed greatly astonished at mamma's influence over Ralph, whispering to me,—

"How queer to hear a grown man acknowledge a fault as though he were a child!"

Ah, she has yet to learn what a precious mother we have, and how impossible it would be to go contrary to her wishes, or to do anything, willingly, that would give her pain.

April 12. Spring, beautiful and blooming, is upon us. The trees are putting on a delicate tint of green, many of the shrubs and bushes are in full leaf, and the little birds are twittering and singing in them all the day long. The meadows are dressed in their richest green, and the daisies and butterflies spangle them with silver and gold, while the little brook sparkles and dances in the sunlight all the day long. In the beech grove the violets and anemones peep up through the dry leaves, the squirrel frisks gayly about, as though delighted that his winter store had lasted till the sunshine came again, and the whole woods are vocal with the songs of the birds, returned from their winter sojourn in a warmer clime. It is spring-time also in my heart, and it re-echoes all their gladness. I can scarcely realize that the winter, the long winter, that I so much dreaded, has indeed gone so quickly. So busy have we been, Gertie, Minnie, and I, among our books, that we have had but little time in which to indulge regrets or think of missing pleasures. Hal has finished his winter's course, and will remain permanently in New York, continuing his studies and practice with Dr. Niles, who is said to be one of the oldest and best physicians in the city. I do not know why, but

I cannot feel quite reconciled to his settling in New York. Raised in the quiet seclusion of our beautiful hills, I have no longing for city life, and fear I shall find it irksome rather than pleasant. Not but that I shall be happy any place with Hal, but it would have been infinitely more to my taste had he settled nearer home, in the retirement of some pleasant little village. Then, too, it is so far from mamma. But, as Uncle Ralph often says, "Sufficient unto the day is the evil thereof." I will not borrow trouble.

There is a secret on my heart to-night, old book, that weighs heavily. I cannot decide whether it is best for me to tell it to mamma or not, since it does not concern myself, but another; so I will even tell it to you, dear old receptacle of all my woes and joys, and if the disclosure brings no relief, I shall at least, perhaps, be better able to decide what it is best for me to do. Walking this evening in the early twilight, I caught a glimpse of Minnie among the trees in the orchard, and thought I would go out and join her; but as I reached the garden gate I saw she was not alone,—a gentleman was with her. "Ah, it is Ralph," I thought, "the sly rogue;" for he has been with her much of late. But an instant afterward I saw my mistake. It was a perfect stranger to me, and Minnie seemed very fond of him, leaning upon his arm and looking up tenderly into his face. I felt myself an intruder, and slipped away unseen. But the thought haunts me constantly, "If he is a friend of Minnie's, why does he not come boldly to the house and ask for her? Why this covert way of meeting?" No one would oppose them. And then, "Who is he?" Somehow, all evening I find myself connecting this stranger with her depressed moods; why, I know not.

Minnie came in shortly after I reached the house, but lingered only a moment before retiring to her room. I said, carelessly,—

"Why, where have you been, Minnie, so long?"

She blushed crimson, and answered, evasively,—

"Only taking a little walk."

"Where?" I persisted, innocently.

She hesitated a moment, and then said, "In the garden;" and went at once to her room.

So she wishes to keep the visit secret; and for all it may be perfectly right and proper (how could it be otherwise with dear little Minnie?), I cannot help feeling restless and uneasy. I wish mamma had seen them, instead of myself, for I feel as though she ought to know it, and yet I cannot bear to betray a secret evidently desired to be so kept. At any rate, I will wait a little and see.

April 28. Minnie's friend has again been here, and, as fate would have it, I have the second time been the unwilling spectator of the interview. I had been over the hill to carry some broth and delicacies to old Granny Weir, who remains very feeble in spite of the pleasant weather, and she detained me so long, telling me, in her rambling, disconnected way, of her sickness and troubles, that it was quite late before I could get started home, and the young moon was throwing a soft light down over the hill-tops as I entered the back gate of the orchard, glad to be so near home. As I ran hurriedly forward, the murmur of voices attracted my attention, and a moment afterward I saw, quite close beside me, Minnie and her strange lover seated upon one of our rustic seats beneath a tree. One arm was about her waist, and the other hand inclosed both of Minnie's, who seemed perfectly reconciled to be so imprisoned. Fortunately, they saw me almost as soon as I did them, and rose hastily, evidently much embarrassed; at least Minnie was so; but the gentleman, with perfect *sang froid*, lifted his hat to me politely, and said to Minnie,—

"I must not detain you any longer, but am very happy

to have chanced upon you so unexpectedly to-night;" and, with a polite bow, he was gone.

I was as much embarrassed as Minnie, for her sake, and walked on slowly toward the house, not knowing what to say. "'Chanced upon her unexpectedly,' indeed!" I thought, half indignant at his attempt to deceive me. Minnie walked beside me in silence till we reached the garden gate; then she said, half pettishly,—

"You will not betray me, Nannie?"

"To whom, Minnie?"

"Aunt Fannie, of course."

"Do you think it right to deceive mamma so, Minnie?"

"No, Nannie; but I love him so dearly," she answered, in a half-whisper that touched my heart.

"Poor little Minnie!" I said; "I can sympathize with you in your love, but not in your wish to conceal it. Why does he not come boldly to the house and claim you?"

"My step-mother opposed him so bitterly that he is afraid to venture again."

"But he cannot hope to win you without coming," I answered. "If he is worthy of your love, he need fear no opposition from mamma, I am sure."

"He is of one of the best families in New York," she said.

"Then, if he is worthy of the name he bears, I am quite sure your fears are groundless. Mamma would never oppose anything that would add to your happiness."

"But you will not tell her of our meeting, Nannie?"

"On one condition, dear Minnie, I will faithfully guard your secret; and that is, that you will meet him so no more, and either tell mamma your wishes yourself, or else let him come up boldly, as he should do, for himself. You must not think me hard, dear Minnie," I said, "for I feel that I am almost as guilty as yourself, in hiding this from mamma; for I must now tell you that this is not the first time that I have accidentally chanced upon you together, and I really feel that it must be the last."

"Thank you, dear Nannie, for not betraying me," she said. "I know it was not right to act so, and I will write to him to-night that he must in future come to the house. We must risk it, I suppose."

And then we said no more, but came into the house together; and I feel greatly relieved; for this thing of keeping a secret from mamma has weighed heavily on my heart, yet I am very thankful not to have to betray dear little Minnie.

May 2. Last Sunday, Uncle Ralph and Ralph came out as usual to spend the day with us, and we all went to the church on the hill together. It was a lovely day, so we preferred walking to riding; and as we strolled along through the green lane we overtook Nettie and her aunt, also going to church. As we walked on together, my mind went back to another Sunday morning, nearly two years ago, the day we first met Ellis Ray, and dwelt upon the changes that have taken place since then. It was a happy group that sat that pleasant morning beneath the maple-trees on the hill-side,—a happy group; but, alas, how is it scattered now! and we can never be so united again. Of that merry group of eight, just half this morning are together, and of the rest no two are in the same place. Ralph, Gertie, Nettie, and I still walk the old familiar paths; Charlie is at Yale, Hal in New York, Ellis Ray at Cambridge studying for the ministry, and Kittie, precious little Kittie, is with the angels. I am afraid I did not hear much of dear old Mr. White's sermon, my mind was so preoccupied by these sad thoughts. I know that he delivered, in his own simple and impressive manner, a beautiful discourse from the words, "And there shall be no night there;" but, in spite of his simple and touching eloquence, my mind would go back wandering to the past, —the beautiful and sunny past,—over which now we can only plant flowers of remembrance.

As we came from the church, I felt Minnie, who walked beside me, give a sudden start, and, following the direction of her eyes, I saw her strange lover standing at a little distance from the door. I don't know why it is, and I regret it with all my heart, but he repulses me strangely. He is a fine, gentlemanly-looking man, and evidently has seen good society, but my heart involuntarily shrinks whenever I think of him. There is an inexpressible something that repulses me, though for the life of me I cannot tell what it is. He came forward at once to meet us, and Minnie introduced him as Colonel Leslie, from New York. He was very polite,—too much so, I thought; and when we had passed the compliments of the day, I dropped back with Nettie and Gertie, and left him to Minnie, undisturbed. Gertie and Nettie were full of curiosity as to who he was, and where he came from; but I said, simply, that he was an old acquaintance of Minnie's, from New York.

"And what in the world brings him here?" said Ralph, a little discontentedly, I thought; for he had joined us while we were discussing the stranger.

"His own inclinations, I presume," I answered, a little maliciously: "they are the motive power in gentlemen's movements generally."

Ralph made a little ugly face at me, but said no more; and Nettie and Gertie soon forgot, or wholly ignored, the presence of the stranger, in the thoughts of their own happy hearts. But not so with me. I was troubled. I did not like this man, I was forced to confess; and then, too, I had an idea that Ralph's interest in Minnie was not simply a passing one; and although I had always hoped it might have been Nettie who should win him, I could not brook the thought of another being preferred to him.

When we reached home, mamma, who was a little in advance of us, waited upon the steps until we came up. She had noticed the stranger with Minnie, and, supposing him to be an old acquaintance of hers, now waited for the introduction, which was given, and then kindly invited him to remain to dinner. This he politely declined, but said that, with mamma's permission, he would call in the evening; which he did. He was very entertaining and agreeable, and I began to think that after all I had been harsh in my judgment of him. He came again the next evening, and then again the next, apologizing for the frequency of his visits by saying he was detained by business in the neighborhood, and had no other acquaintances. Then he took Minnie riding, the last day of his visit, and it was quite late when they returned, and dear little Minnie looked so bright and happy that I blamed myself again and again that I could not enter more fully into her feelings. I said to myself, "It is all because I know of his meeting her clandestinely. But for that, I should probably admire him as much as she could desire;" and I made many resolutions to do better by them in future. But yesterday, as I sat at my desk, writing to Hal, mamma came into my room, and, closing the door, said to me,—

"I want to talk with you a little alone, Nannie."

My first thought was that she had bad news to tell me, and I gasped out,—

"Oh, mamma, what is it? Hal? Charlie?"

But she soon assured me all was right with both; that it was of Minnie she wished to speak. I breathed more freely; and she said,—

"I cannot help seeing that Minnie is very much interested in Colonel Leslie, and, as I naturally feel anxious that she should do well in life, I wish we knew more of his antecedents. Does she ever speak of him?"

"She says he belongs to one of the first families in New York," I answered.

"He evidently has seen good society, and seems to be well educated and refined," said mamma, half questioningly.

"Yes," I answered; but for the life of me I could not speak in his favor.

"Nannie," said mamma, at length, "do you know anything of Colonel Leslie?"

"No, mamma, nothing; nothing indeed," said I, feeling miserable and guilty in the thought that I had to conceal even so trifling a thing from mamma.

"I thought you did not seem prepossessed in his favor; and you know, dear, I have a right to know anything and everything that can in the least affect Minnie's happiness."

"I know, mamma; and indeed I have no good reason for not liking Colonel Leslie. I do not dislike him; only, for some unaccountable reason, he repulses me strangely. It may be only, you know, mamma, because, because—well, because I have a very good excuse for not feeling much interest in any strange gentleman at present," I answered, blushing violently as I spoke.

Mamma kindly overlooked my embarrassment, and said,—

"Yes, dear; but that would not produce the feeling of repulsion of which you spoke, and which, now that you have spoken of it, I must confess I have felt from the first myself, though perhaps not so strongly as yourself. It was that feeling that first prompted me to speak with you about him, to see, if possible, if I stood alone in the matter."

"Minnie told me her step-mother disliked him very much, but did not say for what reason."

"I am afraid he is not a good man," said mamma; "but

we must not pass judgment hastily. I will have Uncle Ralph write to New York and make inquiries concerning him; and in the mean time we must try and overcome this feeling as much as possible, for Minnie's sake. Does she talk of him much?"

"Very little; and that is one thing that seems so strange. You know she is very communicative, generally; and although her heart is wrapped up in him, evidently, she does not seem to like us to ask questions concerning him at all."

"I am afraid she has not chosen wisely; but I shall hope for the best," said mamma, as she again left me alone.

Oh, what would I not have given to be able to tell her all I knew! But for my promise' sake I dared not. I have felt no disposition whatever to betray Minnie's secret to any one, not even to Gertie, who knows all of my own; but the thought of being compelled to conceal anything from mamma, even the veriest trifle, makes me feel guilty and miserable. Dear mamma, whose life has been spent in trying to inculcate principles of integrity and honor in her children, and who has so often said to us, "Whatever you do, never try to deceive or equivocate. Always come to me with the truth,—not a part, but all of it,—and speak up frankly and freely, and the wrong you may have committed will be at least half obliterated by such a course." And so we had always found it. And yet now, when she no longer admonished me as a child but often counseled with me as a woman, my first act was to ignore her former lessons and begin deception. Is it not enough to make me scorn Colonel Leslie, to think he should be the guilty cause of it all?

I finished my letter to Hal in no very enviable mood, and took occasion to speak incidentally of Colonel Leslie in it, to see if he perchance knew aught of him. I am sure if he does he will not fail to mention him in his reply.

Dear Hal! how happy I am to know that he is above reproach! I am sure, much as he loves me, he would sooner give me up than do, or counsel me to do, a dishonorable thing. Our first thought, almost, was to speak with mamma of our wishes and plans; and had they been opposed or forbidden, and argument and entreaty alike failed to overcome the objection, I should only have waited quietly, and am sure Hal would have done the same, until I was of age, or rather until I was twenty-one, and then firmly but respectfully have asserted my rights as a woman to judge for myself. I should have scorned deception, for I do believe that evil alone can spring from it. (There is a time—all under twenty-one, I will say—in which I think it a daughter's duty to yield implicitly to her mother's judgment, especially in matters matrimonial;) unless, indeed, a marriage averse to her feelings should be urged; then she should, at all ages, be immovable as granite. But when she has reached the age of twenty-one her mind should be sufficiently matured to decide for herself, and she should always be allowed so to do. Not that she may not listen to the advice of her friends,—that none are ever too old to do,—but at the same time she is herself better able to decide what will promote her own happiness than another, even though that other should be a dearly-beloved mother.

I once expressed these thoughts to mamma, and she said that I was right; that she thought parents often caused themselves and their children much unhappiness by treating them as children, incompetent to decide for themselves, after they had reached a mature age. I incidentally spoke of these things to Minnie also, yesterday, hoping to influence her to avoid haste in her love-affair; but she answered—somewhat impatiently, it seemed to me—that she thought a woman competent to decide for herself long before she was twenty-one years old: so I said no more.

May 20. Uncle Ralph is going away, to be absent, he says, an indefinite time, but, at the very least, all summer. It is too bad. How can we get along without him? And Charlie and Hal so soon to come, too; for Hal has written that he will spend several weeks at home during the warm weather. How can we do anything without Uncle Ralph, when he is the life of all our picnics and parties, as well as our home-pleasures? He has not seemed quite himself for several months. We have not seen nearly so much of him as usual, this winter, and now that this hateful trip is in contemplation I suppose we shall lose him for the summer altogether. But I am selfish so to speak and feel. Mamma says she fears he is troubled about something,—business perhaps,—and believes the trip will do him good. When he first spoke of it, he was lying listlessly upon the sofa in the drawing-room,—a rather new thing for Uncle Ralph to be listless, but he does not seem quite well of late, I think, —and all at once he roused up, and said to mamma,—

"I have about made up my mind to spend my summer in traveling, Fannie, and think I shall start for Ben's next week."

Mamma looked at him a moment, thoughtfully, and then said,—

"I think you are right, Ralph; rest and change will do you good, I am sure; you do not seem at all well."

"Oh, I am well enough, so far as that is concerned, but I feel so tired and nerveless all the while; I shall accomplish nothing if I stay at home."

"And what are we to do, I wonder, without Uncle Ralph?" I questioned, disconsolately.

"What you will soon have to do all your life long," he said. The first direct reference he has ever made to Hal's and my engagement.

"'Sufficient unto the day is the evil thereof,'" I quoted.

"'The fact of future banishment will not make the present absence a whit more endurable."

"'What can't be cured must be endured,' since quotations are the order of the day," he answered.

"Uncle Ralph, will you write to me when you are away?" I said, drawing up my favorite little footstool beside the sofa, and seating myself thereon. "I don't mean to mamma, and Ralph, and Charlie, with a word tossed gingerly out, now and then, to Gertie and myself, as you would toss crumbs to a kitten; but good, long, bona-fide letters to myself, Miss Nannie Cleve; full of narrative, description, and adventure; not omitting, of course, always the good advice and counsel I shall so much need, and have no one to give me in your absence. Promise me, Uncle Ralph, promise me," I persisted, laying my head down upon the arm of the sofa, coaxingly. I don't know why, but I felt at that moment that I would give anything in the world to have Uncle Ralph speak caressingly to me, as he used to do in the days that, I fear, have passed forever. The thought of his going away for so long a time, perhaps being ill away from us, together with the remembrance of all he had been to us, of his great care and love during the sad weeks attendant upon dear little Kittie's death and Charlie's illness, all rushed over me in a flood of unwonted tenderness, and I no longer felt myself the half-dignified young lady into which I had been transformed for a few months past, but became again the little, dependent, clinging child, whose world was our own fireside, and whose chief idols were mamma and Uncle Ralph.

And here occurred something that even yet sends the blood in a hot current to my face as I think of it. Instead of the caressing word my heart longed for, Uncle Ralph said to me, in a tone so low as to be unheard by any but myself,—

"You should not forget, Nannie, nor permit me to forget, that you have no longer a right to ask, nor I to receive, such a proposition."

The tone was so cold, and the words were so concise, that I felt as though a bucket of cold water had been suddenly dashed over me; but Uncle Ralph kindly covered my confusion by saying aloud, as though in answer to my request, as he arose from the sofa,—

"I cannot promise more than a general letter at first, till I see how I am situated. Fannie, can you give me the number of Ben's house in St. Louis?" And as mamma arose to comply with his request, I made my escape from the room.

I can no longer doubt that Uncle Ralph was seriously displeased at my forming an engagement with Hal, and doubtless thinks I have done a very foolish thing to allow myself to think of such matters at all, at my age. And what can I do about it? It is very possible it was, indeed I am inclined myself to think it was, a little premature in us both; but we love each other, and the thing is done, and now cannot easily be undone; though it might have been much better had we waited awhile before entering into this engagement. Ah! what would Hal think, could he read this entry? It is not that he is less dear to me, that I so write, but that my heart is very sore at the thought of having thus incurred Uncle Ralph's lasting disapprobation. I have always been his pet and favorite, and now for many months he gives me as little time and attention as possible,—indeed, always avoids being alone with me a moment. Even Hal's love, precious as it is to me, cannot wholly compensate for this change. My heart yearns sadly for the thoughtful tenderness of old; and I seriously doubt if I am as happy now as I was in the bright days when we were all children together and Uncle Ralph was our king.

May 22. This afternoon, feeling sad and altogether "out of sorts," I coaxed Gertie away for quite a long ramble. Toward sunset, as we were returning home, winding around the base of quite a high hill, I could not but notice how beautifully the lights and shadows fell across the greensward over which we were walking. Sometimes, upon descending a little, we were quite in the shadow, and again, a moment later, we would come out into the soft, bright sunlight, that fell as clearly and beautifully around us as though there were no shadows in the world. At last we descended quite into the valley, and there it seemed so chill in the shade, that involuntarily we quickened our steps, and I felt a corresponding depression in my spirits, as I said, "How unpleasant it is, since we no longer have the sun!" I looked up; the brow of the hill was still glowing in the warm light, and upon the hill-side lay the flecks of golden light and alternate shadow through which we had so recently passed; and this is what they told me, as we hurried along:—

GATHER UP THE SUNSHINE.

"Gather up the sunshine!
 Sit not idly down,
Dreaming in the shadows,
 Till the day is gone.
Life was made for action—
 Up! with right good will!
Lest the twilight shadows
 Find you dreaming still."

Always in the valley
 Shadows darkest lie;
But look up,—the sunbeams
 Gild a cloudless sky.
And while we sit grieving
 In the shadow's cold,
All the mountain's summit
 Tinted is with gold.

"But the way is toilsome!"
  Yes; but were it not,
All our pleasant dreaming
  Could not change our lot.
Slower steps, and feebler,
  E'en than ours, have trod
Oft the mountain's summit
  And the sunlit sod.

If the goal you're seeking
  On the mountain lies,
Step by step advancing
  Brings you to the prize.
All may find the sunlight,
  If they seek with care,—
For 'tis ever glowing,
  Warm and bright, somewhere.

Gather up the sunshine
  Wheresoe'er it's found,—
Here and there a bright thread
  On the darker ground.
Cast the shadows from you;
  Bid them all depart;
But gather up the sunshine,
  And hide it in your heart.

May 26. I have just had a long, dear letter from Hal, so full of loving words and bright hopes for the future that I cannot regret the chance, whatever pain it may cost me, that linked our fates so closely together. We belong to each other; and let come what will, death only can divide us. I often wish, heroine-like, that something would occur to test our love, just to show how nobly we could bear it. But in our plain, matter-of-fact, quiet life there is little can occur to cause even a ripple in the smooth current of our love, much less to test its strength and depth; so we must even be content with the assurance from one another that, should such trial ever come, we would be immutable, unchangeable, constant to the end.

As I anticipated he would do, he speaks of Colonel

Leslie, and asks how he happens to visit our house. He says, "He is of a good family; but I am sure it will be sufficient for me to say to my Nannie that his acquaintance is no honor to any lady, to cause her to have as little as possible to say or do with him." What strange things impressions are! With no knowledge whatever of the man or his antecedents, I yet had that instinctive shrinking from him that I should have had if his character had been well known to me. How can Minnie be attracted to him, when she is herself so sweet and delicate? I went at once to mamma, and told her what Hal said, and she seemed greatly distressed by it.

"What can I do, Nannie?" she said. "I never was so at a loss in my life before. Poor Minnie! Poor child! Do you think she has any idea of his character?"

"Indeed I cannot say, mamma, but I am afraid she has, she is always so unwilling to speak of him."

May 27. At this point in my diary, last night, mamma came into my room with a letter from New York, in answer to Uncle Ralph's inquiries in regard to Colonel Leslie, in her hand.

"Nannie," she said, "it is worse even than we feared. Listen." And she read:—

"'DEAR RALPH,—Colonel George Leslie, of whom you inquire, is the son of the late Major Leslie, an old and valued citizen of New York, lately deceased; but I am sorry to say he has never been any credit to his honored father's name. He is, by courtesy to the family, received into our best society, but bears in private a most disreputable character; is, plainly speaking, a notorious roué. If I had daughters, I would rather put them into a convent for life than have them thrown into the society of such men as George Leslie.

"'Yours in haste, B. K. LEE.'

"He is an old friend of your Uncle Ralph's, and we can rely implicitly on all that he says. Poor little Minnie! what a blow it will be to her! But she is young, and will, I trust, overcome her preference easily, when she knows Colonel Leslie's true character. How I do shrink from giving the poor child pain! but, like the skillful physician, I must, I suppose, probe deeply, if I would effect a cure."

Before I could reply, I heard a little rap upon my door, which I at once recognized as Minnie's.

"What shall I do, mamma? Invite her in?" said I, feeling quite guilty over the poor girl's troubles.

"Perhaps it were as well to have it over, at once," mamma answered, and I opened the door.

"I have been looking for you, Aunt Fannie," said Minnie, prettily, "and Gertie said she believed you had come in here, so I took the liberty of following you, as usual."

"That was right, darling," said mamma, kindly. "Had you something special to say to me, or did you only feel the drawing of mutual attraction?"

Minnie laughed, and answered that she believed it was a little of both. "I wanted to ask your consent to my spending a few weeks in New York City with an old schoolmate of mine, Annie May. She is very anxious to have me come."

"I am always happy to have you enjoy yourself, dear Minnie," said mamma, "and, if the visit is a suitable one in all respects, can of course have no objection. Who is your friend?"

"Oh, she is one of the pleasantest little ladies imaginable; has a beautiful home, moves in the best society, and I am sure would be unexceptionable even in your critical eyes," said Minnie, laughing,—a little nervously, I thought.

"When do you wish to go, dear?" said mamma, evidently at a loss what to say.

"Oh, in a few days; any time soon, she says."

"What did you say her name was, Minnie?" I asked, only by way of filling up an awkward pause and giving mamma a moment for thought.

"Annie May; and she is charming."

"How old is she?" still by way of giving mamma time.

"Twenty-three."

"Ah! quite a marriageable age!" I said.

"Oh, she is already married, for more than two years," said Minnie.

"Who was she, dear?" asked mamma.

"She is the sister of Mrs. Harvey Linn, who is equally charming with herself. I remember so well the first time I ever saw her,—one day when she came to the school to see Annie." And she dashed away nervously into a long narrative of school-day life.

"But what was her own name then?" said mamma, quietly, evidently noticing Minnie's flurried manner.

"Annie Leslie," said Minnie, driven to the point; "and her father was the finest-looking old gentleman I ever saw," evidently trying hard not to seem embarrassed.

"Is she Colonel Leslie's sister?" asked mamma.

"Yes," said Minnie, with visible embarrassment; and nothing more was said for several minutes. At last mamma said,—

"I am afraid it would scarcely be proper, Minnie, for you to visit in the house of the sister of a gentleman who has shown you such marked attention as Colonel Leslie."

"I am sure I cannot see what difference that would make," said Minnie.

Mamma looked troubled, but said, gently,—

"Where did you first meet Colonel Leslie, Minnie?"

"At his sister's."

"When?"

"Last spring, when papa and I were in the city."

"Did your papa know him?"

Minnie shook her head.

"Minnie," said mamma, after a little pause, "do you know anything of Colonel Leslie's character?"

"I know that he is a gentleman," she answered, somewhat excitedly.

"Did you ever hear of anything to his discredit?"

"Very few people but sometimes have malicious things said of them," she answered.

"My dear child," said mamma, "you know I love you too well to say or do anything that would pain you, but I am afraid you are mistaken in the character of this man. I fear he is not above reproach."

"Yes," said Minnie, "I knew it would come to that! His enemies follow him with these reports wherever he goes; but I will not believe them,—never! never!"

"Darling," said mamma, "it is a dangerous position you are taking, for a young girl, and one that may involve all of your future happiness. If Colonel Leslie is really the gentleman you believe him, I am the last person to throw an obstacle in the way of your marriage; for I infer from what you say that he desires such." Minnie nodded her head. "But if he is not worthy of you, it would be one of the saddest days of my life to see you go to him. Minnie," she continued, tenderly, "you know I love you, darling," putting her arm caressingly about her, "will you not be influenced by Aunt Fannie, and do nothing rashly, but wait a few months at least, until you know the truth of these reports?"

Minnie seemed much affected, weeping quietly as she said,—

"I know you have always been my friend, Aunt Fannie, and I do not desire to go against your wishes; but we love each other, George and I, and everybody talks so hard about him, that it only makes me love him more, because he seems so much to need my love."

Mamma looked incredulous at the last assertion, but only said,—

"Still, dear, if, after all, you should discover the reports to have been true, when it was too late to benefit you, it would wreck your happiness for life."

"I am not afraid: he is always good to me."

"Ah, but lovers and husbands are not always the same, you know. Be warned in time."

"I will not promise you, Aunt Fannie; but I will think of all you say, and try and profit by it," said Minnie, as, evidently much softened, she bade us good-night and left the room.

Mamma said, "We will not discuss this longer to-night, dear," and, kissing me "good-night," left me to my own reflections, which were not of the brightest character.

May 29. Mamma talked with Minnie again yesterday, and drew from her the reluctant acknowledgment that the visit to his sister's was all of Colonel Leslie's own planning, so that he could visit her when he chose. Mamma pointed out to her the lack of principle such a proceeding involved, showed her Mr. Lee's letter, and told her all she asked of her was to wait a few months and investigate thoroughly these reports in regard to his character, and if, after careful investigation, Minnie found him to be the honorable man she at present believed him, then she, mamma, would most willingly consent to their union; but if, on the contrary, the result proved him to be the base character he was represented, then she hoped and believed that Minnie's own self-respect would cause her to cast him from her forever. Minnie at first tried to defend him, but at last admitted that such a course could only be right; and mamma hopes that she will give him no further encouragement. Oh, if she could only see him with my eyes, no more would be necessary.

Uncle Ralph left for the West yesterday evening, and I have felt all day as though some one about the house was dead. He spent two or three hours here in the morning, and once, when we chanced for a moment to be alone, I felt that I could not bear to let him go away without making an effort to reinstate myself in his favor, and said, looking up pleadingly into his face as he passed near me,—

"Uncle Ralph, you will not go away angry with me? Will you never, never love me again?"

"Angry with you? Never love you again? Oh, Nannie, if you only knew——" And then he paused a moment before he said,—softly smoothing my hair in his old caressing way, as I stood before him,—

"Have I indeed been so stern with my little Nannie? No, I am not angry with you, dear child; but my heart is full of care lately; it will soon be all right, I trust. You must not let it trouble you." And, some one coming into the room, no more was said; but when he departed he said "good-by" in his old, tender way, and I believe it made it ten times harder for me to let him go. Dear Uncle Ralph! what is it that troubles him so? Can it be that the fact of my engagement recalls to him vividly his own sad past? It must be! Oh, if I only could comfort him.

June 30. We have all been again to Yale, this time to see Charlie graduate; and the dear fellow acquitted himself undoubtedly with honor. He took the highest honors in his class, and is a great favorite with every one. We reached dear old Beechwood again last night, and I doubt if four walls in Christendom inclosed a happier or merrier group than we. Even Minnie, who has seemed quite drooping and dispirited of late, looked bright and happy; and I am sure Ralph did all in his power to make her so. Why can she not see the difference between Ralph, who I know really admires her, and Colonel Leslie? Perhaps in time she may. Charlie was greatly disappointed at not finding Uncle Ralph at home: and indeed it does seem strange and lonely without him. Mamma had a letter from him a day or two after he reached Uncle Ben's, and since then we have heard nothing more. He said from there he should go still farther west, and that we must not feel uneasy if his letters were not very frequent, as he should be traveling most of the time. Nettie Ray has been in New York for a month past. She returns next week, and Hal accompanies her home. More than six months since we last met. How my heart thrills at the thought that he will so soon be here! Gertie and Charlie are going down to Aunt Katie's in a few days, for a short visit. Now that Aunt Katie has two little darlings of her own to care for, we do not see her nearly so often as we used to. She has only made us one visit in the last two years,—that was when Uncle Ben and Aunt Emily were here last summer. So Charlie and Gertie are going down for a little while, soon. Well, I can spare them better now than at any other time, since Hal is coming.

July 9. Gertie and Charlie have gone,—started day before yesterday,—and last night Hal came. So every day brings and leaves its own record. Hal is little changed, except that he has grown heavier, and handsomer than ever. He has much to tell me of New York life, and prophesies that I will be enchanted some day with it; but I seriously doubt if it will ever be so pleasant to me as life at dear old charming Beechwood. He is coming over early this evening, that we may have a ride before night; and even as I write I hear the quick canter of his horse's feet up the wooded avenue, and, looking from the window, catch now and then a glimpse of the erect figure through the openings in the trees. Joseph, too, is leading the ponies up to the door, for Ralph has promised Minnie a canter upon "Di," his beautiful little filly, and I hear their voices in the hall below. So I must e'en don my habit in haste, or I shall be called a laggard. So, till we return.

July 16. Truly said I, every day has its own record, and some, alas! it were better had never been made. I am so bewildered with the events of the last few days that I scarcely know what to write, or how. Gertie and I have always had a great habit of stealing away into the orchard when we wish to read or study, in pleasant weather; for, besides being so retired and quiet, it is indeed a lovely spot. A beautiful grassy slope, studded thickly with fine old trees, through which the sunlight struggles, falling in golden flecks upon the greensward beneath, the drowsy hum of the bees among the blossoms or fruit, and the musical twittering of the little birds in the branches overhead, all conspire to make it peculiarly inviting to one who wishes to study or meditate. A few evenings ago, as I sat there, thinking, with closed book upon my knee (for I had been reading until the twilight fell), I was startled by a man looking over the hedge near which I sat. It is a very unusual thing for stragglers to find their way to this quiet retreat, but I was greatly startled, as it was growing late, and hastened at once to the house. All evening I kept thinking the face had a familiar look, in the hasty glimpse I had had of it, until suddenly it flashed across me that it was no other than that of Colonel Leslie. How stupid I had been! I went at once to Minnie's room, ostensibly upon an errand, but really to see if she was out, and found her quietly looking over some things in her trunk.

If she had seen him, she had already returned; so I thought I would not worry mamma with my suspicions.

About ten o'clock I retired, and, after tossing about restlessly for some time, I at last dropped into an unquiet sleep, in which I saw Minnie struggling with a great black serpent with a man's head, the face of which was the same that had looked at me over the orchard hedge. I awakened with a terrified start, and presently heard the hall clock strike one. After a little while, for I could not sleep again readily, I heard some one moving cautiously in Minnie's room, and thought, "Poor girl, she is as restless as myself." Then the door leading from her room into the hall softly opened, and I heard her step cautiously without. "She must be ill," I thought, and, hastily rising, I opened my door to see if I could render her any assistance. The full moon shone in through the hall window, and there, directly before me, stood Minnie, fully equipped for traveling, even to hat and gloves, and carrying a small valise in her hand. My first thought was that she was sleep-walking; but my second thought, which proved to be the correct one, almost unnerved me.

"Minnie, are you asleep?" I asked.

"No, Nannie, I am not asleep," she answered. "Why do you watch me?"

"I did not, Minnie. I heard you open your door, thought you were ill, and came to offer you assistance."

"I am not ill. Will you please let me pass you, Nannie?"—for I had gently laid my hand upon her arm as she would have passed me in the hall.

"Where are you going, Minnie?"

"Do not ask me; only let me go."

"I cannot, dear Minnie; for I know the only one who would be base enough to tempt you from your home in this way. Indeed you must not go to him."

"I must and will; you shall not hinder me. He only tempts me thus because he dares not come to me in any other way. We love each other, and nothing shall divide us."

"But, Minnie, do not steal away from us so. Think of the disgrace. If you will marry him, do it honestly in the face of all the world. Mamma will not oppose you, if you are so determined, I am sure; only do not go in this dreadful way." And I held tightly to her hand.

"Do not detain me, Nannie; I am resolute. Go I will!"

"Then I must call mamma. Dear Minnie, hear me! Only do not go, and I promise you I will plead for you with mamma."

"It is too late. I have promised, and my life, my happiness, are now in his hands." And she broke from my detaining grasp and hurried to the door in the lower hall.

"Mamma, mamma," I cried, rushing hastily into her room, "come quickly, quickly, or Minnie will be gone!"

Poor mamma sprang from her bed with a startled, bewildered look, and, catching up a shawl about her shoulders, ran with me, without a word, into the hall. She said afterward she thought I meant that Minnie was dying. Alas! how much better would it have been for the poor girl, I am sure, had it been so! We ran down-stairs, I explaining hurriedly, as we went, that Minnie was going away with Colonel Leslie, and there we found the door open, as she had left it, and reached it just in time to hear the rumble of departing wheels.

"Minnie! Minnie!" mamma called, agonizingly; but soon everything was silent, and we knew that our bright little Minnie had indeed fled from us forever.

When the first moment of terrible suspense was over, mamma sank down upon the hall sofa, and, burying her face in the cushions, sobbed brokenly for several minutes. I was terribly alarmed, for never in my life had I seen her yield thus before. At last she said, piteously,—

"Oh, Nannie! to think how I have loved that dear child all her life, and now she has consigned herself to a living death; for such her union with that man must prove. Oh, how much easier it would have been to have laid her, in her purity, in her coffin!"

We went back sadly to mamma's room, and I remained all night with her, for there was no more sleep for either of us, and I told her then all I knew of their clandestine meetings, and also of seeing the face, that I now was sure was his, over the orchard hedge. Mamma expressed great regret that I had bound myself by a promise not to tell her, from the first, of their meetings, as she might have taken means to prevent so sad an ending. "But," she added, "regrets are now unavailing; only, dear child, let it put you on your guard for the future, never to bind yourself by any promise to conceal anything from your mother."

"Indeed, mamma, I never will again. I have suffered enough all the time for this to make me avoid a like fault in the future. I would have given anything in the world a dozen times to have been able to tell you, without violating my promise to Minnie."

"A young girl may always suspect a thing is wrong that she desires herself to keep, or is requested by another to keep, from her mother; for where will she ever find so loving, so sympathetic, so true a friend as the mother who has watched over her from her infancy? Sometimes her judgment may seem a little stern and cold to the young, impulsive heart; but a child can never go far astray that trusts to the teachings of its mother, especially if that mother is a Christian."

"I know you are right, mamma; but I am sure few

daughters have such a precious mother to go to as have Gertie and I," I whispered, as I nestled my head on to her pillow close beside her own. She drew me closely to her, kissing me fondly, and so we lay waiting for the morning.

Mamma sent Joseph for Ralph early in the morning, and the poor fellow seemed terribly shocked at the news of Minnie's flight. He wanted to start immediately in pursuit, declaring he "would as soon blow the villain's brains out as kill a snake." I thought of my dream, but said nothing. Mamma said pursuit would be useless, since they were doubtless already married; and, besides, Ralph would have no authority to compel her to return, should he even overtake them, which was doubtful. All we could do was to wait till we knew something further. Aunt Martha was shocked and indignant at first, and pitiful and compassionate afterward; while Miss Lane was so sorry and excited over it as to be laid up with a bad nervous headache half the day. She told me the next day that her only sister was enticed away in much the same manner, and, after living a miserable life for a few years, died of a broken heart, at the early age of twenty-three. I did not wonder, when she told me this, that Minnie's flight affected her so deeply.

This was all three days ago; and to-day mamma had a beautiful little pleading letter from Minnie, saying how sorry she was to have done anything contrary to her wishes, but if she (mamma) only knew how happy she was, and what a good, loving husband she had found, she was sure she could not find it in her heart to blame her.

"Curse him!" said Ralph, bitterly, between his teeth; and Aunt Martha sighed, and shook her old head ominously, as she muttered,—

"Yes, yes; a new broom always sweeps clean!"

We were all too sad to laugh, as indeed Aunt Martha

would have been greatly shocked to have had us do; and mamma, as usual, said, mildly,—

"It is very sad; but we can only hope for the best, and, now that she has really gone, try to speak and think as little as possible about it." But she sighed heavily as she spoke; and I know that she will not soon forget the dear girl whose presence for so brief a while brightened our home. Ralph stalked moodily from the room, and we soon saw him flying away on "Di" toward the village, where he will strive to drive away his regrets in the musty old tomes in Uncle Ralph's office. We have all gone back to our daily duties, and so Minnie has slipped out of our quiet life. May God go with her!

July 20. Mamma has answered Minnie's letter as only she can write, combining regrets, forgiveness, and counsel for the future, all in one, and charging her never to forget, in trouble, that warm hearts and welcoming hands would always be ready to receive her at Beechwood.

To her husband she sent no word, not even alluding to him in the letter. She also forwarded the trunks which Minnie had left all ready packed. We all sent our love,— all but Ralph,—but nothing more.

Mamma also wrote to Mrs. Norris a plain statement of the facts, expressing her regret that such an occurrence should have happened beneath her roof. Mamma blames herself much,—which I think is not right; for who would have dreamed of Minnie Norris ever taking such a desperate step? If any one is to blame, it is myself, for concealing, or rather consenting to conceal, his clandestine visits from mamma.

Hal said, "Well, darling, I never should have put your love to such a test: it is all wrong. I should have waited patiently, relying upon your faith and love, until you were of age in the eyes of the law, and then I should openly have claimed you before all the world, and no man would have dared to come between us." And if he had looked as he did when he made the assertion, I do not believe there would!

To-morrow we expect Gertie and Charlie to return; and I am very glad, for more than one reason. I think Ralph needs Charlie, he looks so dispirited and woe-begone, for him, since Minnie's flight. Even Nettie, who has always been a great favorite with him, fails to restore him to his usual spirits. I do hope his heart is not seriously involved, for I so long to have him prefer Nettie above all others. She is so very lovable, and has developed into such a charming woman; you know she is over a year older than I, and I will be eighteen next May. How rapidly the years slip by! I am thinking, if time flies as swiftly with Hal as it does with me, he will not find the two years of our probation so long, after all. It seems but yesterday since we were all children together, hunting for buttercups and chasing butterflies in the meadows, and now we stand upon the threshold of manhood and womanhood, and look back, perhaps a little longingly, to the sunny days of our childhood. Bright and beautiful they truly were, but,—

"Like dew on the mountain, or foam on the river,
They sparkled a moment, then vanish'd forever."

Sept. 1. The summer has passed like a beautiful dream. Hal has returned to New York, and Charlie has gone with him to the city to pursue his medical studies, for he too means to become a physician; it has always been the desire of his heart. He says a man who wishes to do good has a broader field open to him in that capacity than in any other, not even excepting the ministry. For while he ministers to the physical wants of the afflicted, he can also discern more clearly their spiritual needs; for never is human frailty so discernible as when the strong frame is prostrated by suffering, and never is the soul so open to the influence of heavenly teaching as when through bodily affliction it is brought to look upon death as an inevitable something that sooner or later we all must meet. Charlie, with his noble soul, lofty aspirations, and pure and tender heart, will, I am sure, succeed well in the profession he has chosen. He is just the man to win the love and respect of every one, and I am sure he will. He will make a quiet, reserved, and dignified man, but one that no person can fail to love and honor for his own intrinsic worth.

The summer has indeed been full of tranquil happiness. I have written but little in my diary since Hal has been here, for we have been much together, and it would seem like sacrilege to write, even upon your pure pages, dear old book, the record of our interviews. Then our hearts are laid bare to one another, and thoughts and feelings of the soul find utterance meant but for one ear alone, save God's. Enough that we have been together, have been happy, and that the future for us is full of promise. And yet, standing with him in the starlight this evening, waiting for his last adieus, a sad feeling stole over me,—a shadowy fear,—a presentiment that I never should stand thus with him in the soft starlight again. I seemed to see between us a misty form with outstretched hands trying to divide us; and even while his tender words of adieu were yet sounding in my ears, I heard above them all the words of solemn warning, "You hold but a phantom of love to your heart." Whence the feeling came, or wherefore, I cannot tell; but I thrust it resolutely from me; for what are these presentiments but the struggles of the soul, overburdened with some present sadness, to penetrate the misty veil that hides from us the future? Well for us that we cannot look beyond. How could we ever enjoy the present, however bright and joyous it might be, with the certain knowledge that a dark and troubled future lay before us? God indeed is all-wise and all-merciful, I know this; yet

> I cannot still the beating
>   Of my restless, anxious heart;
> I cannot lay the phantoms
>   That into being start;
> They haunt me in my slumbers,
>   They stand beside my chair,
> And whisper, ever whisper,—
>   Trust not Love's promise fair.

This is simply folly. I will no more of it. Never was lovers' future brighter before them than is ours. It is sinful to yield to the forebodings that the prospect of a somewhat protracted absence would, not unnaturally, engender. To-morrow's sunshine will bring brighter, happier thoughts, I am sure: so I will strive, in slumber, to woo them to me now.

Sept. 20. I went yesterday with mamma to pay our weekly visit to Granny Weir, and found the poor old woman very weak indeed. The end is evidently rapidly drawing near. She seems conscious of the fact, and talks calmly and cheerfully of her approaching death. She said her only care was for her little granddaughter Lizzie, who has been nurse and companion for her for the last four years, although she is now but fifteen years old. "Her parents are both dead," she said, "and when poor old granny is gone she will be entirely friendless and homeless." Mamma assured her that Lizzie should not suffer, promising to take her to our own home until a good one could be permanently provided for her. The poor old soul seemed deeply moved, and very grateful to mamma for her kindness. The tears rolled over her furrowed cheeks, as she said, "God will repay you, dear lady, for your constant kindness to the poor and destitute. Now that I know my poor girl will be kindly cared for, I can die in peace."

Mamma said, coming home, that she would write to

Aunt Katie at once about Lizzie, for she was sure she would just suit her for the children; and I think so too. I told mamma, as granny was so low, I would run over again this evening and see how she was, and carry her a little chicken-broth. So, while Milly was preparing it, I have written this in my diary, and now I must run before it is too late, for the days are growing shorter again.

Oct. 12. When I closed my last entry, I put on my hat, and, taking the bowl of broth from Milly, went over the hill to granny's little cottage. But before I entered the house I knew that all was over. The windows were open, and a pile of bedclothes and pillows from granny's bed lay in the yard, and I saw several of the neighbor-women moving busily and noiselessly about. As I entered the house, they all greeted me respectfully, and one of the women said, softly, as she handed me a chair,—

"Poor old soul, she's gone at last!"

"When did she die?" I asked.

"About two hours ago."

I went to the bed, upon which she was laid out decently and tidily, and looked upon the poor shrunken form and pinched features, but for the life of me I could feel no sorrow.

"She died calmly and peacefully," said one; and I could not but think, "What a blessed exchange from her sleepless nights and suffering days, to this quiet, dreamless rest from which there is no waking!" She looked so calm and restful, that I thought in my heart, "It is well with her," as I turned from the bed and asked for Lizzie.

"She is in the inner room," was answered; "and the poor lass is dreadfully broken up over her granny's death."

I entered the little room that served as both bedroom and kitchen, and found the little maid crouching down beside a low fire, rocking herself to and fro and moaning piteously.

"Lizzie," I said, laying my hand upon her head, "do you remember me?"

She stopped her moaning for an instant, and, looking up at me, answered,—

"Yes, Miss Nannie; and granny said to tell you—oh, poor granny!" And she fell to sobbing again more piteously than ever.

"Listen to me a little, Lizzie," I said, kindly, stooping down beside her. "We all know it is very sad for you to lose your dear old granny so; but have you forgotten how dreadfully she suffered when she was alive?"

"Oh, no, miss, nor ever shall."

"Would you be glad to see her suffer so again?"

"Oh, dear, no, Miss Nannie; but who will love poor Lizzie now that granny is gone?"

"Every one will love you, Lizzie, if you are good," I answered; thinking how, with rich and poor, high and low alike, "love, love," is the yearning cry of every heart. "Then, too," I continued, "God will love you and care for you always. See how he has already raised up for you a friend, in my mother, who will see that you have in future everything needful for you. If you are a good girl, as I am sure you already are, you will be very happy; for you are to have the kindest of mistresses, and the prettiest of little children of whom to take care."

I saw that I had gained her attention, for she raised her head and turned her little pinched face, swollen with much weeping, toward me; so I went on, and told her gently of Aunt Katie and her beautiful home and her two lovely children, until, in a measure, I had diverted her mind from its heavy sorrow. I saw that she looked very weary, and knew she needed food.

"Lizzie, have you eaten anything to-day?" I asked.

"No, miss; how could I, when granny was——" And again the tears choked her utterance, though this time she tried bravely to suppress them.

"Yes, I know, I know," I answered, vexed at myself for my thoughtless recurrence to her sorrow; "but I want you to eat a little now for my sake, and then I have something more to say to you."

I went to the pump and brought her a basin of water in which to bathe her face, and reached her the towel, saying,—

"Now bathe your face and brush your hair, like a good girl, and then I will tell you something more of your new home."

She obeyed me mechanically; more because she was used to doing as she was bidden than for any other reason. Then I crumbled some bread into the broth I had brought from home, set it upon the table, and told her she must eat it. It seemed impossible for her to swallow the first few mouthfuls; and at last she said, completely breaking down again,—

"Poor old granny! she will never eat no more!"

"No, Lizzie; she is now where she will never need to eat, and where, too, she will never suffer again. And I am sure it will add greatly to her happiness to see that you bear up bravely under your sorrow."

"Do you think she can see me now, miss?" she asked, eagerly.

"I have little doubt of it, Lizzie."

"Then I will do all you wish; for her last words to me were to mind all that you and Mrs. Cleve told me."

"That I am sure you will do, Lizzie; and now try and eat your broth." And I again drew her mind away to her future at Aunt Katie's, till I had the satisfaction of seeing her finish the last mouthful; then I said, "Now will you go home with me, Lizzie?"

"Please, miss, an' I had rather wait here till Sunday is gone," she said (it was now Friday); "it would break my heart entirely to leave her to-night."

So I said no more, knowing the neighbors would be with her. Mamma sent Joseph over to do all that was necessary for the funeral, and on Sunday mamma and Gertie drove over with Joseph, and after the funeral brought Lizzie home with them. The poor child was quite worn out with her constant weeping, but after a few days brightened up wonderfully, and when she yesterday started to Aunt Katie's, under Joseph's care, she looked quite bright and cheerful, and I doubt not her future will be much happier than her past.

Oct. 24. Ralph came out this morning with a long letter he had received from Uncle Ralph. He was some place in Minnesota when he wrote, and gave some very beautiful descriptions of the fine country over which he has traveled. He says he has no idea when he will return, as he has promised Cousin Ned to take a trip down the Mississippi River with him when he returns to St. Louis from the Northwest, and they will probably make the tour of the Southern States before they return. He says his health is good, and that he hopes to return in good condition for business, some time in the spring. It seems an age since he went away; and I am half vexed to think he can stay away from Beechwood so long with apparently so few regrets. The beautiful autumn is again here, and wood and field and stream seem to have borrowed new beauties from her ever-changing splendor. Oh, what a book is nature for those whose minds are in unison with her in her varying moods, and who can trace in the tender blade of spring, or the fluttering frost-hued leaf of autumn, the similitude to life, from its first tender budding in infancy, to its blighting and decay as it approaches the winter of death. Nettie and I never weary of wandering together through the "pathless woods," and often sit together for hours beneath some old tree, quietly knitting,—for we are again preparing for our annual Christmas-tree,—and often without a word being spoken between us, communing silently one with another and with nature. Nettie and I have the somewhat rare faculty of enjoying each other's society without talking. She often says,—

"How pleasant it is, Nannie, that we can sit together and not feel that we are necessitated to try to entertain each other! I often feel, after we have thus sat silently for some time, that we have held rare and pleasant converse, although perhaps not over half a dozen sentences have been exchanged."

And so it is: our souls commune, although our lips are silent. How much more friends would enjoy each other's society, if they would only converse when they really have something to say, instead of feeling that they must make an effort to talk, when the soul is longing for a communion that words have no power to express. "Perfect love casteth out fear," is a truthful saying, and in nothing do we realize it more perfectly than in the fact that those who understand and love us best are the ones in whose presence we feel a perfect freedom from restraint and act in all things as the heart and conscience dictate. A valued friend once said to me, in a somewhat rare burst of confidence, "Dear Nannie, whatever you do, act always in perfect simplicity and honest faith with those you love. Never allow a false pride to come between your heart and those who are entitled to your confidence." And then she told me how, years before,—for she was much older than myself, and had been married several years,—she had loved and been beloved by one in every way her equal; how she had looked forward with joy to the beautiful future they were to spend together, until, in an unfortunate hour, a slight misunderstanding, a very trifle, arose between them, which she was too proud to explain away, although she could have done so by a single word. And the shadow grew, and deepened, until it became an impenetrable cloud between them, and they parted; parted, bearing away in their hearts the remembrance of a beautiful dream, whose non-fulfillment had shadowed all their future and in a great measure left for both but the wreck of earthly happiness.

"It is true," she concluded, "I have a kind husband, who is worthy of all love, and whom I sincerely respect and honor; but even now, sleeping in his arms, I dream of the past, and awaken with quivering heart-strings at the remembrance of what I have lost. All, all, because of a false pride, that veiled and screened my heart from the loving eyes that should have read its every emotion.

"And for the same reason, I am convinced, marriages often prove unhappy ones, when they are really between congenial hearts. A little misunderstanding arises, which one or the other could easily explain away; but they think, 'Well, if he loved me,' or, 'if she cared for me, it would be understood without an explanation.' And so the first wrong feeling is cherished, and the first cold word is spoken, whose wounds no after-kindness can entirely obliterate. My earnest counsel to every young couple just beginning life would always be, 'Guard carefully against the first unkind word or thought, for therein lies the secret of all domestic happiness.'"

And I am sure she is right. But, knowing the right way perfectly, how difficult it is for us poor erring mortals always to walk therein!

Nov. 12. One year ago to-day since I first laid my hand in Hal's and promised that our futures should be inseparable. How quickly it has sped! and how full of brightness it has been! I have just concluded a long letter to him, and I am sure I shall soon receive one from him, written likewise to-day.

I had another long, dear letter from Charlie this morning. He says life in New York is pleasant for a time, but he would gladly exchange it for the bright fields and wooded hills of Beechwood. He has already made up his mind to settle in our village, where I am sure he will find success, when through with his studies. Ralph, on the contrary, says that when he has once become, in a manner, master of his profession, he is going to some city to live, though perhaps not so far from home as New York. He likes the crowd, the noise, the life, of a busy street: so do not I.

Charlie says he met with an old friend of mine lately who has just returned from a three years' tour upon the continent,—a Miss Sallie Reve, whom I remember as a little, pale-faced, black-eyed girl, whom I once loved very dearly, some six or eight years ago. I met her the winter I spent with Grandma Clifford before her death. Sallie's father was a neighbor of Grandfather Clifford's; and, she being near my own age, about a year or so older, I believe, we soon became fast friends. How I would love to see her again! Charlie seems much struck with her; says she is one of the most fascinating ladies he has ever met; that she had many questions to ask about me, and expressed a very warm desire to see me again. How strange it seems to think of her, little Sallie Reve, as a young lady! She cannot be very beautiful,—although Charlie describes her as very fascinating,—for she was remarkably plain as a child. I must get mamma's permission to invite her, some time, to Beechwood, for her parents were very kind to me the winter

I was at grandma's. But my long letter to Hal has taxed my time and strength so heavily to-night that my entry in my diary must of necessity be brief.

Nov. 18. Just as I have predicted, I have a long, precious letter from Hal, written upon the anniversary of our betrothal. It is full of just such loving words and tender reminiscences as are most likely to touch a foolish little heart like mine: so of course it has been read over again and again, and awakened very happy memories of the past and bright anticipations for the future. I often wonder if anybody else is quite as foolish about the letters of those they love as I am. I read them over and over again, and at every reading find something new and precious that I had not particularly noticed before; and—shall I say it?—I often even sleep with Hal's beneath my pillow, it seems so suggestive of pleasant dreams.

Hal writes me that he also has met Sallie Reve, and thinks her very charming. He says she quite won his heart by her loving remembrance of myself, never tiring of asking questions about me and telling over incidents of our past. He says she has quite set her heart upon my spending the approaching holidays with her in New York; says she will write to me herself about it, and will take no denial. I do not yet know how that would be, whether I should enjoy spending the holidays away from home or not, although Hal says, "I think you would enjoy a trip to the city, and nothing would please me better than to have you make the desired visit. If you conclude to come, of course my holidays will be spent here also; but if you decide to remain at Beechwood, you may confidently expect me on the 24th of December. It would be a cheerless Christmas to me spent away from my darling."

Nov. 30. I several days ago received the expected letter from dear little Sallie, for so I must still remember her, inclosing also a charming little note to mamma, in which she begged so prettily for the pleasure of my own and Gertie's company for the holidays, that mamma's consent was at once given, provided Ralph would accompany us to the city. Her letter to me was full of tender memories of the olden times, and very interesting and pleasant. She told me I must not expect to find her much changed; that she was the same plain little Sallie that she used to be, though perhaps not quite so small in stature as at that time. She spoke of our visit as though everything was settled, and will not listen, she says, to any excuse to the contrary. She adds that "Dr. Ray" (how strange it looks so written!) is quite anxious to remain in New York during the holidays, as it will of course be very gay, but cannot be induced to do so unless we all, Nettie included (to whom she has already written, through Hal), can be prevailed upon to come to New York instead. Nettie has already consented to go if we do, and Ralph is very willing to accompany us; but somehow I cannot quite gain the consent of my heart to go. I feel a strange reluctance about leaving home at this time; perhaps it is because I do not fancy leaving mamma all alone at the holidays. To be sure, Aunt Martha and Miss Lane will be here, but that is not like her children. I wish I knew whether Hal really desires to remain in the city or not: that would of course decide me.

Dec. 2. Well, it is decided that we are to go. I was the only one who seemed at all averse to the plan, and, as I could give no good reason, not even to myself, for my strange reluctance, I was of course overruled; and so we are to go. Mamma herself desired it, saying she thought a little insight into city life would be an advantage both to Gertie and myself. We are to go about the 15th, and remain until after New Year, when Charlie is to return with us for his visit to mamma. Hal, I suppose, will not come again before next summer; and I should not wonder if that thought has something to do with my desire not to go. Seeing him at New York will not be like seeing him at Beechwood. But I must not be selfish: it will doubtless all be for the best.

It seems strange that we cannot hear what has become of Minnie. Only once have we heard from her since her first letter to mamma after her flight. Hal once saw her riding in a carriage with Colonel Leslie, down Broadway. She bowed to him as they passed, and that was all. Mamma thinks her husband will not permit her to write to us; but it seems hard that he should deny her this pleasure. We cannot even hear whether she is in the city or not, though Charlie has tried hard to find out without calling at Mrs. May's to inquire. Poor Minnie! I fear her lot is not all sunshine. But I hear Gertie calling to me, doubtless to help her decide some important trifle (if I may use such a contrariety of terms) in regard to our wardrobes: so, old book, I lay you aside with regret, and obey.

Jan. 20. Our visit is made, and we are once again at dear old Beechwood, never so dear as after temporary absence. I have delayed writing in my diary since my return (we reached home on the 9th) simply because I scarcely know how to record the events of my visit, they were so varied and dissimilar. It was, I suppose, a very pleasant visit,—or, at least, we ought to regard it as such; but, somehow or other, there is an unsatisfied longing at my heart that tells me it was not, with me at least, a perfect success. There were parties and concerts without end, and dinner-parties, suppers, and social days and evenings at home; to say nothing of the art-galleries and thousand and one beautiful things always to be seen in New York. Hal and Charlie met us at the depot, where also Judge Reve's carriage was in waiting to convey us to the house. Charlie took possession of Ralph, and spirited him away, promising that they would shortly join us for dinner, to which the gentlemen had been kindly invited by Mrs. Reve, while Hal rode with us to the house, where he lingered but a moment before he returned to Ralph and Charlie.

We found Sallie ready with a warm welcome at the door, and she bore us away to the pleasant rooms we were to occupy during our visit, telling us we had barely time to dress for dinner, as it was then nearly five o'clock. At dinner we were presented to Sallie's papa and mamma, who gave us all a very cordial welcome, which we could not but see was sincere. A very merry party we formed at table, and Sallie was the merriest of us all. You could not call her pretty; indeed, at first sight you would think her quite plain; but when she once began to converse there was a piquancy and sprightliness about her conversation that was irresistibly attractive and charming. I did not wonder that Charlie called her fascinating. She had seen so much in her travels that she was never at a loss for pleasant topics, and had been thrown so constantly into the best society, both at home and abroad, that the timidity I often feel in unfamiliar society was never felt by herself. We passed a very pleasant evening together; but when it was over and the gentlemen had gone, I sighed to think I had not seen Hal even for a moment, save in the presence of others. He had been very kind and attentive, and once had whispered, when for an instant we stood a little apart from the others by the blazing, cheerful grate, "Hal's darling!" But at that moment Sallie came up with some witticism, and we were no more apart from the others. But even that little word, with the look accompanying it, gave me food for happy dreams; for did it not assure me of his unchanging love? But, when day after day passed in the same manner, I began to long for one little hour alone with him. It seemed, indeed, to be unavoidable, or rather purely accidental; still, it was annoying. I had not seen him for four long months, and my heart was brimful of things, important and unimportant, that I wished to say, and not an hour had we had alone. Hal seemed to be annoyed by it as much as myself, and several times called in the morning hours and asked especially for me; but we were never alone more than a few minutes before we were interrupted in one way or another. At one time Sallie came in in search of her gloves, apologized when she saw Hal, asserting her ignorance of his call, and, standing ready every moment to withdraw, still chatted merrily on until his time was spent and he was obliged to go. I could have cried with vexation; but it was all so innocently done that I could not find it in my heart to blame Sallie. A few mornings afterward he called again; and that time Sallie wanted to ask him the exact street and number of an artist's studio we wished to visit; and still another time for the address of a distant friend that she had forgotten. And so it went from time to time, until I half fancied there was a design in it all, especially since from the inquiries we always fell to chatting all together, and Hal's hour was invariably consumed without my having exchanged with him more than half a dozen sentences. The morning we went to the art-gallery I thought, "Well, now at least I can talk with Hal unheard, if not unseen;" for one is never so much alone as in a crowd, and there are so many quiet nooks and corners in such places where one may sit quietly, apparently examining a favorite picture, all the while listening to or conversing with a friend. But in this again I was doomed to disappointment, for Sallie, anxious to do the full duty of a hostess, stayed with us almost constantly, in order to point out her favorite pictures and bring out beauties that otherwise we might have overlooked; so that, much as I enjoyed the paintings and statuary, I could not help feeling quite dispirited upon my return, and, shutting myself up in my own room, pleaded a severe headache and took a good cry. Here had I been nearly three weeks, and, instead of my usual long happy talks with Hal, had only seen him in the midst of a merry, chatting crowd.

The next evening there was quite a large sleighing-party, and Hal had said to me in a whisper, for he could not but see my disappointment, "Never mind, Nannie; where is a better chance for a cozy chat than under a buffalo robe in a snug little cutter gliding merrily over the snow?" I thought of our ride in the early Christmas morning last year, and was comforted. The party were to start from Judge Reve's door, and, as I came down-stairs fully equipped, Sallie said, "Oh, Nannie, dear child, you must have two veils; your face will freeze through one!" And I ran hastily up to my room for my heavy one.

When I returned, the party were mostly seated in their respective sleighs, and Hal stood holding his horse with one hand, and waiting to help me into his cutter.

"What a pretty little thing it is!" I thought; "so snug and cozy."

As I came down the steps, Sallie was talking merrily but emphatically to the gentleman who was waiting to help her into his sleigh.

"Now, Mr. Raymond," she said, "you know my perfect horror of wild horses, and yet here you have one that I am quite sure will break my neck."

"Indeed no, Miss Sallie," said Mr. Raymond. "He is quite gentle, I assure you."

"Gentle! with that defiant look in his eye?"

"That is his natural look. The poor horse is not to blame for his looks."

"Now you are making fun of me, Nannie," she said to me, as I was about to pass her, "don't you think he looks wild?"

"Why, really, Sallie," I answered, "I don't think he looks as if he would frighten easily."

"Don't you, really?"

"Indeed no."

"Maybe you are not so much afraid of horses as I am, and so would not notice his looks as much."

"I am not much afraid of horses, truly," I said; "I am so used to them, you know." And I started to pass on to Hal.

"Are you not, truly?" she answered, quickly. "Then I shall certainly hand you over to the tender mercies of Mr. Raymond and his fiery steed; for I am sure I should die of terror before we reached home." So saying, with a merry laugh, and without waiting for my reply, she sprang into Hal's cutter, and, seating herself comfortably, looked over her shoulder at me with a merry laugh, saying, "I will not even ask Dr. Ray's consent, for fear he will deny me, and I should in that case be compelled to stay at home."

Hal looked at me wistfully a moment; but what could he do? Turn Sallie out of his sleigh? Certainly not. So I was, after all, compelled to ride with a stranger instead of Hal. He was a perfect gentleman, and for a moment seemed annoyed; then he laughed, and said, "It is just like Miss Sallie! No one ever knows where to find her. But I am sure I, for one, am delighted with the exchange." And he helped me into his cutter gallantly, tucking the robes carefully about me; and away we dashed to the merry chime of his silver bells. My heart was so full for a little while that I did not dare to trust my voice to answer him; but I soon recovered myself, and chatted gayly and merrily all the time, determined not to let him think that I was at all disconcerted by the turn affairs had taken. But my heart throbbed with a dull, heavy throb all the while, and a bitter feeling of resentment arose toward both Hal and Sallie Reve. What right had she always to come thus between Hal and myself? Did she not know we were engaged? If not, she still could not but observe our preference for one another. And Hal himself, I thought, might, if he chose, have been a little more decided. I began to think he was not nearly so much annoyed by these things as I. So thinking and feeling in my heart, yet all the while chatting merrily with Mr. Raymond, we at last reached home. None of the party had yet returned but Gertie, although it was quite late; for which I was thankful. The first thing I did was to bolt my room door, and the next to throw myself upon the bed and give way to my long-pent-up feelings. When Gertie would have comforted me, I cried, vehemently,—

"No, Gertie, it is of no use to talk to me. I knew I ought not to come to New York; and I will never slight such impressions again. What comfort have I had? Only annoyance all the time. Think how different it would have been for me had I stayed at home and seen Hal there instead of here. I will give him back his freedom, and he may marry Sallie as soon as he likes."

"Oh, now, Nannie darling, you are excited, and consequently unreasonable. I admit that this is all very annoying, but you are wrong to blame Hal for it so. I am sure he has called repeatedly at the house and asked expressly for you. Was it his fault if others monopolized his time while here? And then to-night what would you have had him do? Lift Sallie from his sleigh, and insist upon taking you?"

"No, certainly not. But then——"

"Then you must see, dear, that he was not the one to blame."

I could not but see that Gertie was right, and at that moment I heard the other sleighs drive up to the door.

"I cannot see her to-night," I said, and hastily turned down the gas. We undressed in silence, and when at last I knelt beside my bed for my evening prayer, I prayed long and earnestly that I might do only what was right, and be enabled to cast all uncharitable and unamiable feelings from my heart. I felt much better when I arose, and as I lay down upon my pillow I thought,—

"After all, Sallie may be perfectly innocent of any design in this matter. I have never told her of my engagement, and perhaps no one else has. It may be only a little willful preference she feels for him; and she is just the girl not to care who sees it. I will try and think no more about it. If Hal himself is true to me, what does it matter, anyhow?"

So I dropped asleep; and when I awakened it was morning, and Gertie was up and dressed. On first awaking there was a dull, heavy weight at my heart, as of some great grief; but I soon shook it off, resolving to let nothing disturb me on this last day, for on the morrow we were to return to dear old Beechwood, and I was fully ready to go. If Sallie intended to wrong me, which now in my calmer moments I did not believe, she should not know how keenly the blow had been felt.

We were a little late at breakfast, and found the others waiting for us, grouped about the cheerful fire in the dining-hall. As we entered, Sallie ran forward in her own graceful way, and, throwing her arms about me, said,—

"I declare, Nannie, I deserve your eternal displeasure for my rudeness to you last night. I was so frightened at the looks of that dreadful horse, that I was ready for anything, however desperate, to escape riding behind him; and when you spoke so fearlessly, on the spur of the moment I thought it would only be a good joke to let you ride after him, not thinking how rude such a proceeding would really be. I am terribly ashamed of myself; but you will forgive me this once, I am sure?" And she put up her lips for a kiss very temptingly.

Her apology was so pretty and graceful, and at the same time so earnest, that, before she had half done, I had yielded, as usual, and, when she paused, I said,—

"It was certainly not very fair, Sallie, for you to swap me off in that unceremonious manner, without even asking my leave, to say nothing of either of the gentlemen; but what can I do at this late hour but forgive you?" And I kissed the offered lips.

"Oh, thank you, Nannie; you are always so good; and I feel conscious that I do not deserve your kindness so, this morning; but I won't do so again, indeed no." And, laughing happily, she ran back to her seat at the table.

"Ho!" said Sallie's little ten-year-old brother, Joe, "ho! who would have thought of Sallie being afraid of a horse? Why, Sallie, don't you remember how you rode that wild horse of Uncle Ned's last fall when we were at the farm, and laughed at mamma for being afraid he would throw you?"

"That was a very different matter," said Sallie, flushing quickly.

"He is enough sight wilder than Mr. Raymond's horse," said Joe, stoutly.

An emphatic gesture from "mamma" silenced the young gentleman, and breakfast proceeded; but I half suspect, for all her graceful apology, that the ruse was premeditated, and not merely accidental.

After breakfast Sallie and Nettie went out shopping; but Gertie and I remained at home, not feeling disposed to venture into the frosty air. I had just laid the last articles in my trunk preparatory to our homeward trip, and had said to Gertie, "I wish it were to-day we were going, instead of to-morrow," when Gertie, who chanced to look from the window, said, suddenly,—

"Here is Hal, Nannie, just stopping at the door with a sleigh. He is bound, you see, that you and he shall yet have your ride together."

"I shall not ride with him to-day, Gertie, if that is what he has come for."

"Oh, yes, you will, Nannie! you surely will not be more unkind to him than you were to Sallie?"

"I have no wish to be unkind, but I have been thwarted so often that now I have no wish to see him alone. Really, Gertie," I said, seeing her look incredulous, "I mean what I say. All I wished to say to him is forgotten, or long ago become stale; and all I now desire is to return to our own dear Beechwood and poor lonely mamma."

At this moment the servant entered, with Hal's card for me, and Gertie said,—

"Please, Nannie, go with him, if he desires it, just to please me. I am sure it will be best, dear, or I would not urge it."

I found Hal waiting for me, with a half-troubled look; and even when he said, tenderly, "I could not consent that we should be cheated out of our ride altogether, Nannie, and so I came this morning to beg you to accompany me," I could not help feeling that it was done more to pacify me than through any positive desire upon his part, and could not help replying,—

"I scarcely know, Hal. It is so cloudy and cold this morning, I am inclined to think it much more comfortable by the fire."

"You are not offended with me, Nannie? You could not but see the awkward position in which I was placed last night."

"Not in the least offended, Hal," I replied, "but——"

"Then prove it, darling, by going with me at once. I have much to say to you; and to-morrow you go?"

I nodded assent, and without further words donned my wraps and accompanied him. We had a pleasant drive, but it was not like our drives of old. In spite of all I could do, there was a feeling of constraint I had never before felt with Hal, and the many things I had so long treasured in my heart to be spoken when we met remained unsaid. How often it happens that when we have been disappointed, again and again, in the attainment of an object earnestly desired, a perfect revulsion of feeling takes place, and we no longer experience a desire for, or pleasure in, the attainment of it! So it was with me now. I had desired ardently to be permitted to have a good quiet talk with Hal, but had so often been thwarted in that desire that now I had no longer anything to say, and really would greatly have preferred remaining at home. I think, too, that Hal also had something of the same feeling; for, although he was loving and gentle in all he said and did, I could not but feel all the time that it required an effort for him so to be. It is possible my own mood gave coloring to this thought, and I earnestly trust it is only so. Gertie said that when Sallie returned and found we were driving, she remarked,—

"Dr. Ray and Nannie seem to be great friends."

"Yes," said Gertie, in her own quiet way, "it is right they should be; they have been engaged to each other for more than a year."

"Indeed?" said Sallie, in apparent surprise; but Hal told me while we were driving, in answer to an inquiry, that he had told her of our engagement a few days before we came to the city. It is very strange. I cannot quite understand it.

Feb. 3. The more I dwell upon my trip to New York, the more dissatisfied I become with myself and others. Of Sallie's preference for Hal I can no longer doubt; but whether or not he is conscious of it, I cannot say. That he reciprocates it, save in a friendly way, I will not allow myself for a moment to think; for, whatever his faults may be, he certainly would not seek to deceive me, and he writes, since my return, in the same fond strain, and speaks just as confidently of our bright future as ever. But there is an intangible something that I cannot grasp, that makes me constantly restless, and at times even unhappy. There is a change either in Hal or myself, that deprives me of the old perfect freedom of thought in speaking with or writing to him. I ponder more over my letters to him, and often find myself wondering "if Hal will like that expression," whereas I used ever to write just what was in my heart, without fear or hesitation. I don't think that the life Hal leads in the great city tends at all to elevate and purify one's life. This constant round of gayety and pleasure, in which he seems to take infinite delight, leaves but little time for study and reflection, and tends to enervate rather than ennoble the soul. At least it so seems to me. I enjoy life and gayety as well as any one for a little while, but I soon grow weary of them, and long for the old home duties and quiet domestic joys. But Hal seems never to weary of pleasure. According to his own account and that of others, he is never out of the ceaseless whirl that to some seems so fascinating. It is true, a few hours of every day he compels himself to give to study and business, though frequently even they are infringed upon; but all the rest of his time he is in some gay crowd, enjoying only the present. His old tastes and habits seem to have been entirely abandoned, and I often wonder if really for the better. Not that I should ever fear that

Hal, my noble Hal, could ever become addicted to the vices of the profligate; his soul is far above that; but in the ceaseless round of butterfly pleasures, one is so apt to forget the higher and more ennobling pursuits of life. One night at Sallie's, some one spoke of an anticipated visit of Mr. Spurgeon, the celebrated English divine, to America. In the course of the conversation, I asked Hal whose church he attended in the city. The gentlemen looked amused, and Hal seemed a little embarrassed, I thought, as he answered,—

"Why, to tell the truth, Nannie, I have not been very regular in my attendance upon any one church since I came to the city."

"I should think not," said Mr. Raymond, dryly. "I will tell you, Miss Cleve; I called several Sundays in succession to take him out to some of the churches, as he was a stranger, but invariably found him so churlish at being roused at such an early hour from his morning nap, that I generously desisted, and left him to enjoy it thereafter unmolested. He usually has his breakfast on Sundays about the time that honest people are returning from church."

A general laugh ensued, as Hal retorted,—

"It is too bad, Raymond, for you to turn 'State's evidence' in that style, when you well know it is your own fault, by forcing me to keep such late hours Saturday nights that I sleep late of Sunday mornings. I am not so old a stager as yourself, and have to make up for lost time, you know."

This rather turned the tables upon Mr. Raymond, till Mr. Burr, a young gentleman who I fancy is a little jealous of Hal's evident preferment with Sallie, came to the rescue by saying,—

"When you consider Dr. Ray's onerous duties to the ladies, you will be more charitable; seeing how utterly impossible it is for him ever to get much sleep unless he steals it from the morning hours."

"Come, come," said Sallie, "I will not have Dr. Ray maligned so uncharitably in my very presence; let us have 'chess' and 'whist.'" And she led the way to the tables. But I cannot help regretting that Hal's Sundays are spent so differently from what they used to be at home, when attendance not only upon church, but also upon Sunday-school, was considered a pleasure as well as a duty.

Several little things also occurred, mere trifles in themselves, but which showed me either new or perverted traits in his character, that gave me sudden pain. Once he rudely pushed a little thin-faced child aside, who begged him for a penny, and when I threw one back to it, upon the pave, he merely said, "The police should take charge of these miserable vagrants." Once also, the day we were returning from the picture-gallery, we came upon an old, old couple sitting side by side upon the steps of a church. They were very thinly clad and forlorn-looking, though comparatively clean. The old man was totally blind, and his wife had such a pleading, pitiful look, as she sat silently with her poor withered hand extended, that my heart was deeply touched.

"Oh, Hal!" I said, pityingly, "do see that poor old couple!" And I drew my purse hastily from my coat-pocket.

"You must not stop here, on this public thoroughfare," said Hal, impatiently, hurrying me rapidly on: "the city will take care of them."

"Oh, Hal, do let me stop," I pleaded; "the poor creatures,—they are so old and feeble." But he looked so annoyed that I reluctantly allowed myself to be drawn away.

"You must excuse me, dear," he said, "for not letting

you stop; but they are all impostors. I never countenance them."

"Not all, Hal. These were so old; and the man was really blind. And did you not see how pitiful his wife looked?"

"All put on, Nannie. When you once come to the city to live, you will become so familiar with these things you will never think of noticing it, much less of making yourself conspicuous by stopping upon a crowded thoroughfare to relieve it."

"God forbid!" I ejaculated, fervently. "And as to making myself conspicuous by such an act, 'Honi soit qui mal y pense.'" At this moment we reached home, and, after a few parting words, Hal left me upon the steps. I waited till he was out of sight, then quickly retraced my steps to the church, and placed a shilling in the poor outstretched hand; and the low, fervent "God bless you, miss! now we can buy some bread," convinced me that my offering had not been idly bestowed, and I passed on home by another street, with a lighter heart, at least for the moment, though I felt inexpressibly pained that Hal should be so insensible to this kind of suffering, when here in the city he could so often relieve it. Uncle Ralph, I thought, would never have denied me the pleasure of speaking to that old couple and ministering to their necessities. Not that I think indiscriminate giving is always right or best. We often meet with mendicants of strong limb and sinewy frame, whose low, debauched features are evidence of the sinful life they lead, and who beg simply because it is easier than to work. For such as these, I admit, I have only a shuddering pity,—no sympathy. But for helpless childhood, infirm old age, or real distress or suffering in any shape whatever, I have ever a warm heart and a ready hand.

I cannot say how these faults in Hal, trifling as they may seem to others, have troubled me since my return. It grieves, it humbles me, to find my idol, whom I aspired to think so far "above the common herd," whom I had placed upon a pedestal fit even for the gods, is only mortal, stands only upon the earth among his fellows. Yet why should I expect him to be so perfect, while I am so full of faults? It is meet that my vanity should be humbled,— yet it is sad.

Feb. 28. An incident occurred during our stay in New York to which I have never yet alluded in my diary, although we have frequently spoken of it together. But my heart has been so full of Hal, and so troubled by these half doubts and fears, that when I sat down to write I could think of nothing else. But his monthly letter was so full of noble and beautiful thoughts and high resolves for the future, that the old gladness has returned, and I wonder that I ever could have so magnified trifles that may have occurred but once.

But to my incident, which is by no means so unimportant as my negligence would imply. One morning, when Gertie and I had started out alone for a little walk, we met Ralph coming to the door with a letter for us from mamma, and we all strolled off together into a different quarter of the city from any we had yet visited. As we were passing in front of an elegant row of brown-stone fronts, I caught the glimpse of a pale face at a window, that startled me; but before I could speak, it disappeared, and a moment afterward the front door opened, and a light little figure bounded down the flight of steps, and loving arms were about my neck, and warm kisses upon my cheek, and a trembling voice sobbed out,—

"Oh, I thought I should never, never see any of you again!"

"My God! it is Minnie," said Ralph, turning, for the moment, white as death.

"Yes, Ralph, it is Minnie,—or all that is left of her," trying to laugh through her tears, and giving him her hand, while with her other arm she embraced Gertie warmly. "But are you not coming in?"

"Is this your home, Minnie?" I said.

"No; it is Mrs. May's. We are here for a short time only; and this morning I am all alone. No one but the servants are in the house."

Thus assured, we mounted the steps, and entered. Minnie led the way into her own rooms,—a very pretty suite on the second floor. She looked very pale and thin, and in answer to our inquiries said she had been quite ill, but was now well again, only not strong. She did indeed look very frail and delicate.

"Why have you not written to us, Minnie?" I said. "We have all wanted so much to hear from you, especially mamma."

"I hardly know," said Minnie, with such evident embarrassment that it needed no words to tell us she was no longer her own mistress.

"I cannot wait any longer," said Ralph, evidently very nervous and fidgety, after we had conversed perhaps half an hour. "I promised to meet Charlie at one o'clock, and it is now nearly twelve."

"Is Charlie also in the city? How I would love to see him!" said Minnie; but she did not ask for him to call, nor did she invite us to repeat our visit. She seemed nervous, and started at every little sound she heard, and evidently dreaded the coming of some one while we were there, and that some one could be no other than her husband. She either could not or would not tell us of their future plans, saying everything was so uncertain she could not yet tell what they would do. We arose to go, and she herself accompanied us to the street door.

Ralph and Gertie said "good-by" to her and passed down the steps and started slowly along the pave, while I lingered for a parting kiss and word.

"You will not neglect to write to us again, and often, dear Minnie?" I said.

"I will not indeed, if possible. Tell Aunt Fannie I often think of her, and deeply regret ever having given her pain——" She stopped in embarrassment, for at that moment her husband sprang up the steps to where we were standing. With bold effrontery he lifted his hat to me and extended his hand; but, with a contemptuous look full in his face, I bowed coldly, and, with a hasty kiss and a fervent "God bless you, darling!" to Minnie, I ran down the steps, and soon rejoined Ralph and Gertie.

"The contemptible scoundrel!" said Ralph, compressing his lips when I told them of my encounter. "It was to avoid just such a meeting as that—for Minnie's sake only, mind you—that I hastened to leave the house. I am sure, had I met him face to face, that he would have felt the weight of my cane. Any one can see by her pale little face the kind of life he leads her, confound him!"

"I am afraid she is not very happy," said Gertie.

"Happy? Any one can see that she is afraid even to say her life is her own," said Ralph, bitterly.

And so conversing we soon reached home, and the subject of necessity dropped; but poor Ralph wore an anxious, troubled look all the rest of our stay.

Mamma was greatly shocked when we told her of Minnie's altered looks and manners; and she charged Charlie to go to the house at once, upon his return to the city, and bear to Minnie a letter she herself would write, and, if possible, see her himself. He did as mamma requested; but the servant at the door told him that Colonel and Mrs. Leslie had been gone from the city for more than a week, and he really had no idea of their destination. Charlie even went so far as to write a polite request for Minnie's address upon a card and send it to Mrs. May by the servant. Her reply was that Colonel Leslie expected to be traveling from place to place for some time, and she really had no idea where a letter would reach them.

"The truth of the matter is," said Ralph, "he is such a scamp that his family take 'very little stock' in him, and his goings and comings are of little importance to them."

"Yes," said Gertie, "and they all think much less of poor Minnie, now that she is his wife, than they did when she was simply his sister's friend."

"That is very probable," said mamma. "Poor child! she is paying very dearly for her rashness; and the great fear is that she will grieve herself to death away among strangers, with no one to care for or minister to her."

"I do wonder," said Ralph, excitedly, "if it could be a crime to send a bullet through the brain of such a villain! I am sure I will not be answerable for his life if he ever crosses my path."

"Hush, my son," said mamma, calmly. "'Vengeance is mine, I will repay, saith the Lord.'"

"Ay, ay," said Ralph; "I only hope in this case he will not delay it till it is too late to do poor Minnie any good." And he walked impatiently out of the room, but put his head in the door a moment afterward and said, "Forgive me, mamma, I did not mean to be irreverent."

"Poor Ralph!" said mamma; "I am sure he did not."

March 21. To-day mamma had a letter from Uncle Ralph. He says he is tired of traveling, has grown large and strong enough to be "in danger of being run for an alderman" upon his return, and altogether thinks that he has played truant from business long enough, so that we may soon expect to see him in bodily presence at Beechwood. I assure you it made no little stir in our quiet home to hear that one so dearly beloved as he is was again coming into our midst. Uncle Ben has been trying to persuade him to remove to St. Louis, and we greatly feared at one time with success; but he says he thinks he is getting too old (thirty-three this month) to change his residence now,—that he shall cling to our beautiful little village, in all probability, for life. Although Gertie and I laugh at the bare idea of Uncle Ralph being old, we are greatly satisfied with his resolution, for Beechwood would lose half of its attractions if Uncle Ralph were to remove permanently from its vicinity. Mamma, too, drew a long sigh of evident relief at his decision; for since dear papa's death she has looked to him and clung to him as she could to none other. And, indeed, he has filled the place of father, brother, and friend to all of us; and few men have ever been so reverenced and loved as is Uncle Ralph by the inmates, one and all, of Beechwood. Our highest reward when children was his praise, and so, too, now our greatest pleasure is to receive his approbation and love. The idea of living under the ban of his displeasure would be a calamity too terrible for contemplation. Gertie and I have talked of nothing all day but his coming, until at last Aunt Martha said,—

"Well, I declare, girls, one would think, to hear you two talk, that your Uncle Ralph was the only man that ever lived in the world."

"We do not think him the only one, Aunt Martha," said Gertie; "but very decidedly the best."

"I wonder if Nannie sanctions that remark," she said, teasingly.

"I think him at least one of the very best," I said,

laughingly; but I could not but fall to thinking of him and Hal together, and found myself ere long wondering if Hal would be the great, noble-souled man at Uncle Ralph's age that he himself is, and inwardly praying that outward circumstances would indeed influence him so to be. What better prayer could I make for my absent lover? May God mercifully hear and answer. But Gertie is calling me for a walk; I must not detain her.

April 8. Spring, glad and beautiful, is with us early this year, and all nature is dressed in holiday attire to welcome her coming. The air is redolent with the breath of the early flowers, and

> "——full of a strange, sweet calm;
> While the fragrant breath of morning
> Falls like a holy balm."

Beechwood, dear old Beechwood, is never so beautiful as in spring-time. Then she throws off the dark robes of winter, and dons her brightest attire; and truly, to young eyes familiar to her from infancy, she is surpassingly beautiful. I have seen many lovely landscapes and many exceedingly beautiful homes, but, though they may surpass our own in grandeur and extent, yet, for beauties of location, charming views without, and substantial comfort and loving hearts within, give me Beechwood over all the world! Situated upon a little knoll, whose east and south slopes are an unbroken lawn, except only where the trees and shrubbery dot its verdant sward, making cool and sweet contrast to the sunny slopes around, the old house stands. It is not one to strike the beholder with its magnificent architecture or grand proportions, though it is of solid and substantial workmanship. It fronts south, with a wide hall in the centre, cool parlors upon the left, and drawing-room and morning-room to the right; while beyond them, in a unique little wing, is the long, pleasant library, amid whose multiplied volumes one can ever beguile the hours that otherwise would be weary, and find but little opportunity or inclination for ennui or regrets. But, although the house fronts south, the main entrance is from the east; for a long avenue of beech-trees, planted by grandpapa's own hands, and beginning nearly a mile from the house, winds up to the very door of the east hall, which extends just back of the parlors and drawing-rooms, and has always been, in reality, the main entrance. The dining-room and spacious kitchen are in an L, still back of this, and cool verandas encircle almost the entire house. Then, from the windows of the sleeping-rooms above, the view is charming. To the east and front, immediately beneath the eye, are the beautiful lawns; beyond, the winding avenue of stately trees, the little church on the hill, and Pine Grove, Colonel Ray's place, half hidden by its stately pines; and, in the distance, the spires and roofs of the village of M——; while from the south windows we catch a glimpse of the blue Atlantic, about three miles away, and whose angry roar we can sometimes hear above the tempest, when it dashes its waves in mad fury against the rock-bound shore. Just west of the house are the beautiful beech-groves, so inviting to the lover of nature; to the north is the garden, and beyond it the orchard, of whose sunny slope and peaceful shades I have before written.

Such is Beechwood to a stranger. But who can describe it as it appears to the loving eyes that see something to admire in every leaf and spear of grass there growing, or to the loving hearts that cherish every shaded nook, and moss-grown rock, and hidden path, as something almost sacred? Not a room in the dear old house but is hallowed by some past association; not a walk or nook upon the grounds that has not its own peculiar memory or history; and there would be such a hubbub raised about the ears of the unfortunate man who should attempt to inaugurate a change, either in house or grounds, as would cause him to believe Babel itself was reproduced.

April 21. Three days ago Uncle Ralph came home, and such a glad welcome as we gave him! He seems very well and strong, and all the lines of care that shadowed his dear face when he left us have disappeared. He is the same dear, good Uncle Ralph he used to be, except that he no longer treats us as little children,—which I cannot but regret. I would love for Uncle Ralph always to think of me as a little child. On the day that he came, Gertie and I hovered about him all the time; we could not bear to lose sight of him for a moment; and once, as I passed behind the arm-chair in which he sat, with his dear head thrown negligently back, in an attitude of repose, as he talked to mamma and Aunt Martha, I could not forbear bending over and kissing the white high forehead, saying impulsively the while,—

"You dear old Uncle Ralph, I am so glad to have you back with us again!"

He flashed a bright, glad look up at me when I spoke, and raised his hand as though to caress me in the old fond way, but dropped it again presently, as he said, "Thank you, dear child. I assure you I am very happy to be back with you all again," and went on talking with mamma; but the remembrance of the bright look he gave me made me happy all evening, for it assured me that I still held my old place in his heart. But mamma took occasion to say to me afterward,—

"You must try, darling, and be a little less impulsive with Uncle Ralph. You know he no longer looks upon you and Gertie as little children."

"Why, mamma," I said, a little confusedly, "do you think I did wrong to-day? I do love him so dearly, and it is so very difficult not to show it, especially after he has been gone so long."

"No, dear, not wrong. It was very natural that you should show your pleasure at his return; but when you remember that there really exists no tie of blood between you, and that you can no longer be considered a child, you cannot but see that the old childish freedom would scarcely now be admissible."

"I see that, as usual, you are right, dear mamma; but, oh, how I wish I could have remained a child a little longer!"

Yet I could not but think, after I had spoken, how easily mamma might have retorted that Hal and I were in great haste to prove that I was beyond its precincts, when I might easily then have pleaded for a little delay. But mamma never retorts.

Uncle Ralph has much to tell us that is full of interest, of his travels, but which time and space will not permit me here to record. First of all, he took one of the pleasant lake-steamers at Buffalo, and made the tour of the northern lakes,—passing through Erie, and the tiny St. Clair, with its many beautiful islands, then across troubled Huron, stopping for a few days at Mackinac, which lies in its rare loveliness, like a fairy isle, in the straits of the same name. He said that of all quiet and beautiful spots he never yet had seen one that could surpass in grandeur and loveliness this little islet, whose whole circumference, I believe, is but nine miles. They landed just at sunset, and, as Gertie said, it was as good as a fairy-tale to hear him describe the scene as it burst upon him there. The old fort frowning down from its rugged and precipitate height upon the little village, so quaint and old, at its feet; the white beach, upon which the Indian children played, washed by the waters of the straits; the many islets in the distance, and the broad waters of the lakes stretching far away, studded here and there with the tiny white sails of the fishermen or pleasure-seekers; the little harbor, with one or two other steamers besides the one he was himself upon, and over it all the golden light of the sunset clouds and the lengthening shadows of the overhanging cliffs. Then the island itself he describes as one of wondrous beauty and full of many enchanting walks and drives; possessed of many places of interest to the lovers of the wonderful, and having connected with it legends, many of which are full of fearful interest to the inhabitants, who cling to their traditions with superstitious awe. Upon leaving Mackinac, he returned through the Sault Ste. Marie, whose scenery is very fine, and traversed the whole length of grand Superior, visiting the iron, copper, and silver mines, and bringing to us many beautiful specimens of agate and other rare stones. Afterward he visited by rail all the cities of note in the great Northwest; crossed their beautiful prairies, which he says for hundreds of miles are perfectly level, and in the spring covered with exquisitely beautiful flowers, making the earth look as if it was spread with a carpet of brilliant colors, far as the eye can reach. He reached St. Louis, spent a few weeks there, and then he and Ned took a trip, upon one of the palatial Mississippi steamers, to the South, and spent some weeks visiting the principal Southern cities; and now he is once more at Beechwood, and we have resolved not to let him out of our sight for such another trip, very soon again. We need him too much at home. He says Ralph has done wonders in his absence, and he should never fear to trust him in the future with anything, at which praise Ralph looked justly proud.

April 23. This is a lovely spring day, but, like a capricious child, alternate smiles and tears. Gertie and I started for a walk over to Nettie's, but when about half-way there were caught in a violent shower of rain, which so saturated our garments that we were compelled to return home; but before we reached the house the sun shone out merrily, as though laughing at our distress. The little birds are fairly wild with happiness, and the whole earth seems one fairy garden of delight.

Yesterday Gertie and I planted fresh flowers upon dear little Kittie's grave, and trained the luxuriant branches of the white rose we had at first planted, into a perfect little bower above her tiny moss-grown grave. The little form is long ago but dust, but the memory of the precious child is as fresh and green and fragrant in our hearts to-day as the bright tendrils of the rose-tree that ere long will burst into such fragrant loveliness above her narrow bed. Alas! how many such landmarks do we plant by the wayside in our brief life-journey, and how yearningly, as we pass onward, do we look back to them, often, though miles away, bending in spirit above them, dropping bitter tears of remembrance! Happy for us if their bitterness is unmixed with remorse. Eight years have passed since dear papa was laid to rest on the hillock where little Kittie to-day sleeps beside him, and all that the tenderest love can do to beautify the spot has been done. His grave is to mamma a sacred shrine, and ever will be. She was but thirty-two when he was drowned,—in the very prime of a most beautiful womanhood,—and, to my certain knowledge, she has several times been sought by the best of men; but her answer is always the same, that she has no heart to bestow, and that marriage without love is a desecration. She never speaks of these things herself, but Aunt Katie told me that twice the gentlemen had appealed to her for her influence, and at another time I myself was compelled to listen to a conversation not intended for my ears. It was only a short time before little Kittie died, and I, in romping with her, had hidden myself in the cloak-closet that is in the drawing-room, and while there a gentleman, an old friend of mamma's, was shown in, and I, thinking that he would not long remain, and not liking to come out before him, foolishly remained in my concealment. When mamma came in, she sat down only a little distance from the closet-door, and he soon joined her. I sat down on the floor to wait, and fell to thinking of a very interesting story I had been reading, and did not notice the conversation until I heard mamma say, evidently much troubled,—

"You distress me, Mr. Blair. Please say no more on this subject."

"But why is it, Fannie? You used to like me well enough. I once fancied, many years ago, while you were yet free, that had I not been so diffident in speaking I might have won you then."

"Let the past speak for itself; now we have only to deal with the present. I respect and honor you; nay, more, in a certain way I love you. Do not mistake me: it is only the love that one friend may feel for another greatly valued; beyond this I have nothing to give."

"But in time, Fannie,—may I not hope that all these years of patient waiting will some day be rewarded by your love?"

My heart was a-quiver. I could not but hear every word spoken, and the thought of mamma—dear, precious mamma—ever belonging to any one but her children, was dreadful to me. The answer set me at rest, for it was decisive, though low and tenderly spoken:—

"When I married Charlie Cleve, I gave him my whole undivided heart; and when God called him away from me, he took it with him into eternity. It may be right for some persons to marry twice, but for me—never. In the hereafter I wish to stand beside him, and lay my hand with the old trust in his, and say to him, 'I have waited for you;' and nothing must come between us. Another marriage, another love, would be sacrilege; for my whole heart is, not in his grave, for he yet lives in the bright hereafter, but in his keeping."

There was a moment's unbroken silence; then, as he arose to go, Mr. Blair said, evidently much moved,—

"My great disappointment does not prevent my honoring you still more for the sentiments you have uttered. I do not wonder that you were Charlie's idol, while living, for such devotion must ever find reciprocation. I am not a Christian, but I cannot doubt that eternity has for you both untold happiness. May God bless you, dear Fannie, although you have to-night shattered the brightest dream of my life."

A moment later he was gone; and I heard mamma sobbing softly to herself. I felt guilty for not at once coming out when they first began to talk; but it was now too late for regrets. After a moment I tapped softly upon the door, and mamma, not noticing from which door the rap came, said "Come in," and I entered. She did not even then notice from whence I came, the two doors are so near each other, and I sat down beside her, before she noticed my evident agitation.

"What is it, Nannie?"

"Pardon me, dear mamma, but I have unwittingly overheard all that passed between yourself and Mr. Blair." And I related to her the circumstances of my concealment and of their subsequent entrance.

"I regret it, Nannie; for such things are better always known only to the parties concerned. As it is, my darling, you will, I am sure, let it go no further."

"Never, dear mamma," I said; and I have kept my word; only after this long time I am sure I may tell it, dear old book, to you, without fear of betrayal. I have thought many times of this beautiful love, that for so many years has been all that mamma had left of her early dream; and I can better understand the faith in which she here walks daily, and the patient trust with which she looks to the future; for "where the treasure is, there will the heart be also."

As for myself, dearly as I love Hal, I cannot but feel, of late, that there is a depth in my heart still unstirred,—a low undertone in the soul's anthem that has never found its echo. I do not fear that he could not reach the one, that he could not awaken the other, but that he will not, and they will sleep forever. Our love awoke so early, was so early reciprocated and revealed, and has glided so quietly and imperceptibly on, that its inner depths still lie in unbroken slumber. So with the woodland stream whose waters may be tranquil, but deep. While the skies are blue above it, and the storms and tempests visit it not, when there is nothing to obstruct its way, it flows on placid and noiseless forever; and, gazing upon its clear waters, one knows not of their depth or strength. But once let the tempest break above it, let huge rocks be thrown into its quiet bed, let its deep under-current be troubled and broken, and it will bound on with alarming rapidity, and break in angry waves about obstacles that have been thrown in its way. Like love, it must be tested to develop its strength. Not that I wish it otherwise with us: its very tranquillity is bliss unspeakable.

May 3. A long letter from Cousin Fanny, to-day, tells me that she expects to be married in August next, and begs me to come and spend the summer with her, and officiate as chief bridesmaid. They expect to start for

Europe immediately after the ceremony, and Fannie urges me, if I cannot possibly be present at the wedding, to meet her at New York and go with them to the Old World. They will be absent six or eight months. It would be delightful, I am sure, both to go to the wedding and to visit the continent, but I must forego both pleasures for the sake of one dearer. Hal comes home early in June, to spend several weeks, and, foolish little girl that I am, the thought of being with him again in the quiet of Beechwood outweighs all other pleasures, however inviting. It has always been the dream of my life to visit the continent; but how could I voluntarily place the great ocean between us? Perhaps we may some day visit it together. I will try and go to New York, however, and see Fannie before she sails, and wish her "un bon voyage."

When we left New York, after the holidays, Sallie Reve promised to visit us early in May; but she writes now that she cannot come before the middle of the month. I am half sorry, for I want her to make a good long visit, and I must confess that I would rather she should make it before Hal comes, than during his visit, for she is so gay that I cannot see half so much of Hal when we are all together as when we have only ourselves here. That looks selfish, I know; (but when was not love selfish?) Then, too, she can see him when she will, in New York, and I, only during his semi-yearly visits home; for mamma objects to his coming oftener till our two years of probation have expired. It only lacks a few months yet for their fulfillment, and I can scarcely say whether I am glad or sorry. The thought of some day being always with Hal is very precious to me; while at the same time the thought of leaving dear quiet Beechwood forever, for the crowded streets and noise and turmoil of a great city, is very saddening. Then, too, the day that Hal and I were sleighing in New York, as we passed a fine block of buildings in course of erection upon one of the most fashionable streets, he said,—

"Those will be ready for renting next fall, and I have thought several times of securing one of them, they are so pleasantly located. I long for the time to come when I may return at evening and find my Nannie at the door or window waiting for me."

"Ah," I said, blushing, "but not on this noisy street, Hal. A nice little home in the suburbs of the city will be so much more pleasant; and these street-cars do annihilate distance."

"In the suburbs? Excuse me, please. I detest suburbs; and I am sure I shall never want to hide my wife, when I have one, away from all society and enjoyment in that style."

"Suppose she prefers such seclusion, deeming home enjoyments far preferable to any other?"

"Then she must learn, for her husband's sake, to think otherwise. No life so humdrum, say I, as this constant seclusion from society. People soon weary of one another's company when they are always together."

"Granted," I said, with some bitterness, "when they have no higher employment than commonplace compliments and flatteries,—discussions of this party, and that supper, and the thousand and one follies of fashionable life; but with books, and music, and rational conversation, one friend is better company than twenty."

"Pardon me, dear Nannie," he said, gently, for he could not but see that I was a little hurt; "I am sure we will agree perfectly upon this subject when the proper time comes; for my great desire will be to secure your happiness." But, knowing how fascinated he is with this gay life, I greatly fear that he never will be content far removed from it. And I—what could I do, in a constant whirl of excitement? (It would wear me out in six months; and, besides, I do not love it.) My life has been so quiet and happy in my girlhood's home, and mamma has so unfailingly taught us to look for enjoyment and happiness in the higher pursuits of intellect and soul, that I shrink from this fashionable life, whose pursuits seem no higher than those of the butterfly,—pleasure for the present hour. But, then, if Hal will only at first allow me to try my own plan, I shall make our home so charming, that if he loves me, as I cannot doubt he does, he will soon forget to look elsewhere for happiness. Oh, I know that I could make his home very bright and beautiful for him, and so make his wishes, in all things, my own, that the hours would all be golden-hued.

May 16. A little note from Sallie says the presence of friends will delay her coming for a few days, but she hopes soon to be with us. Well, it is all very well; for Aunt Katie came yesterday, with dear little Blanche and Harry. Uncle Harry is to come for her at the end of their visit. We have not seen Aunt Katie for so long, that it is a privilege to be able to give her all of our time, undivided by other guests. Little Blanche, who is two years old, is growing marvelously like our lost Kittie, and of course is a universal pet. She takes wonderfully to Ralph, and he is never weary of romping with her and carrying her when he is at home. Harry is a sturdy little fellow of four years, and he astonishes us all with his quaint remarks and unanswerable questions. To-day he came to mamma as she sat sewing, and said,—

"Aunt Fannie, may Harry have your scissors to play with, a little while?"

"They are so sharp, Harry, auntie is afraid you will fall down with them, and they might run into your eyes."

He stood thoughtfully for a few moments at her knee, as though trying to solve some great problem in his little brain, and then said, quietly,—

"Aunt Fannie, have they feet?"

"Have what feet, Harry?"

"The scissors."

"Why, no, you funny little boy," said mamma, laughing.

"Then," with a look of wonderment in his great black eyes, "how can they run into my eyes?" And when his question was met by a shout of merriment from all the party, he turned away, half indignantly, and said,—

"How can they run, I'd like to know, if they haven't any feet?"

And yesterday, when I said to him, "Look, look, Harry, at the little bird in the cedar-tree," he gravely asked,—

"Do you call it *ced-ar*, Cousin Nannie, because it is so full of *seeds?*"

In the same manner he is constantly playing upon words unconsciously, much to our delight and to Aunt Katie's annoyance, who says she is terribly afraid he will be a natural wag, a character she cannot endure. But he is a noble boy; his little heart is full of generous impulses, and his hand is ever open to the needy. I have often seen him unhesitatingly give all the pennies he possessed to some poor child, and then hasten to bring forth his most cherished toys to bestow those likewise.

Lizzie Weir came with the children, and has improved wonderfully since she went to live with Aunt Katie. She is really now a very pretty girl, and her manners are always gentle and pleasant. The children love her dearly. Aunt Katie says she is a great help to her, and they are all much attached to her. Joseph seems to share in the general opinion that she is a very nice girl, for he never loses an opportunity of speaking with her, when she is out with the children. I said to her to-day, a little teasingly,—

"You and Joseph seem to be great friends, Lizzie."

"Joseph was very kind to me, miss, when I was most friendless; I should be very ungrateful to forget him," she answered, so modestly and honestly that my mirth was disarmed, and I answered her at once,—

"That is right, Lizzie; always hold fast to one who has proved himself your friend. Joseph is a nice boy, and merits your good opinion."

"Thank you, miss: I certainly never can forget any one who was so kind to me as you all were at Beechwood when poor granny died." And the tears sprang into her eyes at the remembrance of the dear old friend she had lost.

"If Mrs. Hall can spare me, I should like to go to granny's grave once, and set out a rose-bush that Joseph brought to me this morning from the village."

"I will take the children out to walk with me this morning, Lizzie, and you can go at once. I am sure your love for your old granny is beautiful and right."

"She was always good and kind to me, miss, and I could not bear to see her grave neglected. She was all I had to love me."

"Joseph shall take care of her grave, Lizzie, and see that it is never neglected," I said, wishing to comfort her.

"Oh, thank you, miss. He promised to-day that he would look after it a little in his leisure."

So Gertie and I went out with the little ones, and left Lizzie at liberty to go to the churchyard, gaining mamma's permission for Joseph to accompany her, and giving her several roots and flowers from our own stock, with which to beautify the grave of her grandmother. She came back, looking sad, but happy, and told me, shyly, that she had promised Joseph to wait for him till he was ready to marry, which will probably be several years yet, as both are very young.

So it is in all conditions of life, congenial hearts seek and know each other; why not as well among those in the humbler walks of life, as among those who tread only upon velvet and flowers? I think Joseph and Lizzie well adapted for each other, and I doubt not that they will be fully as happy, in their humble way, as many who are grander and more ostentatious.

June 12. Aunt Katie returned home yesterday, with her husband and the dear little ones, and the house seems very lonely again without them. Uncle Harry was here but a few days, it is so difficult for him to leave his business long. He is perfectly wrapped up in his wife and little ones; thinks little Harry is the greatest boy alive. He laughed heartily when I related to him his dialogue with mamma about the scissors, and said it reminded him of a similar answer once at the table. Harry was playing with his bread-and-milk, and his papa said to him, "Be careful, Harry; you will make your milk fly all over the table." He looked up a moment in surprise, and then said, "No, papa! How can it fly? It has no wings!"

Lizzie went away very bright and happy, and I hear Joseph singing about his work all day. Truly love lightens labor. How sweet it must be to toil for those we love! I sometimes wish Hal was poor. I believe it would be better for both of us, at first, if he was. Better for him, by giving him a new incentive for exertion; better for me, by giving me something useful to do for others, which I could not set aside at pleasure, as now, and so leaving me less time for thinking of the dear ones at home, when I leave them. He and Nettie both have property from their mother's family that will keep them well of itself; hence Hal, I fear, may sometimes fail to exert the energy in his profession that he otherwise would; although he says it shall never make any difference in his life. Such things often influence us unawares. He and Charlie will soon come now for the summer holidays. I am impatient for the days to pass. I have indirectly heard that Sallie Reve is going to Newport with a party of friends, so that, although she has not written to say so, I shall not look for her before fall. I am selfish enough to be glad that we shall have only the home ones for awhile, much as I am sure I shall enjoy Sallie's visit when she comes.

Later. At this point Gertie came into the room, bringing me a letter from Hal. It reads,—

"MY DARLING,—There is no hour more sacred to me than that in which I sit alone in the twilight and hold thus converse with yourself. I then feel that you are in bodily presence beside me. I can almost touch you with my hand, and, bending, look into the dear eyes that have learned to tell me such precious truths from their depths. Ah! if the future has in store for us one-half the happiness of which I dream, there is no use to talk to me of a future Paradise, for I shall have it upon earth. The months are slipping away into eternity, and but five yet remain to complete our probation. Do you, my Nannie, count them and look forward to their fulfillment with the same restless longing I feel? I would they were now complete. I shall feel safer when you are beside me, in this strange labyrinth of pleasure, wherein are so many siren voices; for I am sure you will be my good angel and guide me aright. I sometimes weary, as to-night, of this maddening whirl of pleasure, but it seems impossible for me to resist its tide. Do not think unkindly of me, dear, if you hear I have been very gay; I am naturally susceptible to pleasure, and its sirens do so entice me. Charlie, dear, prudent Charlie, warned me yesterday that my name was already coupled with that of a young lady of this city, and that in some circles it was confidently asserted we were soon to be wedded. You know its falsity, and will believe me when I say that, whatever I may seem to others, 'I am true to my first and only love.' I regret this report, for the young lady's sake, but am sure I have only paid her the attentions of a friend. My conscience would not let you hear this from any pen but mine. I fear Charlie thinks me imprudent; but he is so unimpressible, how can he understand my temptations? I am writing you a strange letter, I am conscious of it; but I hope so soon to see you, and talk with you face to face, that I will not try to apologize for it till then. You know I love you, my darling, and, knowing this, I feel that you will trust me.

"I expected to have seen you at Beechwood next week, but a party of friends have persuaded me, much against my inclination, to join them in a little excursion, to end at Newport, so that my visit will necessarily be for a little time delayed; but only for a little time. What pleasure could be sufficiently enticing to keep me long from my darling? I will leave them as soon as they arrive at Newport, and fly to your presence. Till that envied time, believe me to be ever, as in the past,

"Yours devotedly,   HAL."

Twice I read the letter through without pause or comment, and then I sat with my hands idly folded upon my lap, dreaming, till Gertie, who sat reading by me, said,—

"What is it, sister? No unpleasant word, I hope."

Her voice sounded strange and distant to me, so completely was I absorbed in my own thoughts, but it aroused me, and I answered,—

"No, oh! no;" for I could not distress her with my vague fears. "Let us go upon the terrace. The air seems close and oppressive; I fear a storm is brewing."

So we stepped from our room window upon the long terrace, and walked backward and forward, with arms entwined, for half an hour or more. There certainly were indications of a storm. The air was close and warm; the heavy clouds hung so low in the west that they hid the tops of the distant hills; the wind sobbed through the tall trees of the grove, and the sullen moan of the distant Atlantic broke upon our ears through the stillness—for night was already falling—like the sob of some great spirit in agony.

"Let us go in," said Gertie, at last; "these wind-sounds are appalling." But they suited my mood, and I replied,—

"Wait a little yet, Gertie; it attracts me to-night. It reminds me of a fearful dream I had last night,—one that Aunt Martha would say surely boded no good. You know her faith in dreams, and one of her worst signs is dark, troubled water. She says it never fails to bring either trouble or death. For my part, I have but little faith in such unpleasant prophecies, but nevertheless I do not fancy the dream."

"What did you dream, Nannie?" said Gertie.

"Do you really wish to hear it? Well, we will turn old women for once, and tell our dreams. I thought I was out upon the ocean, with just such a wrathful sky as this above us, and dark turbid waves rolling angrily beneath. I was in a frail little boat, and Hal was with me. The tempest broke above us, and we knew that our little bark must perish. 'Cling to me, dear Nannie,' Hal had whispered, 'and I will save you.' But just then arose from the midst of the waters a beautiful siren, her long tresses dripping with the sea-foam, her face that of an angel, and her soft eyes, radiant and beautiful, fixed upon Hal. She stretched her delicate white hands, bedecked with costly jewels, toward him, and in a voice sweet as the sighing of an æolian harp, yet which made itself distinctly heard above the tempest, sang,—

> 'Come down to my beautiful home in the sea;
> I have deck'd it with coral and sea-weed for thee;
> And the purest of pearls, and soft-tinted shells,
> Are found in the cave where the mermaid dwells.
> Come, come, come, come, down into the deep with me!
> Come, come, come, come! 'tis the mermaid calls to thee.'

"'Oh, do not look at her,' I cried; 'Hal, dear Hal, hear me. Turn your eyes away from her; listen only to me, your Nannie!' But he had heart and ear only for the wonderfully witching strain; and though I tried to hold him back, as the boat tossed onward toward the beautiful enchantress, he freed himself from my grasp, and sprang into her outstretched arms, just as our tiny boat was dashed to atoms by the waves. Once he turned, and looked wistfully back at me, then vanished from my sight forever; and the cold dark waves engulfed me, closed above me, and I sank down,—down,—until a strong hand seemed to seize me in the midst of the waters, and drew me rapidly upward into a world full of sunlight, and flowers, and all beautiful things; and when I turned to thank my preserver, lo, it was Uncle Ralph! and with a glad cry I awoke."

"Ah!" said Gertie, drawing a sigh of relief, "your dream had a good ending, after all; though it must have been terrible."

"It was. But see, the wind has increased into a gale, and the heavy clouds are drifting seaward; may God be merciful to the poor mariner to-night. Let us enter." And we came within, and closed the casement; and now, while I write, the storm is beating furiously against the shutters, and the loud wail of the wind mingles with the sullen roar of the sea. Gertie is trying to forget it in an interesting book, and I,—I am thinking of Hal's letter, so unlike his usual style, and wondering what can have produced the change. There seems to be something back of all he has written, that he evidently fears will not please me; and a certain constraint pervades his whole letter, that I have never noticed in any of them before. It leaves me restless and uneasy. And for all I laugh with Gertie at my dream, it has left its impress. I cannot shake off a certain uneasy feeling that trouble awaits me; in what shape I know not, but pray it may not be with Hal. Those dark waves haunt me; and the remembrance of his dear face sinking from my view, blended with that of the beautiful siren, is dreadful. Oh, Hal! only be true to your own noble nature and our love, and I fear for nothing. To the report of which he speaks, I attach no importance, for I rely implicitly upon his truth, and he tells me expressly that he is unchanged. I suspect his trip to Newport is all of Sallie's planning; but if he only comes soon, I have no wish to deprive him of so innocent a pleasure. I mean, at any rate, to think and believe that all is right, until he himself tells me to the contrary. Charlie could explain all the hidden meaning of Hal's letter, when he comes, I am sure; but I would not wrong him by going to another for information concerning him, even though that other were precious Charlie. I must be patient till he arrives; and I am determined, come what will, that the "green-eyed monster" shall never find entrance to my heart. If I cannot enjoy love unmixed with that passion, I will have none of it; for of all the passions jealousy is surely the worst and the most inexcusable.

June 20. A dainty little note from Sallie to-day, dated at Newport, reads,—

"DEAR NANNIE,—It is too bad that my visit to your charming home has been so long delayed; but circumstances, which you know we cannot always control, have rendered it heretofore impracticable, not to say impossible, for me to go to you. Mollie Desmonde, who, you remember, was to visit Nettie Ray when I visited you, has about concluded to go there from here, and I shall therefore forego the pleasures of a gay season at Newport for a quiet sojourn at Beechwood, of whose enchantments I have heard so much. See how well I love you!

"Dr. Ray, who forms one of our party, which is quite large, talks of himself going soon, in which case we will probably take advantage of the fact and secure him for an escort. I will drop you a line when we settle upon the day of departure.

"In haste and love, yours always.

"SALLIE."

"Of course," was Gertie's only answer, as she read the letter, and the only comment that passed between us upon the subject. Nor will I allow myself to jot down a single thought, for my heart is full of bitterness, and I would probably write that which afterward I would wish effaced.

July 1. A note from Sallie says we may look for them to-morrow; and a word from Hal excuses his delay by saying that the young ladies expressed a desire for his escort, and he was compelled to wait their pleasure. Of course.

July 2. They have come. Sallie, as usual, has carried the house by storm, everybody, even to Aunt Martha, being fascinated with her. Hal is so gay, and seems so happy to be once more at home, that I already feel ashamed of my suspicions, and will do all in my power to enjoy and make others enjoy their visit. Nettie, Hal, and Mollie Desmonde came over after tea, and we spent a merry, happy evening together. I write this at a late hour in the quiet of my own room, Gertie being already asleep. We are all to go to Nettie's to dinner to-morrow, and in the evening have a canter upon the ponies.

Charlie came home more than a week ago, and is almost as quiet as ever. He is as tall as Ralph, who, I believe, is just six feet, but not so broad-shouldered, and there is a striking contrast between the two. Ralph is so strong and sturdy-looking; his great black eyes are ever so full of fun, and even his short black curls have a mischievous fun-loving way of tumbling all over his head, as though they were wholly unused to comb or brush; while Charlie, with his light, close curls and pale, intellectual face, commands the respect at once of every one. He would be taken for the elder of the two by those who knew them not. He does not seem so fascinated by Sallie as in the winter, although he is ever kind and polite to her.

Nettie told me to-night that old Mr. White, whose health has been failing for some time, has asked for an assistant in Ellis Ray, who has ever been a favorite with him; and he, having completed his studies, is soon to come here permanently. He will be a favorite, I prophesy, and well cared for; for our parish, though small, is wealthy, and the members are ever devoted to their pastor. The only objection that could possibly be urged by some of the older ones was that he is "still young and unmarried," to which Father White gravely replies that "time will soon remove the first objection, and that he doubts not there are many ladies in the parish who will gladly assist him in overcoming the latter."

July 20. The weeks somehow wear away; but, in spite of my brave resolves, I am not happy. It is the same old story of the holidays repeated. Sallie, gay, happy, and apparently without any design, still manages to stand ever between Hal and myself. Go where we will, she contrives to be beside him, or in some way or other to attach him to her party. He may be absent for hours, so long as I am with her, and she is content; but let us be for an instant apart, and he is sure to be in requisition. Yet it is all done so innocently and naturally that none but a close observer could accuse her of immodesty in her advances. She would make a most magnificent diplomat. I think that even Hal himself is but half conscious of the power she exerts over him. I do not believe he loves her; but she fascinates him. I am growing weary of it. He must decide between us, and that shortly. Monday we go to the beach, and, if it be possible, I shall find a chance of talking with him. Uncle Ralph, I think, sees it all, and I know by his restless manner it troubles him much, though he says nothing. Contrary to his usual custom of late, he joins all of our excursions, and contrives to shield me from annoyance all that he can. He even talks much with Sallie, as though trying to afford Hal more time for me. I hope he does not blame Hal, although I myself fear he is too often a willing captive.

July 25. We went to the beach, as proposed, on Monday, day before yesterday, and it came near, so far as I was concerned, having a tragical ending. It was a beautiful day, only a little windy, and we concluded not to go upon the water, but lunched in a little grotto in the rock, and gathered shells and pebbles, and played, like children, in the beautiful white sand upon the beach. The day was wearing away, and we were beginning to talk of returning, when I contrived to say quietly to Hal,—

"I desire to speak with you a moment undisturbed. I have something I much wish to say."

"Shall we walk along the beach a little way?" he answered.

"No; we would be too liable to interruption. I want some of the sea-weed from those rocks," pointing to a cluster of rocks that jutted out rudely into the sea. "Will you help me get it?"

"Certainly I will; but, Nannie, the waves are high, and the rocks are slippery. Is it not a bad choice?"

"No; I fear nothing but interruption."

So we started. Uncle Ralph was talking with Sallie, and I trusted to his skill in detaining her; yet I saw he watched me anxiously as I approached the shore. Hal held me firmly by the hand as we stepped upon the slippery rocks, and I began by saying,—

"Hal, do you remember all that mamma said to us in the library, nearly two years ago?"

"Perfectly well, my darling." And his hand closed more tightly and tenderly about my own.

"Well, the time has come when I think it would be better for both of us——"

Here a piercing scream from Sallie caused us to look around, and we heard her crying,—

"Oh, Dr. Ray, Dr. Ray, please catch my hat! It will blow into the sea; it surely will!" And she started, in her pretty way, running along the beach, after her truant hat, which the wind was rapidly blowing and rolling along the sand toward us. She had been twirling it by one string about her finger, and, holding it too lightly, it slipped from her grasp (Gertie says she threw it down purposely), and the wind bore it rapidly away.

"Stand perfectly still, Nannie; I will rejoin you in an instant," said Hal, thus appealed to; and, springing lightly over the rocks, he secured the hat, and handed it to her. As he did so, I distinctly heard her say,—for the wind was blowing toward me, and I was only a short distance away, —"Please do not go again upon those slippery rocks; for *my sake* do not go!" And, as she lifted her soft eyes pleadingly to his face, her own seemed the counterpart of the siren's in my dream.

Bewildered and maddened, I turned away, and, in stepping across a small chasm, my foot slipped upon the treacherous rock. I lost my balance and fell into the surf, which foamed and dashed about me. I gave one scream of terror, felt the cold waves close over me, and then all became a blank. The next I knew, I was lying upon the beach, enveloped in shawls, of which we fortunately had brought a supply to guard against the sea-breeze, my head in Gertie's lap, and anxious faces bending above me, prominent among them the pale face of Uncle Ralph, with a fierce look upon it I had never seen before. I smiled faintly up to him, heard his low and fervent "Thank God!" and then relapsed into forgetfulness.

Gertie filled in the broken links for me, the next day. She said that Uncle Ralph had already started to go to me, seeing my danger, when I slipped, and that in an instant his coat and boots were off and he had plunged in after me. Just as he reached the water, Hal, who, hearing my scream, had also rushed forward, crossed his path, when, Gertie said, he threw him back fiercely with his arm, saying, "Stand back, young man! there has been enough of this foolery!" and plunged into the surf. Nor would he let any one touch me but himself, till he laid me down tenderly in Gertie's arms. Then they worked with me for some minutes before I showed any signs of life; and Gertie says she believes that Uncle Ralph would have knocked Hal down if he had attempted to touch me. She says that Hal himself was very pale and greatly distressed, and, she doubts not, suffered terribly till I began to revive. As soon as possible they got the horses to the carriages, and, with my head upon Gertie's bosom, we rode home. Mamma had me put into a warm bath at once, then wrapped in warm blankets and put to bed, where I was plentifully dosed by Aunt Martha with hot drinks till I fell asleep.

When I awakened, it was growing dark, and mamma was sitting beside the bed. At first I was bewildered, and knew nothing of all that had passed, but gradually it came back to me little by little, and I shuddered at the thought of my near approach to death, and that too with my heart full of bitter feelings toward another.

"Who saved me, mamma?" I asked, half hoping that she would answer, "Hal." In that case I could forgive him everything.

"Uncle Ralph."

I started. Another coincidence with my dream; only he had brought me back into a world of shadows, instead of sunlight and flowers.

"Is he in the house, mamma?"

"Yes. We insisted that he should remain all night; he seemed so anxious lest you should be seriously ill after the shock. The young ladies both remain at Nettie's to-night."

"May I see Uncle Ralph, mamma?"

"Not to-night, love: quiet is indispensable for you."

"I will not talk, mamma; only please let me see him."

"Early in the morning, dear, if you are no worse."

I lay quiet for several minutes, and then said,—

"Dear mamma, indeed, indeed I cannot sleep unless you grant my request. You may stand right there, and I promise you I will not speak more than a dozen words, nor detain him five minutes. He saved my life, mamma; do not deny me."

She looked a moment at my face, which I know was flushed and feverish, and without further words arose, smoothed my hair and my pillow, arranged the bed a little, and went down-stairs. After a short delay, during which I lay in a half-dreamy state, she re-entered the room, which was growing dim in the twilight, with a tall, dark form beside her, and approaching the bed, said, softly, "Nannie, here is Uncle Ralph," and then stepped to the table to adjust it and ring for a light.

Uncle Ralph bent over me for a moment, with a wistful look in his dear face, and said, tenderly as a woman,—

"Are you better, dear?"

A strange, overwhelming feeling of love and gratitude rushed over me. I disengaged my arms from the covers, and putting them, in my old child-fashion, about his neck, drew his dear face down against my own, and whispered, with a tearful voice, "May God bless you forever!" then hid my face in the pillows and sobbed like a very child.

"Don't, darling," he said, in a tone of distress, smoothing my hair with his hand as he spoke; "don't do so; it will surely make you ill." Then, in a moment, "It was God's great mercy that gave you back to us, not my strength. Think no more of it to-night; to-morrow you will be stronger." And, stooping over, he kissed my hair, that he had been so tenderly smoothing, and went from the room.

Mamma gave me some tiny little pellets upon my tongue, and in a little while I dropped asleep. But I was restless all night, and awakened the next morning with a dull throbbing in my head and a feverish aching all through my frame. I did not try to get up all day, but lay in a half-dreaming state till evening. I rested better last night, and to-day feel pretty well, only very weak and listless.

Sallie is still at Nettie's, and will probably not return before to-morrow. I will go out upon the terrace; the air may refresh me. Gertie left me, apparently sleeping, half an hour ago: so I will steal a little time for reflection;

I need it for the future. Hal has twice called to ask after me, and this morning sent me an exquisite bouquet. I am restless and irresolute, but feel that, in justice to us both, I must remind him that our engagement is only nominal, and trust the rest to chance, or, as mamma would say, to an overruling Providence.

An hour later. After writing the above, I stepped from my low window upon the terrace, and essayed to walk, but found my limbs still trembled beneath me: so I walked slowly to some chairs that stood near the other end of the terrace, and sat down. The air was soft and balmy, for there had been a shower early in the day, and the flowers looked bright and fresh upon the lawn. I was already beginning to feel better, when some one entered Sallie's room, near whose open window I was sitting, and, supposing it was Gertie, and that she would come at once upon the terrace in search of me, I sat still. But in an instant I caught Sallie's voice, in a vehement undertone, saying,—

"No; it is not wrong! I did not know of their engagement until I had already learned to love him; and now the battle is between us; let her win who may!"

"But," said a soft voice, that I instantly recognized as Mollie's, "it will nearly kill poor Nannie; she has loved him so long."

"Bah!" was the retort: "she was nothing but a child when they entered into the engagement. How could he expect to win from a child's heart a woman's love? Believe me, she has never learned the passion."

My blood was aflame, but I was so bewildered and astounded that I knew not at the moment what course to pursue. They had stopped, evidently, at a table a few paces from the open window; and while I remained where I was, it was impossible for me not to hear every word; nor could I pass the long window, had I so desired, without detection. I had no time for thought ere Mollie resumed:—

"But this is a desperate game, Sallie, and your own conscience can tell you if it is right. Has Dr. Ray ever given you reason to believe he loves you?"

"My conscience never troubles me, where my will is involved. As for Dr. Ray, although he has never expressly said in words that he loves me, every glance assures me of it; and but for this hateful engagement, which I am sure he regrets with his whole heart, I should not fear for the result. Were he only free, I should not have to resort to 'these unmaidenly wiles,' as you are pleased to term them, to win him."

I arose from my chair, and, with the blood bounding through every vein, I stepped to the open window, and, in a calm, distinct voice, said,—

"He shall be free to-night!"

And, before either could reply, I swept away into my own room, leaving them with an appalled look upon their faces, as though they had seen a spectre.

Without a moment's delay, or an instant's yielding to the strange throbbing at my heart or the choking sensation in my throat, I wrote a note to Hal, asking his presence in the library as soon as convenient to himself, and, ringing for Annie, dispatched it by Joseph, with the request to give it to no one but Dr. Ray himself; and then I sent for Gertie. I told her nothing, only that I had sent for Hal, and that when he came he was to be shown into the library, and that on no condition were we to be disturbed; I should brook no interference to-day. And now I shall go down and await his coming. May God help me!

It is past; and in the solitude of my own chamber I may look back upon what I have done. My brain reels; my blood is like ice; I must do something to relieve my heart, or it will burst beneath its burden. What better can I do, old friend, than fly to you, as I have for so long done, in joy or in sorrow? And if my narrative is unintelligible or disconnected, who will have more forbearance or compassion than yourself?

I made my way to the library without meeting any one but Gertie, and waited but a little while before Hal came. He advanced at once to meet me, taking both my hands in his, and saying,—

"What is it, dear Nannie? I am so glad to see you better. But are you really better? Your hands are like ice."

I might have answered him that I felt as though my blood was frozen; but I would permit myself no words but to the point in question. So I said, briefly, freeing my hands from his grasp,—

"I am quite well, and only wish to say to you that I do not desire you should forget that our engagement has been but nominal; and whatever in it you may have considered binding upon yourself I willingly free you from, at this moment."

He looked for a moment bewildered, and then said, slowly,—

"Do you wish me to understand that you desire our present engagement to exist no longer?"

"I do."

"For what reason, Nannie? Do you no longer love me?"

"I deny your right to question me. I sent for you simply to give you back your freedom; it may carry you to whom it will."

"It will surely return me at once to yourself."

My heart gave a great, glad throb; but in a moment the dull pain returned, and I answered, firmly,—

"Never!"

"Nannie, what does all this mean? You surely are not jealous? Sallie is gay and innocent, and attracts every one; but I am sure she would be appalled at the thought of causing you a moment's suffering. She loves you tenderly."

I thought of the conversation I had heard that evening, and my heart swelled indignantly that he should defend her. Jealous! My soul revolted at the word. After all that I had borne in silence, to have that hateful word tossed at me thus! I arose and confronted him, and for the moment every atom of love was crushed from my heart. I saw only the beautiful face of the temptress, remembered only that he had no power to resist her fascinations, and said, bitterly,—

"No, Hal, not jealous! But the chain irks me. I will be free! There are no longer flowers to hide it, nor silken cords to bind it. If you will not accept your freedom, I must demand my own."

He became deadly pale, arose, bowed, and said, bitterly, in return, "I have no alternative but to bend to your will," then crossed the room to the door. There he stopped, and, looking at me wistfully a moment, said,—

"Is this final, Nannie? May I not hope that you will grant me another interview to-morrow?"

"It is final, and irrevocable as the laws of the Medes and Persians," I said, firmly; and he withdrew.

When he had gone, I felt as though I was transformed to stone. Every faculty seemed to have left me, and I stood as though transfixed, my blood stagnant and cold. It could have been but an instant that I had thus stood, when he reopened the door, crossed the room to me, and, tenderly folding me in his arms, kissed my eyes, my lips, my forehead, and, murmuring, "God bless you, my darling, forever!" again left the room, to return no more. I had and Gertie, seeing him depart, came instantly to me. I still stood motionless where he had left me, and when she proposed that I should go at once to my room, I mechanically obeyed; but when she would have prevailed upon me to lie down, I said,—

"No, dear Gertie, only let me be this one night alone, shield me from observation and intrusion, and I shall bless you forever."

"Oh, Nannie," she replied, half tearfully, "do not send me from you for the night. Let me come to you when there is no longer fear of intrusion."

"No, my darling; for once hear me,—I *must* be alone." And, with a fond and loving caress, she left me.

I bolted the door behind her, and for hours walked the floor, bewildered and sorrowful, but tearless, thinking, thinking. In that brief space it seemed to me that I lived over every hour that I had ever spent with Hal. A fire consumed my heart and brain, until some tender memory at last unloosed "the flood-gates of my soul," and I wept long and bitterly. I thank God for it, for it has lightened that dreadful pressure upon my brain, and I can think without bewilderment. Now that the act is done, I cannot realize it; I cannot think that the days will come and go, and the seasons come and pass, without this hope, that so long has been the food of my dreams both sleeping and waking. What will life be to me without his love? My soul turns, fainting, from the thought. Yet is it not better that I should suffer alone than that we both should learn too late the mistake we had made? Yet, oh, Hal, my lost love! better, far better had it been for us never to have tasted the sweets of this poisoned chalice than to have discovered at this late hour its hidden bitterness. Our past has been beautiful, but it has faded, and forever!—crushed and broken are the rosy dreams that floated through the love-lit chambers of my soul! Life must wear for me henceforth only the ashen colors of decay. The decree is final. I feel, in the innermost depths of my soul, that the die is cast; that henceforth the future bears for us no joy in common, no grief that may be lightened by the other.

      Once it was not thus.
  There was a time whose memory is embalm'd
  And placed with sacred care within the heart's
  Most pure and holy temple,—an hour when,
  Close nestled to thy side, with quiet joy
  I've heard thee breathe thy low and earnest vows
  Of love unchanging, or, in the serene
  And silent intercourse of soul with soul,
  Have listen'd to the full, harmonious throbs
  Of thy high, loving heart! Alas that e'er
  The hour should come when I should doubt its truth!

Alas, indeed! What bitterness like that of doubt for one beloved! With it we lose our faith in mankind and wonder what in all the world is true. But I will not yield to this morbid feeling; I will not sit with idly-folded hands dreaming of the past and dreading the future. I will shake from my soul this lethargy.

     I will be free; and thou
  Shalt know that woman's pride is stronger e'en
  Than her most fervent love! I will forget
  Thee! Soon the past, like other fever'd dreams
  Of gladness, with its memories of joy
  And sorrow, shall be lost to me forever!
  It may seem hard at first, and I may feel
  Life is no longer life, deprived of thee;
  But still my firm resolve is fix'd,—I can
  And will forget thee! Life no doubt will wear
  A deeper shade of sadness; no glad birds
  Will warble forth their strains of melody
  To cheer my heart; no flowers will spring around
  My future way; and seldom will be seen
  Verdant oases in life's desert waste!
  And oh! when once my spirit shall be free,

Never shall man regain the sceptre thou
Hast lost! Love's dream shall pass forever; while
The chaplet of bright flowers that he wove
Shall hang in memory's gallery of art,
A beautiful adornment, to be look'd
Upon, but never worn by woman more.

Thus I lay down the love that has brightened my life for years; thus chant my last sad requiem above its tomb. It is meet that it should be done in the silence of the midnight; it is sacrilege for other eyes than God's to look upon such hours.

Aug. 1. The days come and go, but, in spite of my efforts to cast from me the influence of the past, I am desolate. My heart steals ever back to this grave of my buried hopes that the flowers will not cover. I sleep to dream of it; I awaken to find it ever uppermost in my thoughts; and yet it is final. I do not deceive myself with the hope of a future reconciliation; indeed, I desire it not. The beautiful cord once broken can never be reunited without a scar. Faith once destroyed can never be perfect again. It is over the ruins of her shrine I grieve. My trust was perfect. I thought no power on earth sufficient to cast even a shadow upon so beautiful a shrine; but it lies in the dust, and on its altars are only now the cold damp ashes of love's fervent offerings. It will some day, I trust, be covered with flowers and ivy; but I shall never forget that the ruined altar lies beneath.

The young ladies returned to Nettie's on the evening of the day of my interview in the library with Hal. For once, no effort was made to disturb us. The next morning a note to Gertie said that they much regretted an urgent summons to join their friends at Newport that day,— would not even have time to make their adieus in person, which annoyed them exceedingly, etc.; and they left upon the afternoon train.

Nettie came over at once, knowing that something was wrong; and her indignation on hearing my story, which, so far as Sallie was concerned, I told to her and Gertie, was unparalleled. She declared that she would go at once to Hal and tell him of her treachery. I pleaded with her not to do so, and finally extorted a partial promise by telling her that I should be seriously offended if she did.

"But you will forgive Hal, Nannie?"

"Heartily and entirely, dear Nettie; but, nevertheless, we can never be the same to each other again. At present any communication is utterly impossible."

She tried hard to overcome my scruples, but finally desisted, saying, with a tender embrace,—

"Well, do as you will, you will always be dearer to me than any other woman, let her be who she may, that he may marry. And I assure you it will not be my fault if he ever brings that unwomanly Sallie Reve into my presence again."

Hal remained here until yesterday, when he returned to New York. He wrote me a day or two ago a beautiful little letter, pleading for a few minutes' interview; but, although my heart bled for him, I was resolute. I simply replied,—

"It would only cause us unnecessary suffering. I shall never forget how dear a friend you have been to me from my childhood, and shall watch with interest your future course. God grant it be a prosperous and honorable one. But it would be wrong for either of us to deceive ourselves with the thought that we could ever be to each other again what we have been in the past. It were impossible. I bid you 'God speed' upon your way, wherever it may lie, confident that it will be in a widely different path from mine."

With this note I inclosed the many letters I had received from his hand, together with my ring, and the many little tokens of remembrance I had from time to time received;

and sent them all to him by Joseph. Yesterday I received a similar package from him, with simply the words to me, "May God bless and keep you! I shall never forget how much sunlight you have woven into my life."

I took this package, together with a jetty curl that I had overlooked in sending the package to him, wrapped them in linen, embalmed them in rose-leaves and jessamine, inclosed them in a tiny enameled box that he had given me when a little child, and, stealing out into the beech grove, buried them beneath a tree, whose whereabouts I am sure I should never again be able to find. With it I buried all future reference to my love, so bright, so transient. Would that I could likewise bury its memory!

Aug. 3. To-day Gertie came to me, and said, kneeling beside me as she spoke, and twining her arms lovingly about me,—

"Nannie, I am sure mamma would let you go to Europe with Fannie, if you were to ask her; for when Aunt Martha said that she did not think you looked quite well, and needed a little change, mamma replied that she thought it would be very desirable."

They all know, of course, of my trouble, but only through Nettie and Gertie, and have all considerately refrained from speaking of it in my presence.

"Ah, darling!" I said, "you are always so thoughtful. Would you go with me too?"

"No, dear, I would rather remain at home; but Ralph or Charlie could go."

"And why not Gertie also?"

She blushed, and shook her head, and said she feared the sea; but if I would like to go, she was sure she could manage it for me.

"I should like much to go, dear Gertie. Any change would be very acceptable to me at present."

She left the room, and in a little while came running back, and, throwing her arms impulsively about my neck, exclaimed,—

"I knew she would let you go! She said if you really desired it, and one of the boys would go with you, she did not think she would have any objection; that she would think about it. That means talking with Uncle Ralph, of course; you know mamma does nothing without his sanction; and I can bring him around very easily, I am sure." And Gertie danced about the room, as delighted as though it were some great favor to herself she had gained.

"Why are you so glad to have me go, Gertie?" I asked.

"Oh, for two or three reasons. One is, I know it would benefit you; then I am sure you would enjoy it; and then——"

"Go on."

"Well, then, I cannot bear that any one else should have more advantages than yourself; especially when you are in reality far superior in every respect."

"Oh, fie, Gertie!"

"I can't help it, Nannie. It tries me terribly to see every one thinking Sallie Reve so smart, when she has not half as much sense in a month as you have in a minute."

I laughed in spite of myself, and, kissing the rosy lips, replied,—

"Well, there is one thing of which Sallie is not possessed, in spite of her talents and beauty."

"What is that?"

"An appreciative and precious sister like mine."

And then we fell to talking of my trip and planning for the future; and so the evening passed.

After we had retired, I could not sleep, but lay thinking for several hours. Gertie slept quietly by my side for a long time, but at last she became restless, and murmured inarticulate words.

"What is it, darling?" I said, thinking perhaps she had an unquiet dream.

She moved slightly, and murmured, lovingly, "Ellis, Ellis."

Can it be possible, I thought, that she loves Ellis Ray? The thought of Gertie loving any one had never occurred to me before, and it awoke a strange tenderness for her in my heart.

"My darling," I whispered, bending over and kissing her.

She opened her eyes, and said, "Dear Nannie." And then she questioned me, and I told her what she had said; and in the quiet of the midnight she confessed to me her love for our young minister, and how he wished her at once to become his wife, but she feared mamma would never consent, she was yet so young,—not eighteen until next March. She said he would willingly wait another year, but his parishioners thought it best for him to marry soon; and he had loved Gertie, and resolved to wait for her, since the first morning he had seen her in the church grove on the hill, years ago.

"And how long has Gertie loved him?" I questioned.

"I do not know," she answered, hiding her face upon my shoulder, as though even in the darkness I could see her blushes. "I only know that when he spoke to me, a few days ago, of his hopes and desires, my heart sprang up gladly to meet him, and I was conscious that it was no new feeling awakened, but one that had only lain dormant till his hand called it into being."

"Well, darling," I said, "set your dear little heart at rest, for I am sure it will all come right, and that very soon." And then we both went to sleep in each other's arms.

Aug. 6. The next morning when I went below I found mamma busy with her flowers, and when I went out to meet her she received me with so bright a smile that I found courage to say, after my greeting,—

"Mamma, will you really let me go with Fannie?"

"Do you really desire it, dear?"

"I do, indeed, if you think I may."

"I should much like you to go,—travel is always so instructive,—if Ralph or Charlie will go with you. Uncle Ralph will be out this morning, and we will see what he thinks of it."

So the result is, that it is settled. I am to go. Fannie is to be married on the 16th, so we will probably sail about the 20th. Ralph accompanies me, as Charlie's studies are yet incomplete.

Yesterday morning I slipped away from the house, for I desired to go alone, and walked rapidly to old Father White's. I found him alone, and very glad to see me, for Gertie and I have ever been favorites with the dear old man. After a little preliminary conversation, I told him I had come to seek his aid on a question involving the happiness of two whom I was sure he loved.

"Ah," he said, "you refer to Ellis and Gertie? Ellis has already spoken to me of their desires, and, although Gertie is still but a child, she has ever been so quiet and thoughtful that I think it would be an excellent thing."

"Then, dear Mr. White, you will speak to mamma, will you not? You know her objections to early marriages."

"I surely will, my dear, this very day," said the old gentleman, beginning at once to look for his boots and overcoat. I bade him good-by, and hastened away to Gertie. But the fates were surely against me that morning, for I found Ellis already closeted with mamma in the library.

"Oh, if he had only put it off for another day," I said. But he had not: so we had only to wait for the bell.

At length it came, and Gertie said, "You will go with me, dear? I cannot go alone." So we entered the room together.

Ellis, always sensitive, looked worried, and only bowed as he set chairs for us, without speaking.

"Gertie," mamma began, kindly, "I am very sorry you have followed so closely in Nannie's footsteps. I dare not consent again to one of these long engagements."

"Nor need you, dear mamma," I began; "Gertie is older to-day in thoughtfulness and womanly wisdom than I, and you would soon have given your consent to my engagement and marriage." I winced as I said the words, but resolved that no sensitiveness on my part should lose Gertie's cause.

"I have spoken to Mr. White, and several of the older members of my congregation, of my desires, and they all approve of my choice, and sanction an early day for the ceremony. And so, I assure you, madam," said Ellis, advancing a step nearer mamma, and respectfully taking Gertie's hand, "if you will only intrust this precious child to my keeping, we will in all things be guided by your superior judgment, and, so far as lies within my power, give you no after-cause for regret."

"Dear mamma," I said, as she sat perplexed and thoughtful, "I will promise to stay with you forever, if you will only give cheerful consent to this. I pray you do not subject dear Gertie to the bitter pangs I have endured, only because she is young." And the hot tears, in spite of my courage, rolled down my cheeks.

"Oh," I exclaimed inwardly, "if Father White would only come! mamma respects his judgment so much."

"My dear children," mamma at last said, "you shake my soul with your pleading. Oh that I knew just what was right! I had firmly resolved that Gertie should be kept free from all such entanglements for years yet; and here, when I least expected it, comes a more resolute attack than the former. Leave me until to-morrow to decide. I must take time for thought and counsel."

"Dear mamma," I said, "I will take all the blame with Uncle Ralph. I am sure he will not be angry, he thinks so much of Ellis. Come, Gertie, come, Ellis," I said, "let us swear eternal allegiance to mamma, if she will only make us happy in this request;" and half playfully, half earnestly, I drew Gertie down beside me. Her pale, pleading face, I think, did more with mamma than all of my words.

"That," said Ellis, "I can do right cheerfully;" and then, more seriously, "If I thought your objections at all personal, dear madam, I could not attempt to parry them; but being led to believe they are only on account of your daughter's extreme youth, and believing that, aside from my own heart's preference, such a union would enable me to be more successful in my calling, I have dared to hope we might be enabled to overcome them."

"I am sure," answered mamma, "were Gertie only a few years older, her choice would please me well; but she is so young to assume such responsibilities. Do you not shrink from them, my child?"

Poor Gertie crimsoned, and then paled, looked pleadingly at mamma, and then at Ellis, who tenderly said to her, "Speak truly the thoughts of your heart, dear Gertie, the same as though I were not present;" and, dropping her head upon my shoulder, she replied, distinctly,—

"Nothing could be unpleasant to me, dear mamma, if shared with Ellis."

A gleam of happiness lit up his face, and mamma had just answered, "Well, well, I am sure I wish to do what is best; but I must take a little time for thought and counsel," when the door opened, and Father White entered.

He understood all at a glance, and when mamma would have risen to greet him, he raised his hand impressively, and said, "Remain for the present as you are;" and, advancing, placed his trembling hands upon the bowed heads of Ellis and Gertie, and said, solemnly,—

"'What God has joined together, let not man put asunder. If any there be who would separate these two loving hearts, let them speak now, or forever after hold their peace.'"

He paused, but the silence of death was in the room for a full minute; then he added, "Then I shall unite them, according to God's holy ordinance, upon the second Sunday in October." And he knelt beside them, and, in his own simple but fervent style, offered up a short petition in their behalf, that melted us all to tears. Once he said, "I ask not for them wealth and honor and worldly aggrandizement, for these are perishable things, that pass as the dew of the morning; but I ask, O Father, that they may be endowed with strength and grace for every hour of trial; that their lives, beautifully blended into one, may flow onward in the arduous but lovely way they have chosen, as the mingling waters of some mighty but placid river; and that they may for their reward see constantly springing up, from the seeds of piety and usefulness that they will have sown, the lovely flowers that perish not, but are only perfected in the land beyond the shadows."

When we arose, for an instant no word was spoken; for from the full heart words come not readily, Solomon to the contrary notwithstanding. Then Gertie turned to mamma, who folded her lovingly in her arms, and kissed her again and again, but did not speak, until Gertie said, tearfully,—

"Speak to me, dear mamma, and say you are content. I cannot be happy without."

"What else can I say, dear child?" said mamma, laughingly, but with a very suspicious quiver in her voice; "for surely the sceptre has departed from Israel." We all laughed, and Father White replied, very meekly,—

"I trust that the royal mantle has not fallen upon unworthy shoulders."

Then Ellis came, and, bending above mamma's hand in his courtly way, said,—

"I trust, dear madam, that my future conduct will prove that I am not ungrateful for the concessions of to-day."

"Only be kind to her, and remember ever that she is but a child, and I can truly give you the place of a son," was mamma's half-tearful reply.

And then, while she and Father White conversed apart, and Gertie had stolen away to her own room, Ellis whispered to me,—

"I shall never forget your kindness of to-day, dear Nannie; for without your aid I am sure your mamma would have been utterly inaccessible."

"I knew that Gertie loved you," I answered, softly, "and I had faith to believe that you would make her happy." Then, as my own blighted hopes arose before me, I turned upon him fiercely, and said,—

"If you ever do cause her one hour's sorrow, I shall be ready to annihilate you!"

"Do not look at me that way, Nannie, as though you believed me capable of such a thing. The hour will never come when I would not willingly sacrifice my life for her good."

I believed him, and answered, penitently,—

"Forgive me, Ellis: I have suffered so much of late that I distrust every one; and Gertie is dearer to me than my own life."

"Never doubt me again, dear sister; for time will but deepen my love, never destroy it."

And I have faith to believe that he is right.

Aug. 12. Now that Gertie is so soon to go to Ellis, I felt that I should not leave mamma; but they would none of them hear of my abandoning my trip; and mamma finally said,—

"Ellis, I am sure, will promise not to take Gertie from the old homestead till your return, and, as Ralph and Charlie will both be absent, a son will not be at all amiss at the old place."

"Indeed we will remain with pleasure," said Ellis, who was present, "if you desire it." And Gertie fairly clapped her hands with joy at the thought. So I leave much better satisfied than if mamma were alone.

I regret that we will not be present at her wedding; and yet it will spare me many a pang. Gertie said last night, throwing her arms about me, and weeping impulsively,—

"Dear Nannie, how can I go through it all without you?"

"Let me stay with you, then, dear."

"No, no; I could not be so selfish; you may never have such another opportunity. I shall feel lost without you; but then, you know, I shall have Ellis."

"Yes, dear Gertie," I answered, "and I believe him in every way worthy of your love."

"Oh, I am sure of that! he is so good and noble."

Dear child! there are no unstirred depths in her pure heart. She not only loves Ellis, but reverences him. He is seven years her senior, and she looks up to him as to a being of superior mould, and hangs upon his words as upon the words of a god. And he? In his eyes she is perfection.

It is beautiful to see them together: they are so admirably suited for one another,—he so grave and thoughtful and dignified, and she so pure and good, and looking up to and trusting him so implicitly, and feeling such reverence for his high calling and pure life.

Mamma seems perfectly satisfied, and Uncle Ralph never offered a word of objection, but shook Ellis warmly by the hand, and kissed Gertie tenderly, saying, "She won't be of much use yet awhile, only to pet; but that gives many happy hours to one's life!" Gertie blushed, and Ellis said he thought she would soon prove herself to be useful as well as ornamental; and I thought how differently Uncle Ralph had received the announcement of my engagement to Hal. But I cannot but think how different my love for Hal was from Gertie's for Ellis. We loved each other more as children love,—as Sallie so scornfully said,—with perfect and beautiful simplicity; but I never looked up to him and reverenced him as Gertie loves Ellis. It never occurred to me so to do. I thought him talented and honorable, and standing far above ordinary men; but, knowing him all my life, playing with him in my childhood, seeing him constantly as he grew to manhood, reverence was a difficult passion for him to inspire; and I have really come to think that love in its perfection cannot exist without it. But it is useless for me now to reason upon this point. I have resolutely put the passion from me; or if at times it gains a brief ascendency, it is known only to my own heart and to God.

Gertie and Uncle Ralph are going with me to New York, to remain till the vessel sails. Mamma prefers to say her parting words at Beechwood, rather than in the hurry and excitement of departure. We will go about the 16th, so as to spend a little while with Charlie. Nettie has promised to spend as much time as possible with Gertie, and assist her as much as possible in her arrangements. What additions she needs to her wardrobe we will get in the city while there. She insists they must all be very plain, as she is to be a minister's wife and must set an example to his congregation. She will make a perfect one, I am sure.

Yesterday she took it into her pretty head that she must put up her curls; that they were inappropriate now for her to wear. So she combed them plainly back behind her ears, and gathered them into a net behind. They are too short to roll in a coil, but they looked beautiful peeping through the net, and here and there one, a little more willful than the rest, breaking away from the restraint and twining about her neck or forehead. At last she succeeded in getting them under tolerable control, and, looking at herself complacently in the glass, said,—

"I am sure Ellis will like it much better; it makes me look so much plainer. Don't you think so, Nannie?"

"Decidedly!" I said, dryly, "if it is the second inquiry you wish answered."

She looked at herself again, and then said, "I am sure it is much more suitable, Nannie."

"Well, let us go into the orchard with our work; Ellis will follow us when he comes."

So we soon were busily chatting there, and did not notice Ellis's approach until he stood before us.

"Why, Gertie," he said, looking at her ruefully, "what have you been doing with yourself?"

"Putting up my curls. Don't you think it much better to wear them so now?"

Ellis saw the smile about my lips, and without more ado stepped behind Gertie and deliberately freed her beautiful hair from its confinement; then, looking critically at her, and readjusting lightly a curl here and there, he said,—

"Wear it, darling, as God made it for you. You cannot improve upon his handiwork."

Poor little Gertie looked half disposed to cry, as she said, "I thought you would like it better so, Ellis. I want so much to look older and more sedate."

He laughed, a free, joyous laugh, as he replied, "I would not change you an atom, my Gertie, either in appearance, age, or manners, if I could. Always be to me your own sweet self, and I will risk all the rest."

I felt confident it would so end, and should have been much disappointed had he evinced a disposition to accede to her proposals. I do not wonder Gertie loves him; I can easily accord him a brother's place in my heart.

Aug. 18. I have bidden adieu to Beechwood. Every nook and corner of the dear old place have Gertie and I visited to-day together. I have laid fresh garlands upon dear Kittie's and papa's graves, and sat with Gertie pensively beneath the trees where we all have sat so often, as children, together. I have given Gertie all my instructions for the future, and wept with her over the ruins of the past; and now, dear old book, I have only to say good-by to you, and I am ready to depart. We leave on the early train to-morrow. My trunk Joseph has already taken to the depot, and my traveling garments are spread upon the chairs beside me.

I start upon this journey with mingled feelings of pain and pleasure. God only knows what it will bring to me! Ah! if it brings but rest to my weary heart, whose unquiet spirit all my reasoning, all my resolutions, and all my philosophy will not lay, I shall indeed be content. I daily argue to myself a thousand reasons why these things are best, but daily again return to my weary regrets for the past and vain yearnings for the unattainable in the future. I had thought never to have spoken again of this, but to-night I am to bid you adieu,—a long, loving adieu. To-night I write the last entry upon your dear pages that I shall ever make. It is meet that this mingled record of joy and sorrow should here have an end. Should I ever open your leaves again, I trust it will be with a lighter heart, and a more hopeful trust in the future, as I glance them over. Now I can only say,—

> Old book, good-by! Full many a pleasant hour
>   I've spent in bending o'er thy friendly page;
> Full many a pang thou'st soothed, with wondrous power,
>   Full many a heavy grief hast help'd t'assuage!
>
> Thou'st shared my sorrows, seen my tear-drops fall,
>   And heard the anguish'd wailings of my heart!
> And now, since I no more may on thee call,
>   I'll drop a tear above thee, ere we part.
>
> Child of my ofttimes fever'd brain, adieu!
>   No other heart will love thee half so well:
> And I, perchance, shall find no friend more true!
>   Companion of my inner life—farewell!

Two Years Later.

Aug. 18, 18—. Two years ago this very day, I laid away my diary, on the eve of my departure for Europe; and, although I have been at home at least six months, I have never looked upon its pages since. But to-night the impulse came so strong upon me, as I sat alone in my quiet chamber, to look on its dear, familiar face again, that I arose, and, unlocking the secret drawer in my desk where it so long has rested, drew it forth and seated myself to glance it over. I read the last entry I then made, and when I had done found more than one tear had blotted its sad record. Tears, not of sorrow, not wholly of joy, but of the two passions, perhaps, combined, together with gratitude, intense and fervent, to the Blessed Father of all, who has brought me safely through so many vicissitudes to this hour of rest and of blessedness. But I will not anticipate. There remain some fifty pages yet unfilled, in the dear old book that I thought I had laid away forever. Upon them I will write, in continuous narrative, disconnected and brief, the record of the past two years. It will form a fitting conclusion to the erratic and broken record on the foregoing pages.

We sailed from New York upon the 20th of August, as I had anticipated, and, after a somewhat windy but otherwise pleasant voyage, landed at Queenstown, in the south of Ireland, and started upon our journey northward. It would be absurd to attempt to record in these brief pages the events of our journey; besides, my note-book of travels contains them all, and it would be folly to rewrite them here. Enough that during our travels in Old Ireland we lived in a perfect dream of bewildering excitement, wandering amid old ruins that for centuries had withstood the war of the elements, and listening to the wild legends with which the country abounds.

From thence we crossed into bonnie Scotland, and spent days and weeks amid the enchanting scenery of the Highlands; came down into Edinburgh, replete with interest of the olden times; visited its castle and cathedral and other places of historical interest; stood in silent awe in the audience- and bed-chambers of the beautiful but ill-fated Mary Queen of Scots, and fancied we saw the fierce conspirators enter through the secret door behind the tapestry and drag from her royal presence the terrified

Rizzio, who vainly clung to her for the protection that, queen though she was, she was powerless to yield. This spot possessed for us more fascination than almost any other in our travels; and we turned from the silent walls with the same feelings we doubtless would have had had we gazed upon the lifeless body of the unfortunate queen who paid so bitterly for the frailties that her persecutors cruelly magnified into crimes.

From Edinburgh we went to Glasgow; from thence to Ayr, where lived and sung the immortal Burns; then through intermediate towns and cities to Stratford-upon-Avon, where sleeps the man whose wonderful dramatic genius towers aloft in the great world of literature. Then on to London, the great Babylon of modern times, to record our wanderings in which would require a volume,—treading with reverence the vast aisles of Westminster, where sleep the royal dead, or standing in the prison-tower, from whence went forth so many noble prisoners to the block of the executioner; ay, even viewing the dread block and axe themselves in all their terror, from which so many beautiful, so many lordly heads have fallen. But it was pleasant to reflect, after looking upon these horrors, that those dreadful days have passed forever. We have fallen upon a more enlightened age and fairer times. No country now is better governed than England, and no monarch lives better beloved by her people than is the good Queen Victoria.

From thence to gay Paris, and all through sunny France and Spain; then over into Italy, with its beautiful skies, reserving Northern Europe until the spring should open, for it was now late in November. Venice we visited, of course, with its once-magnificent palaces and towers, its myriad islands and its massive bridges, its canals and its gondolas. We ascended the Campanile, and rowed in a gondola beneath the Bridge of Sighs, with its terrible history, the greater part of which must rest in the silence of obscurity forever. We visited Florence, with its unrivaled paintings and sculpture, and passed on in time to Rome, the wonderful, the grand, the ancient, and the powerful. It would be simply impossible to describe it; it must be seen, and that for no brief while, to be appreciated. From thence to Naples, with its beautiful bay,—ascending Vesuvius while there, and looking with awe into its crater, from whence such tides of death and destruction have flowed. And then to Pompeii, exhumed after its sleep of seventeen centuries. None but those who have stood in its silent streets and tried to grasp, with man's puny intellect, the history of the ages that lie buried beneath those mighty ruins, can form the slightest idea of the overwhelming awe with which one gazes upon this vast impromptu mausoleum, this mighty "city of the dead."

We had intended to spend the winter either in Rome or Naples; but Mr. Grinnel, ever anxious to please and gratify, proposed that we should spend a portion of it in a trip to Egypt and the Holy Land. You may guess with what avidity both Fannie and I acceded to the proposal; and so was gratified the great wish of my life. We ascended the Nile; we visited the pyramids, and, as we stood beneath their gigantic shadows, felt, as we had never felt before, the utter insignificance of man. His works remain, ofttimes, for centuries, while of him, his very name and lineage forgotten, not an atom even of ashes and dust is left. Mr. Grinnel and Ralph ascended to the summit of Cheops; but Fannie and I were content to sit beneath its shadow and gaze upon the weird beauty of the gigantic Sphinx, and speculate upon the events in the lost ages that its silent lips could reveal, were they animated with life and the massive head endowed with intellect.

But I find I am spending, in spite of myself, too much time and space upon my travels. I will hasten. We visited all the spots made dear to the Christian in the land of the Saviour's birth, knelt in holy reverence in the "Chapel of the Nativity" in Bethlehem, built upon the very spot said to have witnessed the birth of the holy child Jesus, and stood upon the plains of Judea, where the shepherds received the glad news from the heavenly visitant. We went to the "Church of the Holy Sepulchre" at Jerusalem, erected upon Mount Calvary, entered with unsandaled feet the sacred tomb, and knelt with full hearts beside the marble slab whereon reposed the body of our now risen Lord. Ah, no man, be he infidel or Christian, can enter those sacred precincts unmoved. The tomb is of fine marble, some six or seven feet square, and the large sarcophagus of white marble, which it is asserted received the body of the crucified Saviour, occupies nearly or quite half of it. Here also sat the angels who announced to Mary the resurrection of her beloved Master. Forty-two gold and silver lamps, constantly burning, are suspended from the ceiling, and a monk at the head of the tomb reads incessantly in solemn tones the prayers for the dead. This latter we could readily have dispensed with, for nothing in such a place inspires reverence like silence.

We also ascended, by a dark stairway, to the summit of the Mount, where we were shown the hole in the rock where the sacred cross, upon which the Redeemer of mankind expired, was planted; and the chasm across the rock, caused by the earthquake in that dread hour when "the veil of the temple was rent in twain from the top to the bottom; when the earth did quake, and the rocks were rent, when the graves were opened, and the dead came forth." Words could ill describe the sensations of awe and reverence with which we gazed upon these things. It seemed to me that the darkness which then fell upon all nature must return at the very remembrance of the terrible tragedy that once had been enacted there.

But of all the holy places visited, none affected me like the garden of Gethsemane. I had said to Ralph, as we went along, "Dear Ralph, do contrive to let me have a moment in that holy place alone. The eternal talking of these priests and vagrants is intolerable when the heart yearns to be alone with the holy thoughts which the place inspires." So, after the priest in attendance had shown us over the garden, Ralph spoke a few words apart with him, and by the additional argument of a little gold contrived to obtain for us half an hour undisturbed therein. And it was half an hour of such communion as neither time nor circumstances can ever cause me to forget. The garden is inclosed by a high wall, and the priest pointed out to us the rock upon which the disciples slept, who went to watch with the Saviour on the night of his betrayal; the grotto in the rock "a little way apart" where he went to pray; and the spot whereon he stood when betrayed to the multitude by the traitor kiss of Judas. Eight large olive-trees are within the inclosure; and when the priest had left us I wandered off alone, and, seating myself upon the ground beneath one of them, let my mind wander back to that fatal night so full of interest and fearful import to the Christian heart. I heard him say to the disciples who went with him to watch, "My soul is exceeding sorrowful, even unto death: tarry ye here, and watch with me." I saw him with slow steps depart, and watched with sorrow the disciples "heavy with sleep," sitting upon the rock, waiting for, but, alas! not watching with, their agonizing Lord. I saw the tall form, bending beneath the weight of others' sins, wrestling in that dread agony of prayer, that brought redemption to a fallen world. I saw the great drops of sweat and blood that rolled from the massive brow, and heard the earnest, pleading cry, the cry of human agony and godlike faith, "O my Father, if it be possible, let this cup pass from me: nevertheless not as I will, but as thou wilt," and my soul echoed in earnest faith,—such faith as I never before had felt,—"Not my will, but thine!" And with the hot tears stealing down my face, I prayed in that holy place with an earnestness and agony that I never before had felt: "Let me, my Saviour, who in this garden hast wrestled in bitterness for the sins of thy people, bear hence with me a portion of that blessed submission to the Divine Will thou hast here so beautifully taught us; and grant that *I* may never be found sleeping when I should have watched for thy coming."

I went forth from the sacred precincts with a chastened and subdued heart, and, I earnestly trust, more grace to help me in the duties and trials of life.

Jerusalem itself is old, filthy, and dilapidated; and it is difficult to conceive that it ever was the beautiful city so often spoken of in Holy Writ. I could not wonder that Christ, foreseeing its desolation, had wept over it, and cried, in his anguish, "O Jerusalem! Jerusalem! which killest the prophets, and stonest them that are sent unto thee, how often would I have gathered thy children together, as a hen doth gather her brood under her wings, and ye would not!"

But, fascinating as are the remembrances of these scenes, I must not linger. Returning from our trip to Palestine, we came by way of Constantinople, with its mosques and palaces, sailed upon the Bosphorus, and looked upon the giant men-of-war that thrid the very streets of the great Mohammedan city. Then, partly by water, partly by rail, up to Vienna, and on to Switzerland; lingering amid the magnificently grand scenery of the Alps, sailing upon the lakes of Constance and Geneva, and reading beneath the very walls of Chillon's gloomy prison its touchingly beautiful history, made so renowned by Byron's gifted pen; traveled slowly through Germany, so full of history and renown, spent days amid the old castles with which it abounds, and heard legends enough to almost fill a library alone; sailed up the Rhine, reveled amid its magnificent scenery, too grand and varied for me even to attempt a description here, and stood at last in the Imperial Palace at St. Petersburg, unrivaled in its magnificent splendor by any in the world, and looked with awe and wonder on the great bell at Moscow, now used as a chapel, that stands near the base of the immense tower of Ivan Veliki, and is well worthy of its title, "The King of Bells."

At last, after visiting all the most important cities of Northern Europe, we found ourselves again, late in November, in sunny France, and, after spending two months replete with interest in its gay metropolis, took passage for our own sunny land, and were landed safely in New York upon the 21st of February, having been absent just one year, six months, and five days from dear old Beechwood. We had written the ship we expected to sail upon, "The Neptune," and the day we would probably reach New York; and the first person I saw as we drew near the pier was Charlie, swinging his hat aloft to us from a pile of boxes on the dock, and the next, Uncle Ralph, standing, with uplifted hat, serene and smiling, beside him. And then, in spite of my courage, my eyes became so blurred I could see no more, and when the ship struck the dock, and a moment afterward I felt myself enfolded in loving arms, I could do nothing but sob hysterically, and cling to both Uncle Ralph and Charlie, as though I were parting from instead of meeting with them.

Uncle Ralph only folded me to his great warm heart, in

a close embrace, and whispered, "God bless you, my darling!" while Charlie—"still Charlie," as we often called him at home—seemed half wild with joy, principally at seeing Ralph, I think, for never were two brothers more devotedly attached than they.

"How is mamma? And precious Gertie?" I asked, when I could get Charlie still enough to listen to me for a moment.

"They were perfectly well when Uncle Ralph and I left the hotel, about two hours ago," he answered.

"Oh, Charlie, do you really mean that they are in the city?" I cried, delightedly.

"Why, certainly they are," he retorted. "Do you think Beechwood would not turn out in full force to welcome home such renowned travelers? Nettie is with them too, and I expect Aunt Martha would have been, if she had been sure that Millie could have gotten up a dinner sufficiently grand for your reception, without her efficient aid."

"I think Ralph's mantle has certainly fallen upon you in his absence; you are surely more like him than like your old self," I said, laughingly.

"Well, we are going to find mamma. You old folks can follow at your leisure," said he, dragging Ralph away, and looking back laughingly over his shoulder at us as they started. Alas! he looked not at us so again. We saw with horror-stricken hearts the danger, but were powerless to avert it. He was passing beneath a derrick, by which some workmen were hoisting a huge hogshead of sugar into the storehouse above, and, some part of the machinery giving way, it swayed for a moment unsteadily in the air, then fell with its ponderous weight, down, down, until dear Charlie lay crushed and mangled beneath it. Ralph had but an instant before stepped aside, to pick up his hat, which the wind had blown off, and was saved; but Charlie, with the glad laugh and merry jest upon his lips, so beautiful in his manliness and strength, lay bleeding and lifeless before us.

"Oh, my God! my God!" I cried, covering with my hands my eyes from the dreadful sight; and all who were present rushed simultaneously to the spot, to aid him if possible. Poor Ralph was by him in an instant, and his piteous moan, "Oh, my brother! my poor brother!" as he bent above him, wrung every heart.

In a very few minutes Uncle Ralph came, pale, but calm, to say, hurriedly, that he did not think life was extinct, to be brave and hopeful, and he would soon return to us. They soon raised Charlie, and placed him upon a litter, to convey him to the hotel where mamma was staying; and, as they did so, a faint moan apprised us that he lived, and felt the suffering.

"I will hasten at once to Fannie, and, if possible, prepare her for this," said Uncle Ralph, closing the carriage-door upon us.

We drove slowly, and kept close to the curb, while the four men bearing the litter walked upon the pave, with Ralph close by Charlie's side, looking from time to time beneath the cover to see if he yet breathed. I never shall forget that dreadful drive. Fortunately, the distance was not great, and we soon reached the house. Uncle Ralph waited at the door for us, saying mamma desired a room prepared next to hers for Charlie, where she waited to receive us.

We stopped but an instant in the hall while the men readjusted the litter preparatory to ascending the stairs, and at that moment Nettie, who had heard nothing of the accident, entered from the street from a walk with her brother. She caught sight of my face, and flew to greet me, when her eyes fell upon the prostrate form and pale face of Charlie, and, with a cry such as I never shall forget, she sank fainting into my arms. Uncle Ralph lifted her gently, and, whispering the number of mamma's room, bade me run up to her, which I eagerly did, he bearing Nettie after me in his powerful arms, Fannie accompanying him, and the others following slowly with Charlie.

I cannot dwell upon my meeting with mamma and Gertie, and the subsequent events of that dreadful day, they are so harrowing. Upon examination, the surgeon found two ribs broken, and the right arm and leg each fractured in two places, together with a slight fracture of the skull. He said that if it had been midsummer he would have little hope of his recovery, but as we were having clear cold weather he thought it barely possible he might rally. It seemed a perfect miracle that the blow did not kill him instantly; but Uncle Ralph found upon after-examination that a heavy beam had broken the force of the blow, and even when down had kept the greater part of the weight from resting upon him. Only so slight a thing stood between dear Charlie and death, and that, too, in the very hour of our return.

No one can paint the anguish of that night, or the dreadful suspense with which for days we watched the slightest change in his symptoms. His life hung as upon a slender thread which the slightest breath might sever. And this was the return to which we had looked forward so eagerly,—this was our welcome home.

"Nannie," said Nettie, opening her eyes upon me, after her long, deathly swoon, on the day of the accident, and watching me wistfully as I sat beside the bed, bathing her hands and face with cologne, "what has happened? Something terrible, I know; but tell me only one thing: does he live?"

"Yes, dear," I said, soothingly. "The surgeon is with him still, but says there is hope."

"Thank God!" she whispered, the tears stealing from beneath her closed lids. I wondered a little at her deep emotion, although I knew she and Charlie were great friends.

At last she said, softly, "Tell me, dear, did I do anything out of the way to-day?"

"Nothing unnatural, considering the circumstances and your warm friendship for Charlie."

"Ah, Nannie, it is something more than that."

"Is it indeed so, dear?" I said, kissing her tenderly. And then, willing to divert her mind and my own, I added, "I was scarcely prepared for this, pleasant as it is. I have long set you aside for Ralph; but Charlie was ever so quiet, I half doubted his ever wooing and wedding any one."

"We have always loved each other, but agreed to say nothing of it until he had settled in his profession. Ralph has known it all along, but no one else; everything was so uncertain. He has helped to screen our preference."

"And Ralph has known it all the time? That accounts for his thinking ever so much of you, and yet always more as he would of Gertie or me, than as we so earnestly desired."

At this moment mamma entered from Charlie's room, and I eagerly asked for him, while Nettie raised herself in the bed and turned her great eyes wistfully to mamma, but did not speak.

"He is conscious, I think," she said, "although he says very little. Fortunately, the injuries upon the head are but slight." Then she went to the bed and drew Nettie's head upon her breast, and, smoothing her hair back from the pale forehead, and kissing it again and again with trembling lips, said, softly,—

"We must all be brave, my darling, and I trust it will yet be well. What is it the pleading eyes ask so tenderly of me?"

"Oh, Mrs. Cleve," said Nettie, clinging lovingly to her, "I have no mother,—guide me. What may I do for Charlie? Must he lie and suffer without my being permitted to do anything for him? He has told you all; advise me."

"No, dear, my presence will shield you ever. If you will promise to be calm and hopeful and to do nothing to excite him in any way, you may see him daily. You may read to him, bring him flowers, make him refreshing drinks, and cheer him all you can, if God but spares him to us."

"Oh, thank you! thank you!" said Nettie, fervently. "When may I see him?"

"As soon as it will be at all prudent. His life depends upon our care: nothing must be done that will in the least excite him."

"May I not look an instant upon him to-night, as he sleeps?" she asked, so piteously that mamma kissed her again and promised.

And so it came to pass that after the first few days Nettie shared mamma's labors as nurse, Charlie never being satisfied a moment when she was out of his sight. And he gained wonderfully fast, considering his dangerous wounds, a fact which speaks volumes for the power of love over the ills of the flesh.

You are not to suppose, dear old book, that because I have been silent about our Gertie all this while either she or I had been silent long ourselves, when together. She had so much to tell me about home and Ellis and Aunt Martha, and a hundred other things, that we never lost a moment when alone. Ellis, she contended, was the very best man that ever lived, and surely the dearest husband that woman ever had; she only wished she was more worthy of him. He had sent so much love, but Father White—dear old man!—having died in our absence, the labors of the parish had fallen entirely upon Ellis, and it was impossible for him to leave home at this time, else he too would have accompanied her to the city. The parishioners had refitted the parsonage, and it was a perfect little bird's-nest; and now that I had come they should move into it at once. Then she told me how ill mamma had been some months before,—they had never written me a word of it,—and how Uncle Ralph begged that the news might be withheld from us until she was better, asserting that it would be impossible for us to reach home in any event before a change had taken place; how the two doctors that were called both gave her up, and how Charlie all the time felt confident he could relieve her,—having embraced the doctrines of the new school of Hahnemann, so different from their own,—and how, when they declined doing more, he had actually taken the case, encouraged by Uncle Ralph, and succeeded in raising her up, as it were, from the grave itself. No wonder his heart was light and his face happy: to have saved mamma,—precious, darling mamma. And Uncle Ralph, she said, never left the house day or night till she was better. He seemed omnipresent. Surely, next to Ellis, he was the most wonderful, the very best man in all the land.

Fannie and Mr. Grinnel stayed only two days in the city, so anxious were they to reach their Western home and the dear ones therein. At the expiration of ten days Charlie was so much better that it was decided that Gertie and I should proceed with Uncle Ralph to Beechwood, while Ralph and mamma should remain till he was well enough to be removed. Nettie, having friends in the city, was to stay with them, and spend a portion of every day at the hotel with mamma,—a plan which greatly pleased Charlie, who seemed to live but in her presence.

One day, as Gertie and I were starting out for a walk, a few steps from the door we came face to face with Nettie and Hal. I was surprised to find how quietly I took his hand, and how calmly I answered all his inquiries and told little incidents of my travel, as they turned and walked beside us. I had looked searchingly and narrowly into my heart often during our absence, and had become convinced that although I had loved Hal purely and tenderly it was not with the love a woman should accord the man she expects or desires to wed. Again and again had Sallie's scornful words rung in my ears,—"How could he hope to win from a child's heart a woman's love?"— until now I was convinced it was indeed impossible. I was convinced his was not the hand that was to stir my heart's depths. (Perhaps no hand would ever reach them; but, if so, I should surely live alone.) But, in spite of my convictions, I half feared I could not stand the test of meeting him face to face. I trembled lest the old yearning should return, and leave me helpless and miserable as before. But I touched his hand, I walked beside him, I looked with confidence into his eyes,—the same deep eyes that so often had looked love into mine,—and felt I could walk thus calmly in his presence forever, without one quickened heart-throb, or one sigh of regret for the past. My idol was shattered. My eyes no longer looked upon things as I desired they should be, but as they in reality were. I saw in him no longer the noble being I had worshiped, but the gay man of the world, handsome, and courted by all, finding his highest pleasure in the world's mad whirl, and making fashion and pleasure his chosen divinities. What he felt I know not, I do not desire to know; but Nettie told me only yesterday she believed he would yet marry Sallie, though for months after my departure he could not bear to enter her presence. My only reply was, "It is well: we never were suited for one another," and the subject dropped between us, I trust forever.

We found dear old Beechwood the same as ever, only, if anything, more beautiful. All the beauties and fascinations of the Old World had only made us cling with more fervor to our own sunny home in "the land beyond the sea." Gertie and I ran, like eager children, to every nook and corner in the place, the first day, which was sunny and warm, a regular harbinger of spring. We visited the lawn, the orchard, the grove, the spring under the hill, the ponies, and finally returned, much to Aunt Martha's delight, laden with fresh-laid eggs, that we had pilfered from the poultry-yard.

"Well, I never!" said that good old dame. "I expected you would return a grand lady, with your head so full of furren travel that you would have eyes and ears for nothing else; and here are you and Gertie romping about like two bright children, and coming back to me with your dainty aprons full of eggs, just as you used to years ago."

"Never fear, Aunt Martha, that anything can ever make me indifferent to Beechwood or any of its beloved inmates, much less to the delicious rolls that I am sure your skillful hands will manufacture from these same eggs, just as you used to do in the olden time."

"Deary me! the child forgets nothing; not even my rolls!" was her gratified reply, as she patted me lovingly upon the shoulder.

"Oh," called Gertie, joyously, "Ellis is coming!" and away she bounded down the avenue to meet him. We had not written him the day of our return, and, when we reached the house, found, much to her grief, that he was away attending to his duties; and now when she saw him coming she was like a bird freed from its cage. Nearly two weeks since she had seen him: no wonder she was glad! He quickened his steps to meet her, opened his arms and caught her to his heart, and, bending his tall form-lovingly above her, whispered in glad surprise that which was enough to brighten her eyes and bring the roses to her cheeks as she came to me, leaning upon his arm, with her hand tightly clasped in his own. He gave me a warm, brotherly greeting, and before the evening was half spent I was fully satisfied as to the wisdom of Gertie's choice. Let him converse of what he would, his eye followed her movements and his hand was ever ready to anticipate her wants. Uncle Ralph gave him the utmost confidence and love, which I felt assured undeservingly he could not have obtained.

And so the days sped on, full of pleasant hours and incidents, that I may not take the time to record here, until, one balmy day in spring, when all nature was full of gladness, Charlie walked in, leaning a little heavily upon a crutch, but otherwise well and happy. The surgeon had warned us that he would probably be lame for life; but this we were thankful to accept, so long as his life was spared.

"Oh," said Aunt Martha, sitting down with her apron to her eyes, and crying, half in joy at his return and half in sorrow at his misfortune, "to think of his ever being brought to this! So comely and beautiful,—to go upon a crutch for life! Ah, it is dreadful, dreadful!"

Gertie and I had often spoken of how brave we meant to be, for Charlie's sake, when he returned, and never let him see us grieve at all over his misfortune. So now I spoke up bravely and said, "But see, Aunt Martha, how well he looks!" and then I too broke down and could say no more. The sight of the dear, handsome fellow standing there before us maimed for life was too much for me: my eyes blurred, my voice faltered, and if mamma and Ralph had not entered just then, I know not what I should have done. Gertie too, and Ellis, entered at the same moment from another door, and there were happy greetings from every side; only I saw poor Gertie's heart was as full as my own when she looked upon the tall, manly form standing so quietly leaning upon his crutch.

"Do sit down, dear Charlie," I said. And Ralph wheeled a great chair to his side.

"Thank you; I have a fancy to sit over there by Aunt Martha upon the sofa," said Charlie, gayly, at the same moment dropping his crutch and stalking boldly and independently across the room to her side. Oh, what a joyous shout arose as Gertie and I, aided and abetted by Aunt Martha, clung to him, hysterically laughing and crying by turns, till at last, after returning our caresses most fondly, he called aloud to Ralph,—

"See here, Ralph, have you no compassion for a man, to let him be suffocated in this manner, even though it be with sweets, here in your presence?"

"Ah," said Aunt Martha, "how true it is that 'the darkest hour is just before day'!"

"But who," said Gertie, laughing, "would have believed our Charlie such a 'gay deceiver'?"

"Who indeed?" said Aunt Martha. "And practiced upon his old aunt too! I really believe he cannot have any of my cream muffins for tea," a dish of which he was particularly fond.

"Now, dear Aunt Martha, you surely would not be so

cruel! You know I only wanted to find out how well you loved me," said Charlie, standing in little awe of her threat, well knowing that the house and place would be ransacked, as well as her brain, to conjure up delicacies with which to tempt him.

"Saucy boy!" she answered, shaking her finger at him as she disappeared through the door leading toward the kitchen, going, we all knew, to prepare for him the very delicacy she had threatened to withhold.

"Oh, how good God is to us!" I said to mamma that night, as I sat talking upon the side of her bed for hours after she had retired,—the first really good talk I had had with her since my return. "How good he is to spare you, precious mamma, to us in our absence, and now to raise dear Charlie to us again!"

"And to bring my loving daughter back to me," she added, "and happy too, I trust."

"Very happy, dear mamma," I whispered, softly; "or, at any rate, not in the least unhappy. I am perfectly sure the past throws no shadows over my present life."

"Oh, darling, you cannot tell how happy your words make me!" she said. And then I told her all my convictions and my doubts, and finally of my meeting with Hal when in New York, and the effect produced.

"It is true, dear mamma," I said, in conclusion, "that the past has left its scar upon my life. (Such things cannot occur and leave us as though they had not been, for memory remains, and she is a stern warder) but I am thoroughly convinced that I am happier thus than if all had proceeded in the original course marked out. It is but one more grave to look back upon in life's journey; but it is one above which I shall never weep."

"God is indeed good," whispered mamma, as she kissed me good-night; and my slumbers were sweet and dreamless.

Uncle Ralph spent much of his time at Beechwood, coming and going, as in the olden times. Especially while mamma was absent, he came daily to see that all was well, —sometimes staying but a few moments, sometimes lingering for hours. I had written to him frequently in my absence, feeling that the ban to my so doing was removed, and receiving ever in reply pages of such lofty sentiments and kind advice as could but purify and elevate my heart. I never was so happy as when listening to and conversing with him; and Gertie and I craved no greater pleasure than to steal him away for a ramble with us over the hills, or a ride in the early morning upon the ponies.

One evening, a few weeks after mamma had come, he came out to me in the garden, where I was sprinkling the flowers, and said,—

"Come, Nannie, get your hat, and let us improve this balmy air, by a walk over to Gertie's." She was then living in the parsonage, about half a mile distant from us.

"With all my heart," I answered, running to fetch my hat.

Mamma and he were conversing beside the gate, when I returned; she kissed me tenderly as I passed forth, and handed me a tiny basket of delicacies for Gertie. Uncle Ralph's face wore such a look as I had never seen but once before upon it; the tender, wistful look with which he bent above me on the evening of the day he had rescued me at the beach.

"Oh, Uncle Ralph," I said, clinging to his arm, and looking up gratefully into his face, "you never will allow me to speak to you of the day you saved my life; but tonight you must, indeed you must. My heart is so full of love and gratitude that it will not be denied. Where would I have been but for your strong arm and loving heart? Food for fishes,—and my bones, miles away, bleaching among the coral."

"My darling!" he said, shuddering a moment convulsively, and taking the hand that lay upon his arm in his own strong one.

We walked on a moment in silence; then, as we drew near the stile that leads across the field to Gertie's, he stopped in the thick shadows of the overhanging trees, and, laying his hands upon my shoulders, and looking me earnestly in the face with his great, wistful eyes, said, softly,—

"I did more for myself, darling, than for you. At least I trust time will so prove it."

The tone, the manner, the words, were all unlike Uncle Ralph, or at least unlike his way of speaking to me; but, before I could find words to answer, being myself a little confused by his manner, I saw the fragile form of a woman, that I had noticed creeping slowly along toward us from the village, approach and sit down languidly upon the stile near us. The face had a familiar look upon it, yet for the life of me I could not say to whom it belonged. It had once been beautiful, I could plainly see; but now the lips were compressed and colorless, the eyes were sunken and languid, and over it all was a look of such inexpressible sadness that my heart was at once deeply touched.

"Who can it be?" I whispered to Uncle Ralph.

"A stranger; but one evidently in need of friends. Let us approach."

We did so, and I said, kindly, "Are you ill, my poor girl?" she looked so young and helpless.

She looked at me searchingly a moment, with a glance that made my heart throb strangely, and, burying her face in her hands, sobbed aloud,—

"Have you indeed forgotten me?"

The voice confirmed the impression the glance had conveyed, and in another instant I had her folded in my arms, dropping hot tears above her, as I said,—

"Oh! is it indeed precious Minnie, returned to us at last?"

"Yes, Nannie," she answered, through her choking tears, "returned to you to die."

"No, no, darling; we will soon make you well at Beechwood. Won't we, Uncle Ralph?"

"I am sure nothing will be left undone to accomplish that end. But have you walked far to-day, my child? You look weary and languid," he said, kindly, taking her hand.

"Only from the end of the avenue here. I rode that far in the coach, but it goes no farther this way."

"Do you feel able to walk to the house? or will you sit here with Nannie till I go for the carriage?"

"Oh, I can walk," she said, eagerly; but I replied, emphatically, seeing her pallid looks,—

"No, it will take longer for us to walk than if the carriage came; and you are already weary. Then Uncle Ralph can tell them you are coming, and mamma will have a little fire made; for the evenings are chilly."

"Yes," said Uncle Ralph, "that is best; and, as I can walk much faster without my coat, and you may feel chilly, sitting so long, if you will allow me;" and he drew off his coat and adjusted it carefully about Minnie's shoulders. She looked up at him gratefully, but did not dare to speak.

When he had gone, I drew forth Gertie's little basket, so carefully prepared by mamma, and said,—

"Come, dear Minnie, I am sure the walk has made you hungry, as well as myself; we will eat Gertie's delicacies, and to-morrow, together, carry her more."

I spoke gayly, for I saw her heart would bear no tenderness; and I also saw, by the eager look in her eyes as I opened the basket, that she was faint from fasting.

"Let me see,—here is some blanc-mange, and a glass of currant jelly; and, as I live, some of Aunt Martha's cream muffins; do try one, Minnie;" and I handed her out the dainty cake. She ate it eagerly, and I pretended to do the same. "Now try another; and I will make an impromptu spoon for the blanc-mange, for here is a little bottle of vanilla-cream all ready for it, you see." I went on, by way of explanation, and to keep her from trying to talk: "Gertie has just gone to housekeeping; and, at the rate mamma and Aunt Martha furnish her table with delicacies, she will never learn to make them for herself. She lives just over there, in the little cottage amid the trees. There!" showing the wooden spoon I had rudely carved from a beechen chip with my penknife, "there, I guess now we can have the blanc-mange! You eat that, while I devour my muffin. I don't care at all for blanc-mange;" a righteous fib, for which I trust I may be forgiven, under the circumstances. By the time she was done eating it, Uncle Ralph came with the carriage, and expressed himself delighted at seeing her looking so much refreshed.

"Oh, you see," said I, laughing, "we had nothing else to do, so we broke into mamma's basket to Gertie, and devoured its contents. My walk had made me ravenously hungry. It was well you were not here to share the spoils. I assure you, you would not have had the lion's share, by any means; would he, Minnie?"

Minnie smiled faintly and shook her head, and I rattled away merrily till we reached the house. Anything, I thought, to give the poor weary heart time to compose itself.

Mamma, Aunt Martha, Ralph, and Charlie all met us

at the gate, and gave Minnie a joyous, happy greeting,— the same as though she had come to us in happiness and splendor; but nothing could quiet the overwrought nerves. She clung to mamma, and sobbed and moaned upon her neck, until every heart was wrung at the sight of her anguish. But after a little the storm of grief gave way, and she became more calm, and allowed herself to be led into the house, where everything possible for her comfort had already been done.

For several days after her arrival she was unable to leave her room, but then she began to rally, little by little, till at last she could come, for part of the day, with us, below-stairs.

Her story was a sadly pitiful one, as gleaned from her; though she still strove not to throw any more blame than she could not possibly avoid upon her miserable husband. After the first few weeks, it seems, he became arbitrary and unkind, compelling her to do many things against which her womanly pride and delicacy rebelled,—taking her to places of low amusement, from which she shrank, and compelling her to go to his sister's, after he had recklessly spent her own small fortune, to ask for pecuniary favors that he knew would be refused to himself. And then, at last, when a little daughter came to them, near the close of the first year, he seemed jealous of the attention she lavished upon it, and would often take it from her arms and send it away from the house, by the nurse, when she knew it was suffering for sustenance. At last his family, utterly worn out with his low life, threw him off altogether, and would listen to no more appeals for aid; and after that he would often go away for months together, leaving her with no means of sustenance whatever for herself and babe. Then the poor child worked, early and late, with her needle, gaining the merest pittance thereby; and when a second little one came, at the end of another year, her health failed completely under her cares, and consumption, hereditary in her father's family, began its work upon her vitals. Her children were her only comfort; and when, a few weeks previous to her appearance among us, her husband brutally threatened to take them from her and send them to the orphan-asylum in New York, she stole from home during his absence, with her little ones, determined to die rather than return to him. She had a little money, from the sale of her mother's jewels, to which she had clung to the last, and, going about fifty miles from Boston, where she had fled from her brutal husband, she left the train at a little village and under a feigned name sought employment. But it was hard to get work, encumbered as she was with her two children; and when at last a kind-hearted farmer's wife took them in, the little ones were so ill from fatigue and exposure that they grew rapidly worse, and died within a few days of each other.

The people were very kind to her, it seems, caring for her and her little girls and aiding her in giving them decent burial. She stayed and worked all that she could for the good woman of the house, until she found her life was waning, and knew that she had but a little while to live. Then a yearning desire to see us all once more took possession of her, and she one day unfolded her history to the kind woman who had so befriended her; and she was so touched with her misfortunes that she gave her money for her journey and started her to us. But the money was not quite sufficient; and when she reached our village she had eaten nothing for nearly twenty-four hours, and was ready to fall when she met us. The mail-coachman had kindly brought her from the village to our avenue, a distance of perhaps two miles; and she had started to walk alone the other mile to the house. How she would have fared had we not met her, God only knows.

She seemed to rally considerably for a time; and every pleasant day Ralph would come from the village and take her, sometimes with mamma, sometimes with me beside her, for a short drive; and it was touching to see how tenderly he would lift her from the carriage,—often, when the ground was at all damp, bearing her in his strong arms into the hall. She greatly feared that her husband would learn her whereabouts and come and claim her. I said so one day in Ralph's presence.

"Never fear," said Ralph, impetuously: "if he ever comes about this house, he will not long have life enough left in him to carry her away."

"'Thou shalt not kill!'" said mamma, solemnly. "I cannot bear to hear you talk thus, Ralph."

"Well, mamma, for your sake I shall say no more, and shall try my best to restrain myself, if he ever does come; but I do hope you will not object to my at least trying upon him the strength of my boot."

But her fears were not to be realized; for we received word from Charlie, who had gone to New York on business a little while before, that Colonel Leslie had been found dead in his room, his brains blown out by his own hand. We did not tell Minnie the manner of his death, but only that he had died; and her piteous cry, "May God be merciful to him!" was sad to hear. She asked no questions, and never spoke his name after the first hour, seeming to wish to forget his errors, and, if possible, his very existence.

She seemed for a time to rally, but it was a deceitful strength. It began to fail, little by little, till at last she scarcely left her room at all; and then we took to sitting with her there, sometimes one of us, oftener all; for when alone she fell into the deepest melancholy. She often spoke of her parents and her dear little girls in the tenderest manner, and expressed a wish that her children could have slept beside her. This mamma promised should be, if she did not recover; they could easily be moved to Beechwood; and it seemed to gratify her much.

One day it was sultry, and she slept, and I, weary with reading aloud, threw myself upon a lounge that stood in one corner of the room, and dropped asleep also. When I awakened, she was sitting in her easy-chair beside the window, evidently unconscious of my presence, for she sat with clasped hands looking sadly out upon the beautiful clouds in the west that waited for the sunset. I was about to speak to her, when she arose, and, pacing the room with feeble steps and with hands clasped tightly together, began in a low, weird voice to sing the following strain:—

> Lonely, lonely! my heart sobs the livelong day;
> Lonely, lonely! it whispers and moans alway.
>   Buried are all my heart held dear,
>   In dust and ashes they lie,
>   While lone I pursue life's pathway drear,
>   Alone, alone must I die.
> Lonely, lonely! my heart sobs the livelong day;
> Lonely, lonely! it whispers and moans alway.
>
> Lonely, lonely! once I was blithe and gay;
> Lonely, lonely! the sunlight has fled away.
>   Grief o'er my spirit her pall has flung;
>   Shadows encompass my brow;
>   And of all I held when life was young,
>   Nothing is left me now.
> Lonely, lonely! my heart sobs the livelong day;
> Lonely, lonely! it whispers and moans alway.

It is impossible to describe the touchingly wild music that accompanied these verses. My eyes were full of tears, and my heart of sympathy; for it was evident that both words and music were deeply felt and wholly impromptu.

For a moment her song ceased, and she paused in her walk; then with indescribable pathos she sang the next verse, standing with uplifted hand, form slightly bent, and eyes fixed and earnest, looking with that far-away look, as though striving to pierce the veil that hides us from the beautiful, the unknown land of shadows.

> Weary, weary! thus must it ever be?
> Weary, weary? *no, there is rest for me.*
> For in that land of love and light,
> Far o'er the crystal sea,
> Where loving hearts are waiting to-night,
> There, *there* is rest for me!
> Weary, weary! thus must it ever be?
> Weary, weary? *no, there is rest for me.*

I shall never forget her as she then stood, thinking herself alone in her solitary chamber, the fragile form slightly bent, the long white robe flowing loose and free about her, her hand uplifted, the pale, spirituel face, with that far-away look upon it, slightly raised, and the great, earnest eyes, so brilliant and beautiful with life's decay, seeking to penetrate the unknown future,—singing, in those wild numbers, the strange burden of her heart. It formed a picture I shall carry with me all through life.

"Oh, Minnie," I said, tenderly, going toward her, "cheer up, darling! Life has, I trust, much of happiness yet in store for you."

She started a little at my unexpected approach, and said, "No, Nannie; the page is almost written,—and it is well."

"You are so young, dear; you must not despair. You will soon gather strength and health," I answered.

But she only shook her head sadly, and held her frail little transparent hand between me and the light.

"See, dear Nannie, there is no life-blood there. You must not seek to deceive either yourself or me longer. I have ambition and will, and trust I shall not sink long before the last hour comes; but it is not far distant now. I shall soon rest by my precious little Fannie and Matie. Oh, to think how much happiness I might have had within these walls, had I not, like Eve, banished myself from Paradise!"

"Do not think of the past now, my Minnie. We are all so happy to have you with us again."

"Yes; you are all too kind to me,—when I have brought nothing but disgrace and sorrow to you all."

"Tell me, Minnie," I said, leading her to her couch and anxious to divert her mind,—"tell me where you found those touching words you sang so sweetly as you walked the floor."

"I do not know, Nannie. They came to me as I walked. I never heard them before. The thoughts they embodied were in my heart as I sat by the window, but clothed themselves in words and melody without any effort of my own."

"It is a rare gift, darling. Came it ever to you thus before?"

"Once only; when my little Matie died. Sorrow alone —intense and fearful—brings it to me."

"Will you let me read the words? Have you them?"

"Yes, if you so desire. Soon after little Matie died, I sat alone beside her grave and that of my darling little Fannie, and my mind, in the midst of my sorrow, went back to my childhood. I saw again my father and mother and little sister; remembered their tender care of us, and their sorrow at her death. My mind ran hurriedly and sadly on up to the then present. It seemed but a day's journey I had come since I stood at my mother's knee; but, oh, so long and wearisome, so full of graves, both of lost friends and lost hopes, so full of trials and sorrows! And the thought that I must still press wearily onward and leave my little ones to rest among strangers seemed the bitterest of all. I had ever been willful, and, few bearing with me as my parents had done, after their death the only happy hours I had known were those I spent here with you in your quiet home. Would to God I had listened to your pleadings, and had not flown forth from such a sheltered nest!"

"But the poem, darling," I urged, as I saw her again yielding to the sad present.

"Ah, yes. Suddenly, as I thus sat thinking, the same weird spirit that came to me to-day seized upon me,—a dreamy sensation of mingled sadness and peace stole over me, and I arose, and, with clasped hands, paced slowly to and fro amid the graves and chanted to a low, sad melody the following words." And she handed me from her portfolio a paper, from which I here transcribe them:—

"So weary. All the livelong day
I've struggled o'er the toilsome way;
And now, when evening shades steal on,
Weary and sad I stand alone,
With cold hands to my hot brow press'd,
And sadly cry, 'Is there no rest?'

"Along the way my feet have trod
There rest, 'neath many a verdant sod,
The forms I've loved, the hands I've press'd,
The lips that I've so oft caress'd;
Whilst I, alas! must still press on,
Nor even by their graves kneel down!

"Yet this I know, that far away
There is a clime of beauteous day,
Beyond the toil, beyond the stream,
Beyond life's weary, fleeting dream,
Where—oh that I may be so blest!—
'He giveth his beloved rest.'"

I could not speak when I had finished reading the words, my heart so fully appreciated the strain to which the poor torn heart must have been subjected to call them forth. I could only bend over the low couch upon which she lay, and kiss the pale forehead, the sunken, tearless eyes, and the flushed cheeks again and again, while my own hot tears fell upon the pallid, upturned face, which my heart told me would soon be hidden from our sight forever.

She lived only about three weeks from this time, and now lies quietly sleeping by dear little Kittie and papa; and as soon as the weather becomes cool enough her little children will be removed to her side. Her last days were calm and peaceful. She seemed willing to go, trusting in the merits of Christ's blood for acceptance with the Father.

She sat up a little every day to the very last. Once, only a few days previous to her death, Ralph, at mamma's request, lifted her from the chair to the couch upon which she usually lay in the daytime, and, as he laid her down, she smoothed, with her little transparent hand, his cheek, and I heard her say softly to him,—

"Ah, dear Ralph, you are always so tender and good to me. My heart tells me you are one of the best of men."

"Would it had told you so years ago, little Minnie!" said Ralph, brokenly; and mamma and I stole out upon the terrace beyond the sound of their voices; and presently I went below, through our own room, on to the lawn.

Ralph lingered but a little while in her room; but when he came below, the traces of not unmanly tears were on his cheeks, and, walking to the gate, where "Di" stood impatiently waiting her young master, he mounted and rode away to the village,—pausing first to say to me, in broken tones,—

"Don't send for me, Nannie, when the time comes, unless she wishes it; I could not bear it."

"Dear Ralph!" I whispered, by tone and look assuring him of my earnest sympathy; and, pressing my hand in token of his appreciation, he dashed away, as he ever does when unpleasantly excited.

She died so quietly and hopefully that we could scarcely realize that she was indeed gone. It was just as the sun was setting behind a great mass of purple and golden clouds in the west that the messenger came. She had asked that her bed might be drawn in front of the open window, and she lay, with her little white hands crossed upon her breast, looking out quietly upon the sunset,—the last she was ever to behold on earth. Aunt Martha had said, hours before, that she believed her dying, but she seemed so calm and cheerful we could not think it. Gertie, mamma, and I were in the room, when all at once she said, distinctly and clearly,—

"The hour has come."

"Dear Minnie," said mamma, as we all approached her bed, "not yet, darling, we trust."

"It has come, Aunt Fannie; and my last request is that you will remember how much better it will be for me than if I had lived as I have for the last three years. God is merciful."

"My darling," said mamma, solemnly,—for the expression upon Minnie's face told that her impressions were but too true,—"shall I send for Ellis, to pray with you? He is below-stairs." He had the day previous administered to her the holy rites of the sacrament.

"Yes; it would be sweet to go upon the wings of prayer."

Gertie ran hurriedly below for Ellis and Aunt Martha. Uncle Ralph, Ralph, and Charlie were in the village.

"Kiss me, dear Nannie, and hold my hand as I pass into the valley. It will not be so much like going alone."

I bent beside her and kissed her, and for a moment I thought her breath was gone. At this instant a thrush, on one of the trees beside the casement, burst forth into a song full of melody and gladness, and, with a smile upon her lips, she opened her eyes a moment languidly and looked out upon the sunset, then closed them upon the world forever. Ellis made a short, appropriate prayer, during which she once responded audibly; but, when we arose, it was over,—her spirit had indeed gone upward on the wings of prayer. Her hand still clasped my own, but loosely; and, as for a moment we gave way to our sorrow, a soft ray of sunlight struggled through the trees and the open window, and, as it rested upon her beautiful upturned face and soft golden hair, she looked indeed as though a stream of light from the celestial city had fallen upon the lifeless casket of clay as the glad spirit passed through the open gates into the presence of the Eternal. We looked upon the dear face and thought of her earnest words of parting, and the remembrance took from us much of the bitterness of death. We have had carved upon her tomb simply,—

Minnie Maud Norris.
She hath rest.

Giving her thus her girlhood's name; ignoring her husband's altogether.

And so, nearly three months ago, passed from our lives, but not from our hearts, our precious Minnie, for the second time. To-night, as I sit thinking over her last hours,—so beautiful, so full of quiet peace, exerting over us all the chastening effect such suffering ever brings,—my thoughts involuntarily weave themselves into the following simple strain commemorative of her death-scene:—

MAUD.

Our Maud, our darling, was dying,
   So beautiful and so fair,
With the sunlight softly lying
   On her silken, shining hair.

Her robe, in its dainty whiteness,
   Fell soft from her throat away,
And she look'd like an angel waiting
   To enter the gates of day.

A moment the blue eyes sadly
   Look'd out on the summer sky,
As a thrush his song trill'd gladly
   In the branches swaying nigh.

Then the white lids, drooping slowly,
   Closed over the beauteous eyes;
And the calm was so deep and holy,
   We stifled our tearful sighs.

Like an infant gently sinking
   To sleep on its mother's breast,
So she, without fear or shrinking,
   Pass'd into her dreamless rest.

And, although our hearts were breaking,
   Our sorrow we set aside,
When we thought how her awaking
   Would be with the glorified.

And soon, with the pale flowers twining
   In her soft and golden hair,
We left her, without repining,
   To the angels' tender care.

For we felt that the hand that led her
   So gently across the stream
In its tenderness would guide her
   To the land of which we dream.

It is more than a month already since I began these entries, I find so much to call my attention elsewhere. But they are so nearly complete, I will persist a little longer.

Charlie, dear Charlie, is perfectly well again, except that his right arm is not, and we fear never will be, so strong as formerly. He has been established for some time in our village, and, as I predicted he would be, is a general favorite. He and Nettie expect to be married in December; it is now the last of September. They are very happy, and I doubt not her choice was better than mine for her would have been, although I always thought she would suit Ralph admirably.

Gertie and Ellis are fixed up so snugly in their cozy little bird's-nest of a cottage, it does one good to look in upon them, especially as Gertie assumes such matronly little airs and presides so prettily at her dainty tea-table. It was only yesterday Ellis told me that he did not think she had her counterpart in all New England. Nothing with him is wrong that Gertie does; nothing is quite good enough to lavish upon her.

I believe I have failed to mention that Miss Lane, having lost both of her pupils by my absence and Gertie's marriage, herself married a very worthy gentleman whom she had long loved, but from whom she had been kept by untoward circumstances, and is now living in Brooklyn, very pleasantly situated.

I have tried to give the leading incidents since my return as much as possible in the order of their occurrence, although many of them were weeks apart. And if I have said but little of my own individual thoughts, feelings, and plans for the future, it has only been because all others seemed of more importance than my own, and were, perhaps, more easily narrated.

After Minnie came, the most of my time was spent with her: yet I will not deny that strange thoughts and feelings crowded into my heart in regard to other matters. I could not help thinking of, and speculating upon, Uncle Ralph's strange words and stranger manners the evening we had met her in the avenue. But the more I speculated, the more my thoughts became inextricably involved. What good had he done himself more than me in saving my life? There was one interpretation to the words and look that sent the blood in a hot torrent to my face, and a wild thrill to my heart; but I dared not believe it the correct one. Still, I could not but think of it and dwell upon it, till at last, fearful of betraying, by blush or look, that my heart ever harbored such utterly impracticable dreams, I came to seek refuge ever in Minnie's room at his approach and busy myself for her comfort while he remained. But he never, by word or look, referred to the conversation alluded to, until at last I became ashamed of ever having for an instant cherished such a thought, and met him in the old accustomed way. Then came to me the most terrible ordeal of my life,—so terrible that my heart shrinks back appalled from its remembrance. Yet must I make its record, or my story is incomplete.

One sultry day, near noon, several weeks after Minnie's death, I felt nervous and unhappy, I scarcely knew why. I found no companionship in books; music was utterly out of the question; the weather was entirely too warm for me to go either to Gertie's or Nettie's, and mamma and Aunt Martha were busy in the mysteries of jelly- and preserve-making in the basement kitchen. I felt lost and unhappy, and finally went to my room, and, after a refreshing bath, began slowly to comb and arrange my long hair, which, for want of something better to do, I dressed with unusual care, in coils and curls innumerable, over a beautiful comb of gold,—Fannie's gift to me when abroad. I completed it, for a wonder in my mood, to my satisfaction, and, arraying myself in a thin, flowing robe, went below just in time to meet Uncle Ralph and Ralph entering the hall door together.

"Upon my word, sis," said Ralph, stooping his tall form to kiss me, "you are the prettiest, coolest little body I have seen to-day. Isn't it so, Uncle Ralph?"

"She certainly does look enviably cool," he replied, passing on into the drawing-room.

Now, I did not expect him either to caress me or to call me pretty, yet I was just in the mood to feel the least slight, and thought at once, "Oh, yes! he thinks, I suppose, I have spent hours before the glass," and the fact of its being literally true, for once, did not tend to dissipate my ill humor.

"Where is mamma, sis?" said Ralph, lightly catching me up in his arms, to the imminent peril of both hair and dress.

"Oh, Ralph, don't be so rude!" I cried. "Put me down, and I will tell you."

"Oh, that is it?" he said, teasingly. "Well, there you are!" carrying me into the drawing-room and dumping me down into a great arm-chair, thereby putting the finishing touches to my disordered attire.

"I declare, Ralph, you are too bad!" I said, impatiently, seating myself by the open window, picking up a piece of light work, and beginning to sew industriously. "If you want mamma, I think I will let you go below yourself to find her."

"Fie, Nannie! The idea of your telling any one 'to go below.' Do you not know such language is altogether unbecoming from such rosy lips as yours?" And he disappeared from the room, shaking his head deprecatingly.

Now, I ought to have known that the worst thing I could possibly do, when Ralph was in a teasing mood, was to let him see that I minded his raillery. The dear fellow had shown but little disposition of late to indulge in it at all, and I should, under ordinary circumstances, have welcomed its return; but I was "out of sorts," as Aunt Martha would say, and resented it accordingly. Then, too, Uncle Ralph sat reading his newspaper as complacently as though the mercury did not stand at ninety-five degrees in the shade out-of-doors; and his composure only added to my evident discomfort.

Presently Ralph returned, and with him mamma, who was saying, as they entered,—

"I am half afraid for you, too, Ralph; it is so sultry, we shall surely have a storm."

"Not a bit of it, mamma. And then, you know, I swim like a turtle." He had stopped just behind my chair, and, as I was about to ask where he was going, he said, thoughtfully,—

"This is a beautiful comb, sis. Where did you get it?"

And he pulled it out of my hair, as though innocently to examine it. Of course down tumbled curls and coils about my shoulders, and my afternoon's work was lost, and I in no humor to renew it. My eyes filled with tears of vexation as I said, impetuously, "I do wish you would never return, Ralph, till you can learn to behave yourself," and started up-stairs to my room.

A few moments afterward I heard him calling to me, penitently, on the stairs,—

"I am very sorry, little sister, that I was so naughty. Come down and kiss me good-by, please. I am going away till to morrow, fishing." But I pretended not to hear, and he finally went away with Joseph in the little spring-wagon. Then, when I saw he had really gone, repentance came, as usual, and I sat down and cried away my shame and anger. I twisted up my hair in its usual great coil, and, feeling languid and miserable, threw myself upon the bed, and, ere I was aware, dropped off into a troubled slumber.

The air was very heavy and sultry, and I must have slept at least two hours, when I was awakened by some one coming into my chamber. I aroused myself, and saw mamma hurriedly closing the shutters and sash; and when she saw I was awake she said, nervously,—

"It is as I feared. A terrible storm is coming up. Oh, if Ralph had only not gone!"

I sprang from the bed, and, hastily adjusting my dress, ran down-stairs. Great masses of black and leaden-hued clouds were sweeping over the heavens, while a long, low line beneath them, in the west, was green, and swept fearfully fast up from the horizon.

"This cloud is most to be feared," said Uncle Ralph, as I joined him where he stood upon the lawn watching the heavens. I looked in the direction he pointed out, and saw out over the bay a tall, funnel-shaped cloud, pointing downward, sweeping rapidly eastward, or from the beach out to the open sea. "Such clouds are sure to carry death and destruction in their track. God forbid it cross the track of any ship!"

"Oh, Uncle Ralph, do you believe that Ralph has had time to reach the island?" I asked, in alarm. They usually went to fish to a small island about five miles away from the mainland.

"No, I think not; but I trust he saw the storm arising before he went upon the water. There were two or three others besides himself, and they would naturally delay a little."

"Has the storm been long in coming up?" He looked at me curiously a moment, and I added, "I fell asleep; the day was so sultry."

"You are a little feverish," replied he, taking my hand. "Go and bathe your temples; it will refresh you."

I went with childlike submissiveness, and did as he

directed me, and by that time the wind was blowing so furiously that we fastened all the doors and windows, and went into the great hall, that place seeming the most secure from danger. Through the shutters and the glass beside the great door we could see great branches of trees whirled like feathers through the air, which was thick with dust and leaves. The domestics had also gathered into the hall, and sat in silent fear.

"Please come with me a moment to the upper hall," I whispered to Uncle Ralph, who sat upon the wide stairs. He arose without speaking, and accompanied me. "I was afraid to come alone; and I felt as though I must see the bay."

We approached, and through the shutters looked out to sea; but the storm was so intense we could see nothing, for now the rain and hail began to fall in torrents: we could hear the mad roar of the waves, however, and knew they must be terrific. We crossed to one of the rooms which looked out upon the grove, and saw great trees snapped off as though they had been tiny saplings.

"Oh, if Ralph only were at home!" I said. "And to think I was so cross with him!" And the hot tears flowed silently over my face as I turned to go back to mamma.

"Try to forget it now, Nannie; pray to God to care for him in this peril, and to give you more strength for the future."

One reason I so love and reverence Uncle Ralph is, that he never screens my faults. He never says, "It is nothing;" but ever points me to the better way.

We found mamma sitting, pale and motionless, with her head resting upon her hand; and when I crouched down beside her, and pressed my lips to her hand, she said, in a tone that revealed the depth of her agony,—

"Oh, Nannie! I shall never see my brave boy again!"

"Dear mamma, say not so," I pleaded; though my own heart beat fearfully at the thought.

"It is impossible that he could live through this fearful tempest. Just so my Charlie perished years ago. Oh, why do I ever let them leave me to go upon those treacherous waters?"

Then Uncle Ralph soothed her as no other could have done. I do not remember to have ever seen her so fearfully agitated before. And ere long the violence of the storm abated.

"Joseph will soon come," said mamma; "he was only to drive Ralph to the beach; and then we shall know more of them."

In a very short time Joseph did come, and sent in word to Uncle Ralph that he would like to see him.

"No, no," said mamma, in an imperious manner, wholly unlike her usual mild demeanor. "No, tell him to come here; I must hear at once all that he knows of my boy."

"Dear Fannie," said Uncle Ralph, "it will be much better to let me speak with him first alone."

"No, Ralph; forgive me, but I must know everything now: this suspense is worse than death!"

Uncle Ralph looked troubled, but said no more, and Joseph came.

"Joseph, what of your young master?" said mamma, eagerly, as soon as he appeared.

Joseph looked at Uncle Ralph, uncertain how much to tell.

"Tell, briefly, all you know," he said to him. So he began:—

"The other gentlemen were waiting for us when we reached the beach, as Mr. Ralph had stopped a little in the village, which you know is considerably out of our way, to get his fishing-tackle. Then there was considerable discussion as to whether they should start or not before the storm. It seemed so distant, they at last decided that they could easily reach the island before it broke: so they put off."

"Be quick, Joseph," said mamma, sitting rigid and pallid, with clasped hands; "be quick; did they reach it?"

"Why, you see, my lady, they had not noticed the strange-looking cloud that came up so suddenly,—the one, your honor," turning to Uncle Ralph, "that looked so much like a sugar-loaf upside down."

A silent shudder ran over us all, but Uncle Ralph only nodded, and Joseph went on:—

"I had started back to the village with the team when I first saw it. It struck the ground about half a mile from the shore, and demolished everything in its track; tore up great trees by the roots, as easily as I would tear up a weed; unroofed barns and houses, and completely tore to atoms the old tenantless house that stood near the beach."

"But the boat, Joseph, the boat?" cried mamma; for, like most servants, he was very tedious in his narrative.

"Yes, my lady: the boat was about three-fourths of the way to the island when it struck her. I had stopped, for I saw she was just in its track. It lifted her clear out of the water, as it would a leaf from the ground, then turned her completely bottom upward, throwing the young gentlemen into the midst of the great whirling waves."

Uncle Ralph had risen, when he saw what was coming, to prevent, if possible, so terrible a history; but it was too late. Mamma put out her hand appealingly, and said, faintly,—

"And what then?"

"I saw them all struggling, for a moment, together, in the water; and then the rain and hail blinded me so, I could distinguish nothing any longer; so I rode to the village as rapidly as possible, and Mr. Charlie started at once, in company with several others, to go to the beach, and across to the island, to learn the truth. He sent me home to tell Mr. Ralph, here, all I had seen, and to say to you, my lady, not to give up, for they should doubtless find them all alive on the island, as they were all good swimmers, and not far from it when the boat capsized."

"No, no! I shall never see my boy again! Oh, Ralph, my darling, my first-born! And grown so much of late like my own buried Charlie! May God give me strength for this trial!" And she buried her face in her hands, and moaned aloud again and again, in her anguish.

"He will, dear Fannie; trust him," said Uncle Ralph, tenderly. Then to Joseph,—

"Go at once to the beach, upon the best horse, and bring us the first definite word you can receive."

"I will, sir," said Joseph, bowing himself respectfully out of the room, at the same instant that Ellis and Gertie, having in some way heard the news,—for ill news ever travels fast,—entered the hall.

I had heard all, as in a dream, while an iron band seemed binding heart and brain. I had not moved or spoken during Joseph's narrative; but the whole scene arose vividly before me as he narrated it; and I fancied I could see Ralph's pale, ghastly face looking from the troubled waters, the dark hair lying in tangled wet masses about it, and the pale lips whispering the words, "Please come and kiss me good-by, little sister," as he had called to me from the stairs that morning. I saw poor mamma's pallid, sorrowful face; I heard Gertie's low sob of anguish, as the story was briefly repeated to herself and Ellis; I heard Uncle Ralph and Ellis both speaking cheerful words of hope and courage; but their voices sounded afar off, as dream-voices, and I half fancied I would soon awaken from this, as from other feverish dreams of terror and distress.

At last I arose, went out upon the veranda, and walked slowly to the end looking toward the grove. The storm had all passed; the sun shone out brightly, and the little birds twittered lovingly in the branches. But the sunshine had a peculiar look, as though it shone through a dark mist; and the notes of the little birds, like the human voices, sounded afar off. A beautiful ash, that papa had planted when Ralph was a baby, had been twisted and torn, until the trunk was shivered into a thousand pieces, some ten feet from the ground; and it now stood shattered and desolate, with its beautiful head of verdure upon the ground at its feet. I shuddered as I looked at it, and the iron band seemed tightening around my brain. "It is Ralph himself," I thought, with a cold, creeping sensation pervading my whole frame,—"Ralph himself; cut off in his manhood's early prime; broken and wrenched from us with all the verdure and nobleness of manhood fresh upon him."

Soon Gertie came, pale and tearful, and, clinging to me, said,—

"Oh, Nannie, do you believe it possible that Ralph is indeed lost?"

I looked at her with the same calm with which I had heard everything else, only gathering her a moment closely to my heart, and saying, soothingly,—

"We will know better, dear, when Charlie comes."

I pointed to the shattered tree, and said, "Do not let mamma know of it; and, dear, if you can, stay near her: I cannot, now."

My voice sounded as strange to me as had her own, and I do not think I could have spoken so calmly much longer.

"Oh, Nannie," said Gertie, tearfully, as I pointed to the tree, "it is Ralph's own tree. I know from that he must have perished." And she clung to me, sobbing hysterically.

"Be calm, Gertie; you were always good to him," I said, stoically. "Go to mamma, please, dear." And I passed through the hall back into the kitchen. There I stood a long while in the back door, watching the bees among the honeysuckle-flowers. Then I remember stooping down and stroking the back of a pet cat, that came rubbing and purring about me; then I walked slowly out to the garden-gate, counting, mechanically, the paving-stones as I walked along, and, remembering now that my limbs trembled excessively beneath me, wondering why they had not left the bench beneath the bee-hives long enough for a person to sit down upon. I had not changed my clothes since the storm, the air was cold and damp, and I was thinly clad.

"Do go and put on a heavier dress, child," Aunt Martha had urged, and, seeing I showed no evidence of so doing, had finally brought a light breakfast-shawl and thrown it over my shoulders. I drew it about me, for I was very chilly.

The hours slipped away, and finally I heard the tramp of horses' feet, and looking from the kitchen-window, near which I stood, saw Joseph and Charlie riding together up the avenue. The lamps were already lighted in the dining-room, where supper had long been waiting, and the twilight was deepening in the grove. I turned mechanically, and went into the drawing-room.

Mamma still sat, pale and tearless, in her chair, with Gertie still beside her, and Uncle Ralph and Ellis near. She looked at me wistfully as I entered, and held her hand out to me. I went to her, kissed her hands and forehead and lips, and heard her tender voice saying to me,—

"We must not lose our trust in God's mercy, dear."

"No, dear mamma," replied I, listening all the while for the sound of Charlie's footsteps. Uncle Ralph had evidently heard them; for he arose, and went out. I walked to the table and adjusted a book or two, then closed the piano and straightened the cover, feeling all the while as though I were walking upon the deck of a vessel in a troubled sea, and finally sank down into an easy-chair, waiting to be awakened from this terrible nightmare that had seized upon both mind and body.

Finally Uncle Ralph returned, and said tenderly to mamma, "Charlie has come, Fannie;" and as she started from her seat excitedly, he entered. One glance at his pale, troubled face, terror-stricken and awed, was enough; there was no need of words. He walked directly to mamma, and, folding her tenderly in his strong arms, said, brokenly,—

"My poor mother! may God comfort you!"

A low wail, as from a broken heart, for a moment escaped mamma's bloodless lips, as she sank swooning upon his breast. He laid her gently down upon the sofa, and Aunt Martha and Gertie, and Nettie Ray's aunt,—who at that moment entered with Nettie,—busied themselves for her recovery. I saw them all working with mamma, without feeling for an instant that my presence in the group was at all necessary or desirable; felt Nettie's kiss upon my forehead as she sat down close beside me, and the pressure of sympathy as she took my hand; heard Uncle Ralph telling Ellis, in a low voice, that two bodies had been found upon the island beach, washed ashore by the waves,—the bodies of young Maitland and Leonard, from the village,—but the other three had doubtless been washed farther out to sea. Ralph's hat had been found in some brush near the shore, and the boat, still bottom upward, and much shattered, floating on the waves. No boat was in sight, save one far out upon the open sea, that could not possibly have been near enough to render any assistance.

I heard it all with tearless eyes, and this terrible stricture increasing constantly upon heart and brain, until I felt that reason was tottering upon her throne.

"Oh, dear Nannie," said Gertie, coming and kneeling down beside me, her sweet voice choked and her face bedewed with tears, "dear sister, do not look so! you frighten me! Ellis, Charlie, speak to her, do!"

"Darling," said Charlie, tenderly, "it is a terrible blow; but we must bear it together. Think of dear mamma: it falls heaviest upon her; let the thought of her sorrow lighten our own."

"Think of mamma?" I said, almost fiercely. "Think of dear mamma? Ay, God help her! But she sent him forth from her with blessings and caresses. They parted with their hearts full of love and tenderness, and her last words to him, I doubt not, were a blessing. And I? My parting words to him were, '*Never return till you can do as I wish!*' or that in substance. I sent him from me with anger in my heart and scorn upon my lips, for a little harmless pleasantry; and God has taken me at my word: he will never return! Oh, if I could only weep as you do, Gertie! but I have no tears; the fountain, I think, is dried forever."

They talked with me; they reasoned with me; they tried to comfort me; but it was of no avail. My heart was ice, and my brain a ball of liquid fire. At last I lay upon the library sofa, only to hush their pleadings; and when for an instant I was alone, I stepped through the open window into the veranda, and, in the deepening twilight, flew to the grove. I felt that I should die in the house; I must have air; I could not breathe; and I must go where there were none to speak to me. Chilled and bewildered, I wandered about through the wet leaves and grass. I saw the stars coming out through the trees above me, and thought how they looked down upon the waters beneath which my brother lay. I tried, again and again, to pray; but my lips could only frame the words, "My God, my God!" to be followed ever by the terrible ones, "he will never return!" It seemed impossible that he had that morning left us in health and spirits; it surely had been a month ago.

How long I had been out I know not,—perhaps only a few moments, perhaps an hour: I could never tell,—when, as I stood with my hands vainly striving to undo the fiery band that I felt encircled my head, a tall form stood beside me, a kind hand rested on my arm, and Uncle Ralph spoke soothingly, though firmly, to me:—

"My dear child, this is wrong, all wrong; this is open rebellion against the will of our kind All-Father, who never sends affliction but in mercy."

"No, no!" I cried. "It was not mercy to take him from me, when I had sent him away in anger. Why should He?"

"To teach you the sad lesson, perhaps, to be more forbearing with those you love."

"Oh, my God! my God! Have I not tried for years to conquer this great sin, until I felt of late that I held it in complete abeyance? and now, like a demon, its last struggle has been its worst, and I shall go through life crushed and desolate. My God, be merciful!" And again my hands were pressed upon my burning temples.

Uncle Ralph said afterward that he was completely at a loss what to do. He saw that brain-fever was inevitable, unless I could be made to weep. He tried to draw me to the house, but I would not go; then he recalled little tender incidents in Ralph's life, or in my own, but to no purpose: I had no tears to weep. At last he said, softly, and, oh, so tenderly,—

"Darling, do you remember Caryl Carrington?"

The name had ever a peculiar fascination for me, and I listened.

"Do you remember—" and he went on, delineating in the most touching manner some passages in that fearful night of which I have already spoken, and his own overwhelming grief when he found she had died in his arms. For a moment my grief was absorbed in his. I had tears for his sorrow, but not for my own, and they slowly trickled down my cheeks.

"Would you like to have me suffer such sorrow again?" he asked.

"God forbid!" I said, earnestly.

"Then listen to me. For a long while another has been as dear to me as ever was she. Shall I have to mourn that death has snatched her also from my arms?"

"God forbid!" I reiterated.

Then, slowly and earnestly, and bending slightly over me, he said, "Then, unless she herself casts me from her, I must now protect her," and drew me gently to him.

One earnest, pleading look into his face, and I lay sobbing out my sorrow upon his breast. It was a strange time, a strange place, for such a scene, but, as he has since said, he had no choice of remedies. I remember no feeling, save one of rest and protection. Indeed, all that I have narrated of this terrible time seems dream-like and unreal. I remember it all, but in a shadowy, indefinite way.

For a little while he let my grief have its course, knowing it was that which my weary brain most needed. Then he said, smoothing my hair gently away from my heated forehead with his soft, cool fingers,—

"Now you will go in with me, my darling, I am sure; and, for my sake, you will let them get you warmly into bed, and will try earnestly not to think, but to sleep."

I let him lead me like a child. I did as he bade me, without question, only kneeling a moment tearfully by mamma to receive her kisses and mingle my prayers with hers.

He gave me in charge of Aunt Martha; and I am sure I cannot tell what she did with me, so completely had my violent weeping, after my nervous system had been so overwrought, prostrated me. I believe I went to sleep under her hands. Nor do I remember, save in a very indistinct manner, anything of the next three or four days, lying in a kind of dream-like stupor all the time, suffering untold agony with my spine and brain. I recollect, very indistinctly, seeing light forms flitting silently about me that I dreamed were visitants from the shadow-land; but they all had familiar faces, some like Gertie and Nettie Ray, but more like Aunt Martha and mamma. And several times Charlie and Uncle Ralph appeared among them, and I looked eagerly for Ralph also, but he never came.

At last, one morning, I heard a robin singing beneath my window, and thought how sweet it was, and wondered that everything seemed so still; then Gertie stole softly to my bedside from an open door, and set a little vase of violets on the table near me.

"Thank you, dear," I said, softly, and with a low cry of joy she sank beside my bed.

"Do you know me, darling?" she said, with tearful voice.

"Know you? why should I not, Gertie?" I asked, but found I spoke with great effort.

"Oh, you have been so sick, and talked so wildly, I feared you never would know me again. Ah, and they said I must not let you talk," she said, with tears and kisses; "go to sleep, darling sister, do."

I closed my eyes and tried to think. Had I indeed been so sick? If so, why? At first I could remember nothing. Then slowly, one by one, the links in memory's chain came back, until I remembered all,—all. The scene in the grove was less distinct than any; indeed, I was not quite sure that I had not dreamed it, after all. But I was too weak to think, almost to care, so I soon dropped asleep again, and slept until the doctor came, two hours afterward, from the village. He was our old physician, whom Charlie insisted upon calling when I became so ill, distrusting his own abilities. He seemed delighted at the change, and said I would do nicely now, with care.

And so from day to day I gained a little strength, until at last they carried me down-stairs and let me lie upon the sofa in the drawing-room. No one spoke of Ralph, and I could not question them. All strove to appear cheerful in my presence, but poor mamma looked at least twenty years older than before that fatal day. The color had left her lips, her cheeks were sunken, and her beautiful eyes had lost their brilliancy. She seemed but a wreck of her former self; and, although she was ever kind and gentle, I knew her heart was breaking.

One morning—it was the second I had been carried down-stairs—I took a whim that I wished to sit in the library; so they wheeled my easy-chair before the bay-window, and clustered everything around me they thought would amuse me or add to my comfort. The window was open to the floor, and the fragrance from the dew-covered flowers was delicately sweet. But I could enjoy nothing with mamma's patient, suffering face before me. Oh, I thought, if I could only lay down my own life to recall dear Ralph's!

At last we were a moment alone, and calling her to me, and winding my arms about her lovingly, I said, as I laid my head upon her bosom,—

"Dear mamma, tell me, for my soul is in doubt, why

does God so afflict you? His reasons for myself I can easily understand; but for you, patient, lovely, and godly,—it seems inexplicable."

"Hush, darling; question not. 'What we know not here we shall know hereafter.' My faults are many, and I doubtless need the discipline. I try to submit cheerfully; but a mother's heart clings with wonderful tenacity to her children; and when death suddenly snatches them from her embrace, it wrenches the tendrils of the heart with a violence that is worse than death to herself."

"Ah, mamma," I said, tearfully, "it will surely kill you; you know not how you are failing."

"No, darling. The storm often crushes the flower that it does not break. But, dear Nannie,"—with trembling voice,—"I can only say, like one of his servants of old, 'Though he slay me, yet will I trust in him!' Can you not also trust in him thus, my darling?"

"I will try, dear mamma; indeed, indeed, I will try!"

Mamma kissed me tenderly, and left me to my own thoughts, which were full of peace, in spite of my sorrow. I felt that my mother's faith should indeed henceforth be mine. I remembered Gethsemane, and thought how I had there resolved to lead a better life. I remembered the tears I had there shed, the prayers I had there uttered. I looked back upon my life since then,—my earnest endeavors to do right, and my ofttimes yielding to unexpected temptations,—and felt that constant watchfulness, and earnest, abiding faith in my Saviour, could alone lead me aright through the many temptations of life. For this I earnestly prayed, and thought with a chastened sorrow upon our present affliction. "He hath led me by a thorny path," I said to myself, with tearful eyes; "but I trust it is into a better way."

As I lay back in my easy-chair, thus thinking, and drinking into my soul the beautiful view from my open window, I saw a man coming up the avenue. "It is Charlie," I thought; for he came daily, now, for a little while, and Uncle Ralph was already in the drawing-room with mamma. Intent upon my own thoughts, I forgot his coming, until I heard the click of the gate; then I again looked up. A tall, manly form was entering the gate—but it was not Charlie's. My heart gave a great throb, as I wiped the mist from my eyes and looked again. Then, with the frantic cry, "It is, it *is* my brother! it is Ralph!" I sprang through the long, open window and lay sobbing and panting upon his breast.

"Precious little sister," he said, kissing me again and again, as he strained me to his great warm heart and wiped the tears from my white cheeks. "So pale and thin, too! Has she indeed grieved for her brother so?" And the hot drops from his own eyes fell upon my forehead.

I could only cling to him and sob, convulsively, "Oh, Ralph, Ralph!" I did not lose consciousness; I did not faint; but the strength all departed from me. A languor stole over me like death; and I remember thinking in my heart, "If it be death, let me dream on thus forever!"

It was but an instant before mamma and Uncle Ralph, having indistinctly heard my cry and come to look for me, stepped out upon the veranda. Then, when they saw Ralph bending over me, the cry that went out from my mother's heart I never shall forget while I have being. It roused me; it nerved me; and I cried,—

"Go to her, Ralph! Oh, my God, the sudden shock will kill her!"

"No," said Uncle Ralph, circling my trembling form with his strong arm, and crying in spite of himself, "no, it will cure her, I trust."

But he was but half right. No one who heard that cry

could ever forget it. It was not a scream of terror, it was not a cry of distress, but it came welling up from the depths of the poor bleeding heart, like the strange, sweet discord produced by a rude hand tearing asunder with one grasp the chords of a lute. No one could doubt that the long-lacerated chords of her heart were wrenched by that thrilling cry. Ralph sprang to her with outstretched arms, and she sank in a deathly swoon upon his breast.

Then such a scene as ensued! Ralph, still holding mamma to his heart—he would resign her to no one—and kissing and caressing her and talking with us alternately, was a hero, and a real royal one. He carried mamma into the house, laid her upon the sofa, still holding her in his arms, only allowing Aunt Martha—who could scarcely do anything for crying and ejaculating between every breath, "The Lord save us! Miracles will never cease!" or, "The Lord love us! I cannot yet believe it is himself!" —to unloose her dress a little and bathe her temples and hands with cologne. He himself held a vinaigrette to her nose, but said he was sure his kisses were the best restorative, which I do not in the least doubt; for when at last she opened her eyes and found herself still in his arms, with his warm kisses falling upon her eyes and lips and forehead, she smiled up to him, and the silent tears stole from beneath the lids that had again closed, and the pale lips moved, we all knew, in fervent thanksgiving.

Then Joseph was dispatched for Ellis and Gertie, and to leave word also at Mr. Ray's; and then Charlie came galloping furiously, having heard the news in the village, where Ralph had stopped, but failed to find him. And such an embrace as they two gave! Mamma, who was much better and was lying upon the sofa then, cried and laughed hysterically; and I believe all of the rest of us followed her example.

And how had it all so come? The sail in the distance, in trying to make the shore, *had* passed across their track, and succeeded in saving two, Ralph and one other, but was driven by the storm so rapidly out to sea and so badly injured that she was forced to put in at a little island many miles distant, and it was several days before she was again fit for the water. She was a very slow-sailing vessel; but the officers and crew were very kind to them, and landed them at the nearest port as soon as possible, from whence they came directly home,—not, alas! till we had long tasted for him the "bitterness of death."

The day passed, as all days will pass, be they sorrowful or glad, and the twilight was closing about us. The house had been full of friends all day to see our hero; but now they had departed. Mamma, pale, but with a face radiantly happy, moved slowly about; and I lay quiet, but happy, upon the sofa I had occupied most of the day. My heart was full of a quiet joy, and none the less so that it had bent that morning so submissively to the divine will before Ralph came.

While they were at supper—for we keep old-fashioned country hours in our meals at Beechwood, having dinner at two and supper at seven—I arose and crept to the easy-chair beside the west window, and sat looking out upon the lingering sunset, when I heard a step, and Uncle Ralph sat down close beside me. I do not know why,—it had never been so before,—but I felt the day had still something to record for me. He took my hand quietly in both of his, as he said,—

"The day has been full of happiness to us all, Nannie."

"It has indeed, Uncle Ralph."

"There still lacks one thing to make it complete with me."

"And that?" very softly.

"The assurance that the hope I have cherished since that fearful night in the grove is not without foundation. Can you give it me to-night, dear Nannie?" And he bent forward to look with his earnest eyes into mine, as though he would read the secrets of my very soul.

"Then it was not a dream?" I said.

"Yes, darling; but one which, I trust, is to last through life. You once said to me, years ago, that you felt if I could only always be near to guide you you would never go astray. Will you trust me still? Will you walk with me and let me hold your hand all through life's journey? We will help each other, dear Nannie, that neither fall."

"Oh, Uncle Ralph," I whispered, "you would not deceive me with this hope? It is not that you wish to promote my happiness and good, but really that you love me?"

"My darling child, for years you have been dearer to me than my life."

"Yes; but as Gertie? Or—your other love?"

"Little doubter," he said, "I could have flung *your* 'other love' into the sea, so wroth was I, when he came between me and the pure young heart I was watching and training that I might win it in the future."

His tones, his eyes, the pressure of his hands on mine, all carried conviction; I could no longer doubt. The man I so long had looked upon as one of the noblest of God's creation, who stood so "head and shoulders" above all other men, whom I so long had worshiped and loved with my whole heart, yet never dreamed of daring to aspire to, had stooped to lift me to his sphere,—poor, little, unworthy, erring me! I had no words to speak; I only laid my weary head upon his shoulder,—its future blessed rest,—and, half bewildered by my weight of happiness, nestled within the loving arm that now encircled me. He laid his cheek against my forehead, as it rested on his shoulder, and we both sat looking out upon the purple clouds,—for the sunset was fading,—and saw the evening star come out, and let our souls converse through silent lips. Then mamma came, with loving eyes, and said,—

"I found a son this morning."

"And Nannie has given you another one to-night," said Uncle Ralph, finishing her sentence for her. And so, with blessings and caresses, closed this eventful day.

"Mamma," I said, with many blushes, a few days after the events last recorded, "did you ever suspect that Uncle Ralph loved me?"

"Never till the day I told him of your own and Hal's engagement. Then he told me how he had hoped for years some day to win you, and spoke the only unkind words he has ever spoken to me, for allowing you to enter into an engagement while yet too young to know your own heart."

"Oh, mamma, why did you not tell me of it then?"

"What good could it have done, when you were so bound up in Hal?"

"Ah, dear mamma, at that moment I worshiped Uncle Ralph as a superior being, and daily prayed that Hal would grow like him. I did not dream it was love I had so hidden away in my heart for him; but now I know it by its true name. I have always loved him."

"And what," said mamma,—the least little bit maliciously, I thought,—"and what, pray, was the feeling you had for Hal, then?"

I laughed a little, as I said, "Simply a reflection of the true passion, I suppose. I could not aspire to reach the sun, and so I took an object that it shone upon and tried to think it the real planet."

"Bravo, my little girl! that was indeed well defined!" said Uncle Ralph, stepping through the open window.

"Oh, Uncle Ralph, how could you?" I cried, in confusion, springing to my feet.

"It was a little rude, Nannie, I confess," he said, as he held toward me a beautiful cluster of white japonicas he had brought to me from the village; "but I heard your mamma's last question, and could not refrain from listening to your reply. Won't you forgive me this once?"

Always a little emboldened when I am embarrassed, I said, laughingly, "On one condition."

"Name it."

"That you will tell me, if you really were so fearful of some one else stealing my heart, why you were so long in declaring your own wishes in regard to it."

"Ah," said Uncle Ralph, half dramatically, half seriously, "the poet must answer for me, when he says,—

> "He that loves deep and well blurts it not forth
> Unto the eager crowd; but in the calm
> And hush of wood and vale, whispers it soft
> Unto the solitude.'

"But seriously, Nannie, do you never mean to call me anything but 'Uncle Ralph'? I think it is time half of the cognomen were dropped."

"Never," I said, demurely; "lest I forget the reverence due to your age and position."

"You are a saucy puss," he said, laughing. "I will have my hands full to keep you straight, I see."

"Ay, that you will," said Ralph, catching the last remark, as he entered the door. "I have been all my life trying it, and have at last ended by being in complete subjection myself."

"Ah, Ralph, you are a privileged character now, and may say what you please. I am only too happy to have your teasing tongue at work again," I responded.

"There! do you see? She has conquered me even in this,—taken my vocation from me completely; I shall never be able to perpetrate a joke again,—never!" which remark he instantly proved by picking up a kitten at his feet and depositing it in my work-basket, where it was soon completely entangled in the meshes of bright Berlin wool which I was weaving into a shawl for mamma.

And so, old book, my narrative draws near its close. The time has slipped away in bright dreams and brighter realities since I began this last continuous narrative, until it is now late in October; and early in December I shall lay my hand in Uncle Ralph's, to be led by him forever. My soul has found its destiny, my heart its rest. There are no longer restless yearnings for the unattainable; there are no longer unstirred depths within my heart; for his hand has touched the innermost recesses, and brought music from the chords I dreamed would lie in silence forever.

And so, I close your lids, dear old book, as I would close the white lids over the sightless eyes of a beloved friend whose heart had ofttimes looked into my own. I shall hide you away in some safe recess, as I would lay my friend's lifeless form away beneath the cool sods of the valley,—feeling that much in my life that was sad, much that was beautiful, is hidden away forever in your tomb. And as I would whisper tearfully above the grave of the beloved one, so say I now within my heart for you,—

"REQUIESCAT IN PACE."

Written on the Fly-leaves of the Old Diary.

This morning, at breakfast, Ralph asked me for some old receipts and deeds he had years ago given me to put away for him, and, being very busy, I directed him where to find them himself, in the secret drawer of my old desk, that had not been opened for years. He stayed so long I feared he had not found them, and went to look for them myself, when, lo, there he sat, so intently reading he did not even hear my approach. I stole to his side, peeped over his shoulder, and looked upon the pages of my own "Diary," that twelve years ago I had interred in this tiny sepulchre, I thought, forever.

"Well, well!" I said; "have you no more respect for the buried past than thus to disinter its ashes?" The book was open at the last page, and Ralph, looking up with moistened eyes, drew me down upon his knee, and said, earnestly,—

"I thank God hourly for the gift of my precious wife, who for so many years has been all to me that my heart could crave."

"Oh, Ralph," I said, always touched by his loving praise, "if I have only been half worthy the blessed place you have given me in your great heart, I am content."

Into what lover-like channel our conversation might have run I know not, for at that moment a shout of merriment was heard, and two sturdy boys of nine and seven years burst into the room unceremoniously,—for it was the old school-room and their favorite resort,—headed by my brother Ralph,—now "Uncle Ralph,"—with a saucy little miss of four summers queening it grandly upon his shoulder, and all in high glee.

"Well, I declare! Pray, good people, how long do you expect your honeymoon to last?" he asked, laughingly.

"As long as your love of fun; and that will be forever," I said, blushing a little in spite of my matronhood.

"Try it yourself, Ralph," said my Ralph, "and you will not have so much curiosity upon the subject."

"Not I!" he laughed. "When I am at home [he now lives in Philadelphia, but spends a month with us every summer], my business engrosses all of my time; and when I am here, between these young rogues, and Gertie's and Charlie's, I hardly get time to swallow my dinner. What could I do with a wife, pray? I am the only old bachelor uncle left; and Beechwood would not be Beechwood without an 'Uncle Ralph.'"

"Yes; and I doubt not," I said, half teasingly, "that some young lady in embryo is hidden away for you, as for the former Uncle Ralph, until you are ready to accept her for your destiny. You old bachelors are not so unimpressible as you would have the world imagine."

"I only hope," said Ralph the First, with a merry twinkle in his eyes, "if that is so, Ralph, that she will not prove as unmanageable a case as mine. I have had my hands full, I assure you."

"I believe you," he assented, with a solemn nod of his saucy head. "My own former experience teaches me to sympathize most heartily with you."

"Well," I retorted, "as I am a woman and entitled to the last word, I can only say that, according to your own statement, you are both in subjection, yet *my* hands are not half full yet. So much for woman's superior skill in the art of managing." And I made good my escape before either could reply.

I found, when I reached my room, that I still held the old loved diary in my hand; so here, upon the fly-leaves, I make this brief record, after the lapse of so many years:

We were married, Ralph and I, upon the 6th of December following my last entry; and Nettie and Charlie were also married at the same time. We lived two years in the village, and then mamma declared she could no longer live alone at Beechwood. Ralph had gone to Philadelphia, to practice law; Charlie was compelled to remain in the village, to build up his practice; Ellis and Gertie were so pleasantly situated that it seemed a pity to disturb them; so Ralph and I came back to the old homestead, much to my joy and mamma's evident satisfaction. And so Beechwood, beautiful Beechwood, which has been my home from infancy, is, I trust, to be my home forever. Here I first opened my eyes upon the light of earth, and here I hope to close them when "life's fitful dream" is ended.

Mamma, dear, precious mamma, is as good and patient as ever; a little older, perhaps, but if anything healthier and happier than I ever saw her. We often tell her— Gertie and I—that she is younger than either of her daughters. She says she renews her youth in our children; and if that is so she certainly ought to be very young, for they have life enough to supply a household.

Ralph and Charlie, our two brave boys, are the pride of our hearts, so full of noble and manly impulses; while our little Fannie rules the house in her own pretty way, and is the pet of every one,—even bringing a twinkle of mirth into her papa's eyes, when he is gravely reproving her for some petty fault, by her cunning way of arguing the point. Her Uncle Ralph and she are choice friends, and she will fly hatless and shoeless—if she chances to be dressing at the time of his approach—down the avenue to meet him. He says he cannot but feel it is Kittie's own bright little self restored to us; and indeed her sunny head and laughing eyes are not unlike those of our lost darling. We did think some of calling her "Caryl," but the name seems too sacred to be lightly taken on our lips; and so we call her "Fannie," for mamma, and keep as a sacred legacy the name and memory of "Caryl Carrington."

Then Gertie's two fair daughters, Fannie and Ella,—for Ellis's mother and mamma,—of ten and twelve years respectively, are ones to make any parent's heart throb with pride and joy, and are especial favorites with mamma; while Charlie and Nettie are surrounded by a circle of bright little ones unequaled anywhere. Ralph, Charlie, and Hal are manly, brave, and fun-loving, and little Matie Mae, just three years old to-morrow, is charming as a fairy.

Charlie and Nettie are very happy. They have a beautiful home in the village, but, in pleasant weather, we welcome them often and gladly to Beechwood. We have so many Ralphs now that we are compelled always to say of the younger ones, "Ralph Clifford," and "Ralph Cleve;" while brother Ralph is now, unquestionably, "Uncle Ralph," and *my* Ralph is content to be simply "Ralph," or, as "Uncle Ralph" will persist in calling him, "Ralph the First."

Ellis is beloved and respected by all; while Gertie, the same sweet Gertie of old, is the idol of his congregation.

Poor brother Ralph, true to his lost love, will never marry, I believe; but he is happy and content; gives us the holidays ever, and a month in summer, and is the darling of us all.

Aunt Martha, hale and hearty still, only a little rheumatic, sits much of her time by the fireside, knitting,— she has so many little feet to cover now, you know,—and is the honored guest with us ever.

Joseph and Lizzie, years ago, were married, and live in a little cottage Ralph built for them, just back of the orchard. They have no children, but Lizzie, faithful and pretty as ever, has taken care of mine respectively, and loves them, I verily believe, as though they were her own.

Aunt Katie, poor Aunt Katie, has been five years a widow. Uncle Harry's death was a severe blow to her, but she wears her widowhood meekly and with Christian submission. Since Colonel Ray's death, three years ago, she has removed to Pine Grove, his old place, and is now our near neighbor. Harry is a manly youth of nineteen; and Blanche is beautiful and lovely as a dream. They are Aunt Katie's life.

"And Hal?" Hal still lives in New York, married about a year after I was, to Sallie. They come occasionally to Charlie's, but not very often; and then, of course, we all unite to make their visit as pleasant as may be. I was in New York, with Ralph, last spring, and Sallie called upon me at the hotel and invited us to dinner. We went, of course. They live in elegant style on a fashionable square, and are as gay and fashionable as ever. But Sallie already looks faded and broken, and, Nettie tells me, is very languid and insipid, except when in a gay crowd, surrounded by gentlemen, when she is still charming. She says her health is not good, and that she seems nervous and petulant much of the time. They have two delicate-looking little girls, of six and eight years, who are brought into the parlor every day a little while after dinner; the only time, I believe, their mother sees them during the twenty-four hours. She sent one of them back to the nursery, to have her dress changed immediately, the day we were there, because she had disarranged it a little by sitting upon the floor to hunt for a ring she had lost; and, as she went pouting from the room, Sallie said she thought "children the bore of one's life."

"Oh, dear!" I answered, quickly; "they are the sunlight of our home."

"Sallie does not see ours often enough to know what they might be," Hal said, a little bitterly.

I thought of our two manly boys, and our bright little Fannie, at home, dressed neatly and comfortably, and allowed to live in the fresh air as much as possible; and I thanked God inwardly that he had given me the warm mother-love so fervently for my little ones, and taught me so well how to care for their health and comfort.

I looked at Hal, as he and Ralph stood talking together, and felt pained to see how worn and old he looked. Ralph looked, as they stood together there, at least ten years the younger. "Oh, how mercifully God has led me!" I thought; and when in the evening we returned to our room, I stood by his side as he sat talking with me, and, pressing my lips upon the high, white forehead, said, half tearfully,—

"Oh, Ralph! Into what a blessed world of sunlight and love and flowers you have indeed drawn me! My dream, after all, was prophetic."

And so life passes with us. If it is not all sunshine, we meet the clouds together, and they pass more quickly. And as we press onward, and the gray hairs come to mingle with the dark tresses of the one and the golden threads of the other, and the shadows of life lengthen behind us, we will only walk more closely by each other's side till we reach the end of the journey, if haply it may be granted us to reach it together. It is a beautiful hope, one of which we often speak, that we shall be permitted to take our last dreamless rest in one and the same hour; that we shall pass hand in hand through the chill waters, and together enter that beautiful land "where there comes to the heart no sorrow, neither shadow of parting."

A tear drops on the page from above me, and a deep, manly, loving voice, that I well know, says, fervently, "AMEN!"

THE END.

www.ingramcontent.com/pod-product-compliance
Lightning Source LLC
Chambersburg PA
CBHW032103220426
43664CB00008B/1114